IMAGES
of America

CUTCHOGUE AND NEW SUFFOLK

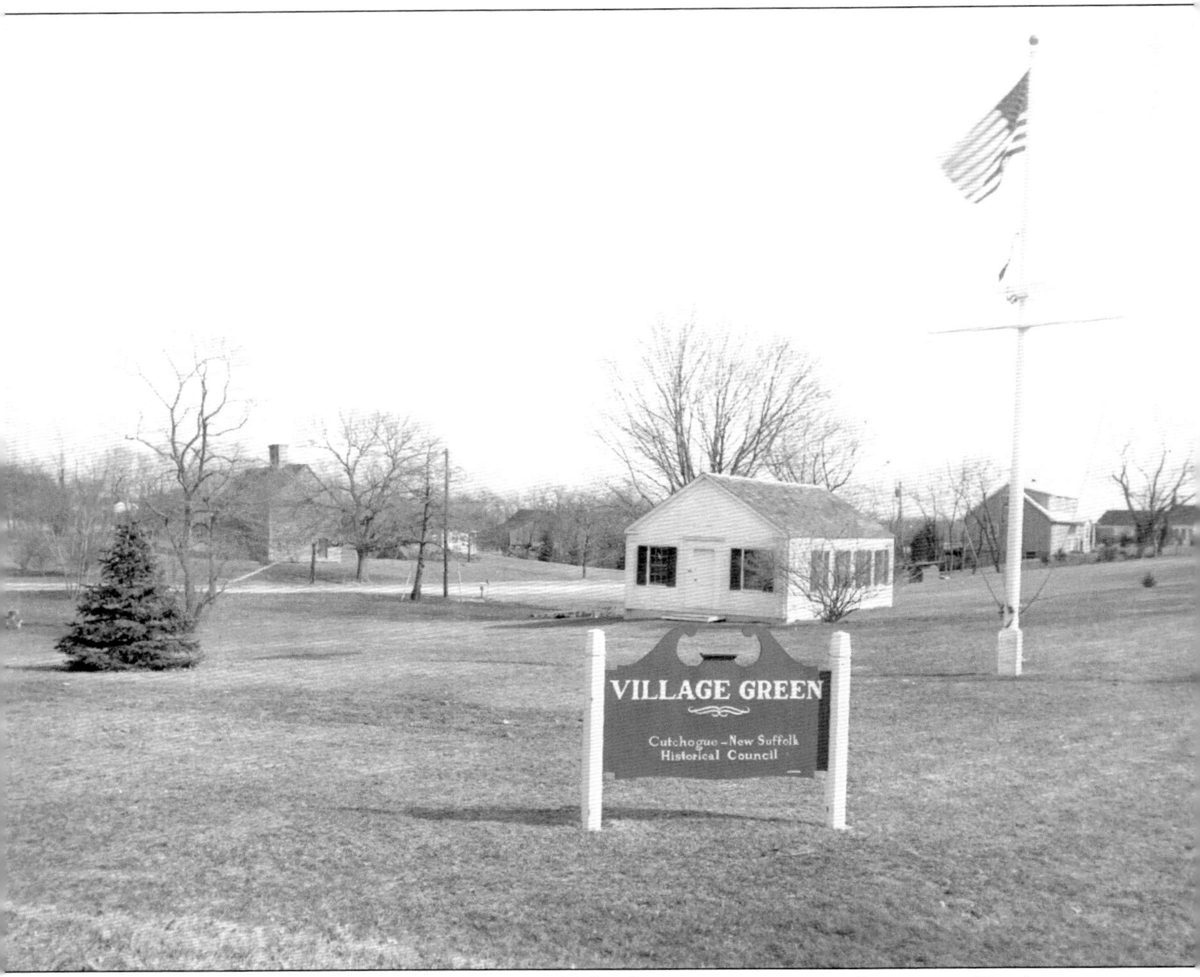

The Village Green, Cutchogue, 1965. The large, open space in downtown Cutchogue was transformed in 1960 into the Village Green, where historic buildings could be preserved for public enjoyment. Since that time, the Old Schoolhouse, the Wickham Farmhouse, a barn, and a carriage house have joined the Old House across Case's Lane to form the Cutchogue–New Suffolk Historical Council's compound of historic structures. The buildings are open to the public during the summer months. (Courtesy of the Southold Historical Society.)

On the Cover: The Old House Dedication, July 1, 1940. Southold Town residents gathered along Case's Lane in Cutchogue to witness the formal dedication of the Old House, which was chosen to symbolize the 300th anniversary of the town's settlement in 1640. Ironically, it was not until the hurricane of 1938 and the loss of trees masking its ancient profile that the iconic dwelling was discovered and restoration undertaken. Today, the Old House forms the centerpiece of the Cutchogue–New Suffolk Historical Council's complex of restored buildings on the Village Green in the hamlet of Cutchogue. (Courtesy of the Southold Historical Society.)

IMAGES
of America

CUTCHOGUE AND NEW SUFFOLK

Zachary N. Studenroth

ARCADIA
PUBLISHING

ISBN 978-0-7385-9828-4

Published by Arcadia Publishing
Charleston, South Carolina

Printed in the United States of America

Library of Congress Control Number: 2012947174

For all general information, please contact Arcadia Publishing:
Telephone 843-853-2070
Fax 843-853-0044
E-mail sales@arcadiapublishing.com
For customer service and orders:
Toll-Free 1-888-313-2665

Visit us on the Internet at www.arcadiapublishing.com

This book is dedicated to all of the trustees of the Cutchogue–New Suffolk Historical Council who contributed in so many ways to the growth of the organization since its founding in 1960.

Contents

ACKNOWLEDGMENTS

Many people contributed to this book, from archivists and historians to preservationists, collectors, and photographers. Without their enthusiastic support, the book's completion would not have been possible. First and foremost, I wish to thank Mariella Ostroski, librarian and archivist in the Local History Room at the Cutchogue–New Suffolk Free Library, whose collection of historical images and knowledge of their significance was an invaluable aid in the preparation of the book. Mariella also assisted in processing many of the photographs for publication. Her dedication, perseverance, and good humor cannot be overstated.

The collectors of family photographs and memories deserve a special word of thanks. As keepers of their family legacies, they preserve the history of our communities for future generations. Contributing to this publication were James Grathwohl and Emily Victoria, Virginia McCaffery, Mary Holland, Roberta Jaklevic, and Norman Wamback. From public collections came many of the Charles H. Meredith photographs held by the Southold Historical Society, Southold, New York, and early views of firemen and apparatus held by the Cutchogue Fire Department. To these contributors, both public and private, many thanks are given.

In this era of fact-checking and the phenomenal range of research tools offered by the Internet, it remains essential to share the text with those whose memories and historical interests encompass the subjects under review. James Grathwohl and Virginia McCaffery provided invaluable help in this regard, reading the text and sharing their insights into the people, places, and events that form the history of Cutchogue and New Suffolk. Finally, special thanks are due to preservationist and educator Kurt E. Kahofer, whose editorial assistance brought the text into clarity and cohesion.

Unless otherwise noted, all images appear courtesy of the Cutchogue–New Suffolk Free Library.

INTRODUCTION

The history of Cutchogue and New Suffolk, twin hamlets located on the North Fork of eastern Long Island, spans over three centuries of recorded settlement in a unique region of New York State. It begins with the Corchaugs, one of the last of the surviving Long Island Indian tribes, who left their legacy in the Cutchogue name as well as artifacts that fascinated farmers tilling their fields in the 1800s and archeologists a century later. The remains of a Native American fortification on Downs Creek, said to be the most complete archeological discovery of its type, is memorialized as Fort Corchaug, now a National Historic Landmark.

But the recorded history of the area begins not with the "Contact Period" between Native Americans and the English settlers who founded Southold Town in 1640, but with Cutchogue, the first colony that split from the original community in the 1660s. Typical of its colonial origins, the Cutchogue settlement was sustained by agriculture and other natural resources, including timber, salt hay, wild game, and seafood. As such, the community prospered for nearly two centuries until its companion village, New Suffolk, was laid out in the 1830s by an enterprising businessman who was eager to capitalize on its waterfront location. Together, the villages shared another century of growth, the one continuing as an agricultural enclave and the other as a center of maritime interests, until the two drew together before World War II to share such community resources as a volunteer fire department, commercial district, and religious institutions.

The images in this book span over 100 years of growth and change, from the early one-room schoolhouses, churches, and public houses that defined Cutchogue and New Suffolk in the early to mid-1800s, to the bustling waterfront, commercial districts, and truck farms in the mid-1900s. Chapter one features the remarkable structures and the people who built them, starting with the c. 1649 "Old House," New York State's earliest surviving dwelling and now a museum house operated by the Cutchogue–New Suffolk Historical Council. From the vernacular dwellings of the 18th century to the elaborate Victorian summer homes of the 19th century, the chapter provides a glimpse into the way Cutchogue and New Suffolk responded to architectural trends across the decades. Along the way, churches and houses were built, rebuilt, and repurposed; schoolhouses grew to accommodate a growing population; old-fashioned dry-goods stores became more specialized in their offerings; and new forms of commercial buildings—gasoline stations and diners—were invented.

In chapter two, the essence of these twin communities is captured in photographs of the expansive farms and waterfront activities that define their histories. Cutchogue's ancestral farms are legendary; from Henry L. Fleet's productive fields, so profitable that they enabled the proprietor to develop his own horse-breeding and racing stables, to the potato and cauliflower fields that yielded crops so plentiful they spawned their own truck farming industry. Not to be outdone, New Suffolk became a center of commercial fishing, pleasure boating, and experimental boat-building. Its location on a peninsula bounded by protected bays attracted maritime activities of all kinds, including scallop and oyster dredging, that brought world renown to the tiny hamlet.

New Suffolk also attracted its share of "summer people" who enjoyed sport fishing, rowing, and bathing; some would build seasonal homes and cottages, leaving a legacy of resort architecture enjoyed by current residents.

Chapters three and four look at people going about their daily lives in the 19th and early 20th centuries. Young people gather at schoolhouses and churches, firemen display their fraternity and volunteer service, and community members celebrate significant events in local and national history. Life in these villages is also seen in the faces of immigrants who came seeking work, from the Irish, Germans, and Poles of the 19th century to the African Americans and Hispanics of the early to mid-20th century. All came to make a better life; many stayed, contributing to the diversity of modern life in Cutchogue and New Suffolk. And as the face of Cutchogue and New Suffolk evolved, so too did local businesses, responding to the needs of a dynamic American populace. As the blacksmith shop gave way to service stations, new markets came to town with goods and services representing national brands. Much of this transformation was recorded by Cutchogue's own photographers, Charles H. Meredith and Linnaeus Allen, who for many decades captured daily life and special events.

Two of the most remarkable transformations of daily life in the 19th century came about from the construction of the railroad and the invention of the automobile. In chapter five, the impact of the Long Island Rail Road and its station on Depot Lane is recorded in a series of photographs portraying the stations and loading docks that provided quick transportation to and from New York City for both farm produce and vacationers. And by the end of the century, a new mode of motorized transportation made its impact on rural life, as seen in the horse-drawn coaches and buggies that gradually gave way to the "horseless carriages" and trucks that hauled vegetables from the fields and eventually to metropolitan markets. Automobiles and trucks required road improvements, and with them emerged a new generation of recreational travelers who "rediscovered" quaint, rural settings such as Cutchogue and New Suffolk.

In chapter six, vacationers and local residents alike find time out from their daily chores to gather at picnics, social clubs, on the beach, and at parades and other festivities. Leisure time, always a part of the American scene, witnessed a steady increase in the 19th century, especially for the middle class, which could now afford the luxury of spending time away from work, a concept formerly reserved for the rich. Cutchogue and New Suffolk witnessed this trend and prepared for it by building hotels and summer camps for urban visitors. A country club opened in the early 1900s, and the Fleet Farm offered a racing track and polo fields. Meanwhile, locals created their own exclusive clubs like the Pequash Recreation Club and The Old Crows, with membership restricted by invitation and offered to old-time residents only.

Finally, the surprising "firsts" of Cutchogue and New Suffolk are covered in chapter seven, which examines several remarkable events that impacted national and international affairs. Beginning with Benjamin Franklin's granite mile markers—a complete series of postal milestones set by the inventor/statesman in the 1750s—and concluding with the launch of the Long Island winemaking industry by Alex and Louisa Hargrave in 1973, Cutchogue and New Suffolk have witnessed extraordinary things! These "firsts" also include America's first submarine base, a letter that changed the course of world events, and a musical composer who brought fame to his native Cutchogue.

The following pages illustrate the history of two remarkable Long Island communities, Cutchogue and New Suffolk, that have witnessed great changes to the American scene in the 1700s, 1800s, and 1900s. It is the author's hope that you will read and enjoy the book and derive a new appreciation for these special places.

One

Building a Community

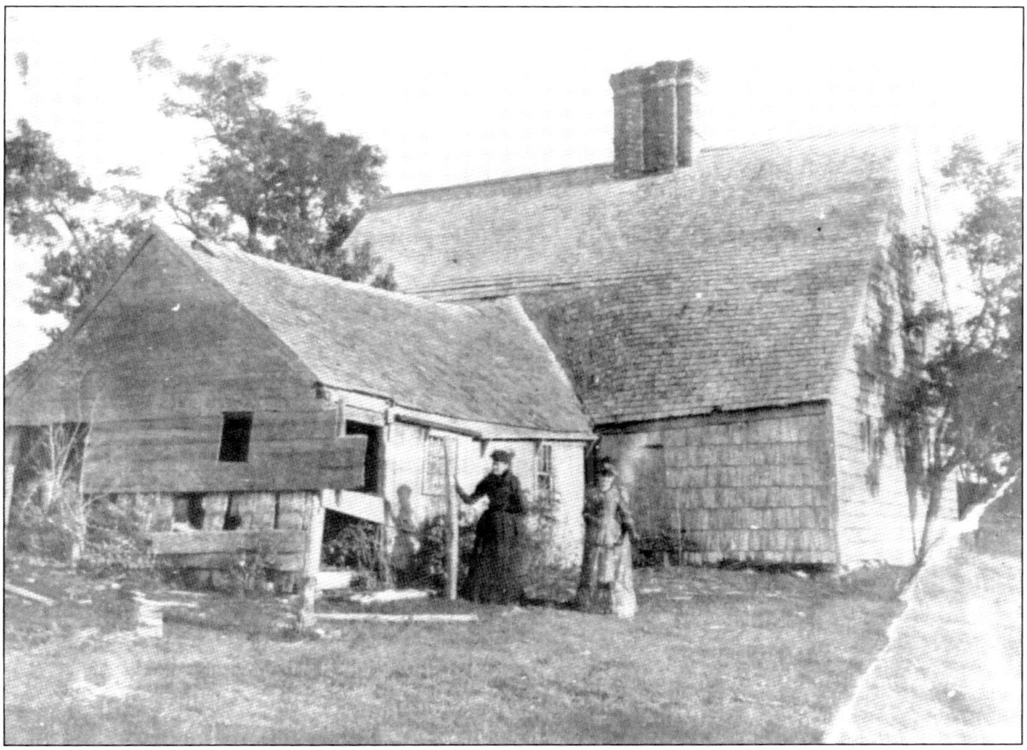

The Old House, c. 1900. Recorded by the Historic American Buildings Survey (HABS) between 1938 and 1940, the Old House or "Horton-Wickham-Landon" house, as it was then known, was an iconic symbol of Southold Town's 17th-century settlement period. Built in Southold in 1649, the house was relocated to Cutchogue in 1660. The ladies are believed to be Mrs. Frank Case and her daughter, the last owners. (Courtesy of Library of Congress, Prints & Photographs Division, HABS, NY-546.)

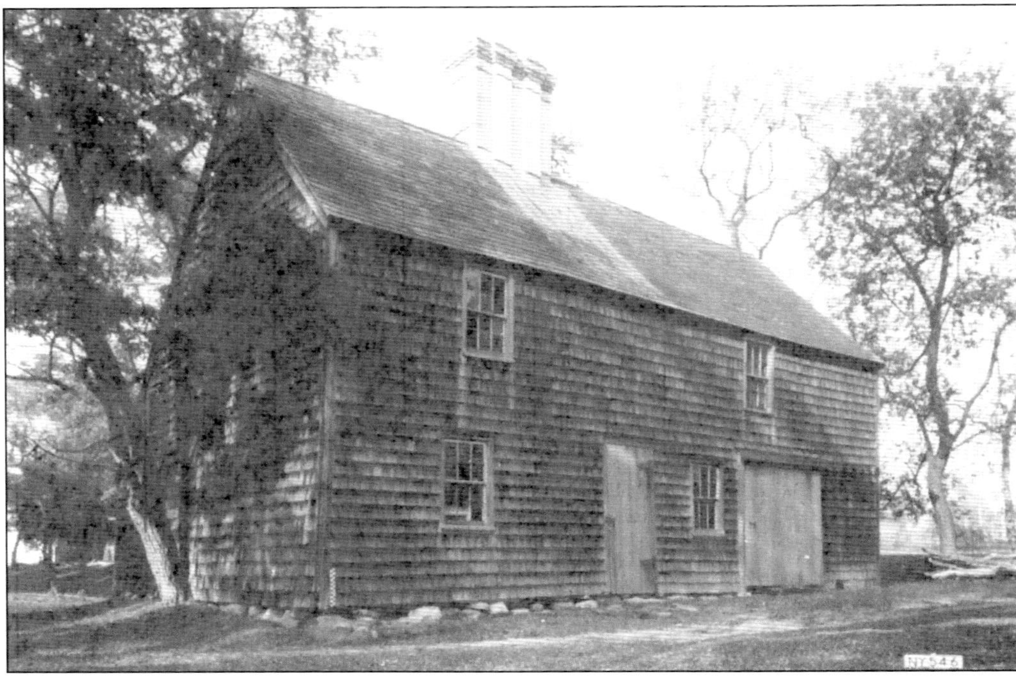

The Old House, c. 1938. The medieval-style Old House was discovered by architectural historians in 1938 after a hurricane flattened many of the trees surrounding it. Converted into a barn in the 19th century, alterations included newer window sashes, barn doors, and shingle siding. The massive brick chimney was not altered, however, and is characteristic of mid-17th century architecture. (Courtesy of Library of Congress, Prints & Photographs Division, HABS, NY-546.)

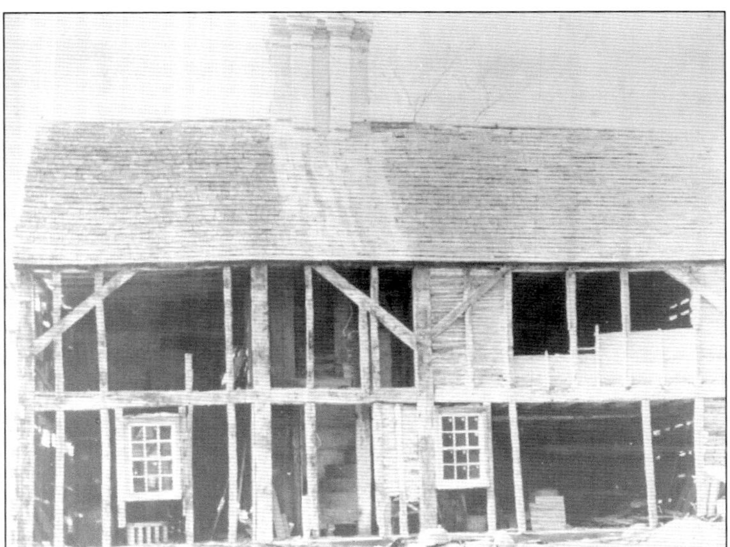

The Old House, c. 1939. The Old House was restored by architect James Van Alst in 1939 and became the centerpiece of Southold Town's tercentenary celebrations a year later. The removal of wall shingles from the front façade revealed the intricate timber framing of the house, with its massive posts and angled braces that are characteristic of 17th-century construction practices. The wall studs missing at the right were later replaced.

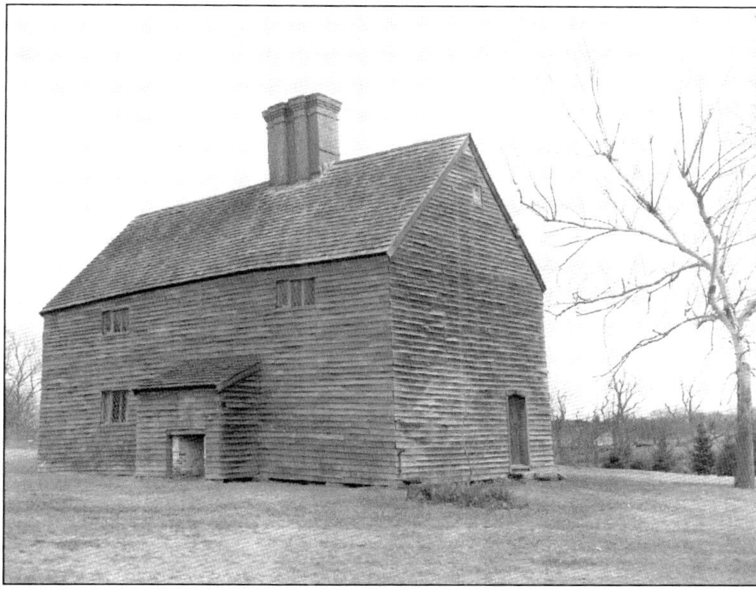

The Old House, c. 1940. The restoration of the Old House returned the exterior and interior to its 17th-century appearance. The kitchen wing—a later addition—was removed and replaced with a covered bake oven, wood shingle siding was replaced with oak clapboards, and doors and leaded casement windows were restored.

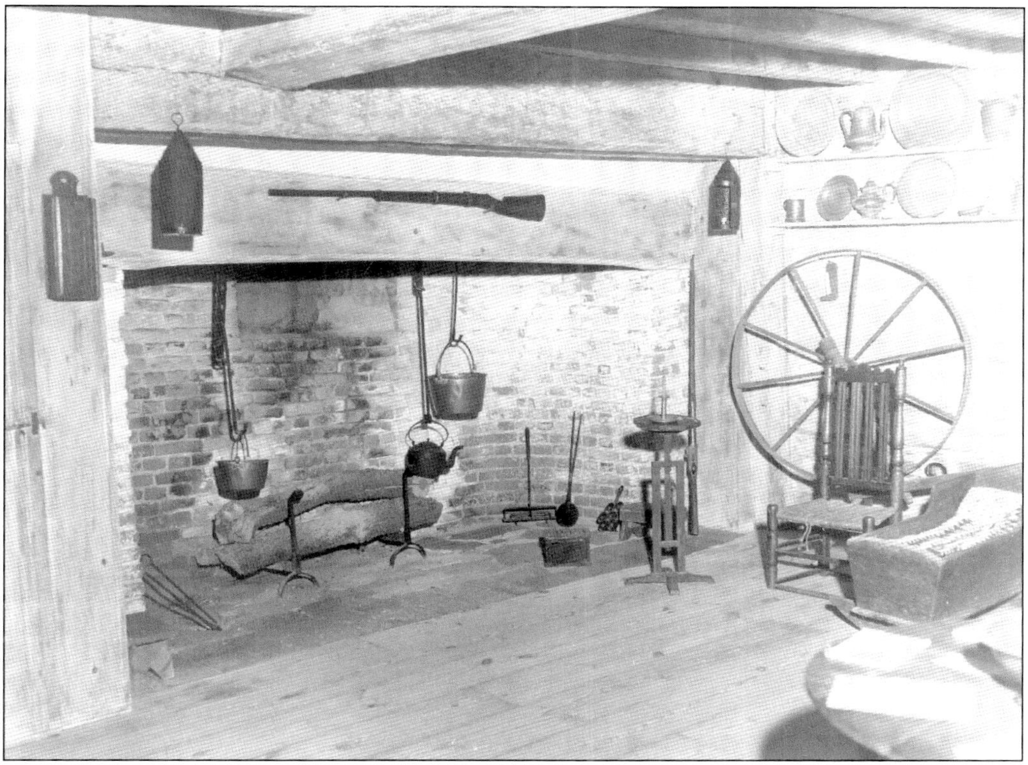

The Old House, Interior, c. 1940. The restored interior of the house displays the extraordinary timber framing of First Period workmanship. Featured within the principal room on the first floor is the characteristic summer beam, which dominates the ceiling, while the wide fireplace opening and brick hearth provide ample room for displaying kitchen utensils. The house is now interpreted by the Cutchogue–New Suffolk Historical Council.

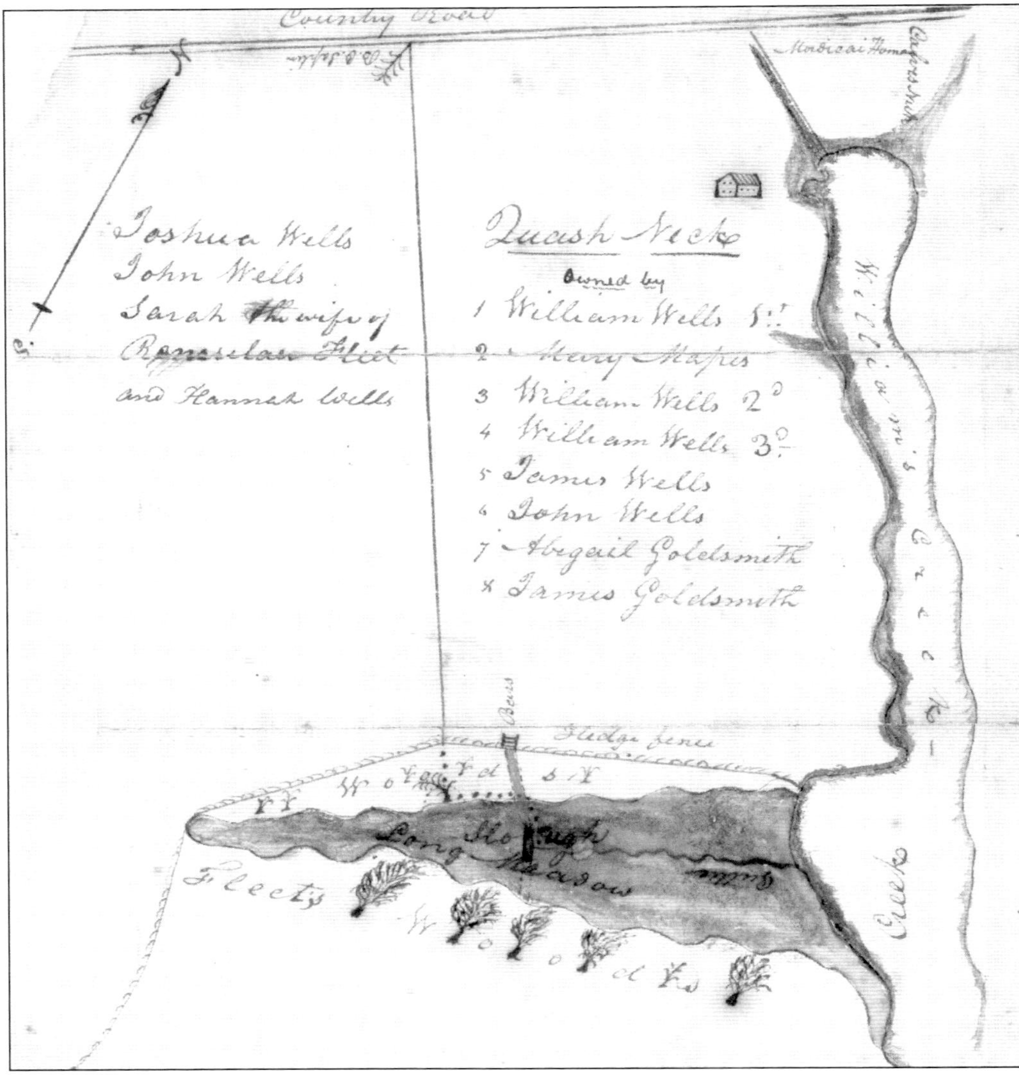

QUASH NECK, C. 1825. The old Country Road that ran through Cutchogue (today's Main Road, also known as the King's Highway) skirted numerous necks of land, marshes, and inlets that characterized the shoreline of Peconic Bay to the south. Quash Neck (now known as Pequash Neck) was one such land mass that figured prominently in the original Cutchogue settlement. The first owner, William Wells, received the land in return for negotiating a treaty with the Corchaug Indians in 1667. Ownership of Pequash Neck descended in the Wells family until it came into the possession of the Fleet and Goldsmith families in the early 1800s. The value of this and other "necks" to the early settlers lay partially in the natural salt grasses or "hay" that furnished feed for their livestock. The fertile upland, much of it previously cleared by Native Americans, was ideal for growing the crops that sustained the original Cutchogue settlement.

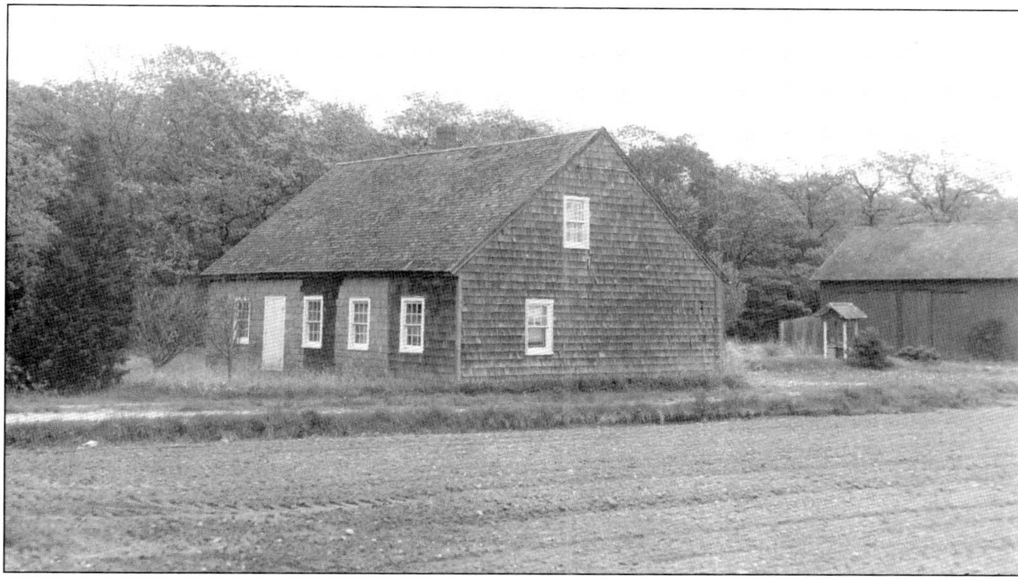

WICKHAM FARMHOUSE, 1963 AND 1965. Compact and devoid of outward decoration, the old Wickham Farmhouse looks abandoned in the above photograph, taken by Charles H. Meredith in 1963. The house stood at the time on the North Road, its back wall facing east. But the Cape Cod–style farmhouse was deceptive in its simplicity; concealed within were the architectural features and structural framing associated with 18th-century design and building practices. The Wickham Farmhouse was donated to the Cutchogue–New Suffolk Historical Council by the William Wickham family in 1965 and was moved to the Village Green in Cutchogue (below). The house was restored by the Cutchogue–New Suffolk Historical Council, and architect Orville Beebe and builder Corwin Grathwohl supervised the renovation. Moving historic houses on Long Island has become a local tradition in itself; even the Old House, built in Southold in 1649, was moved in 1660!

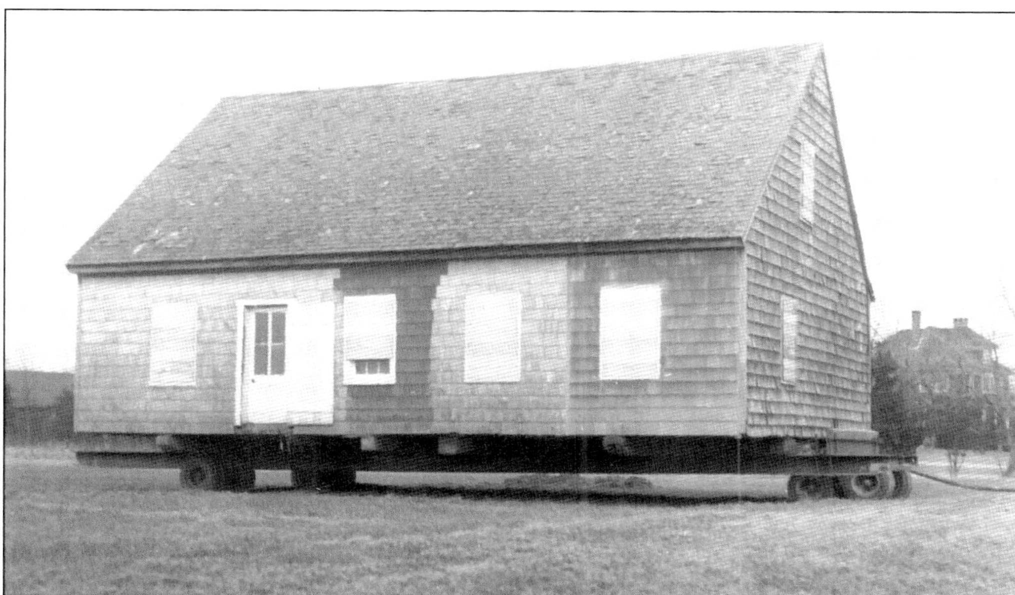

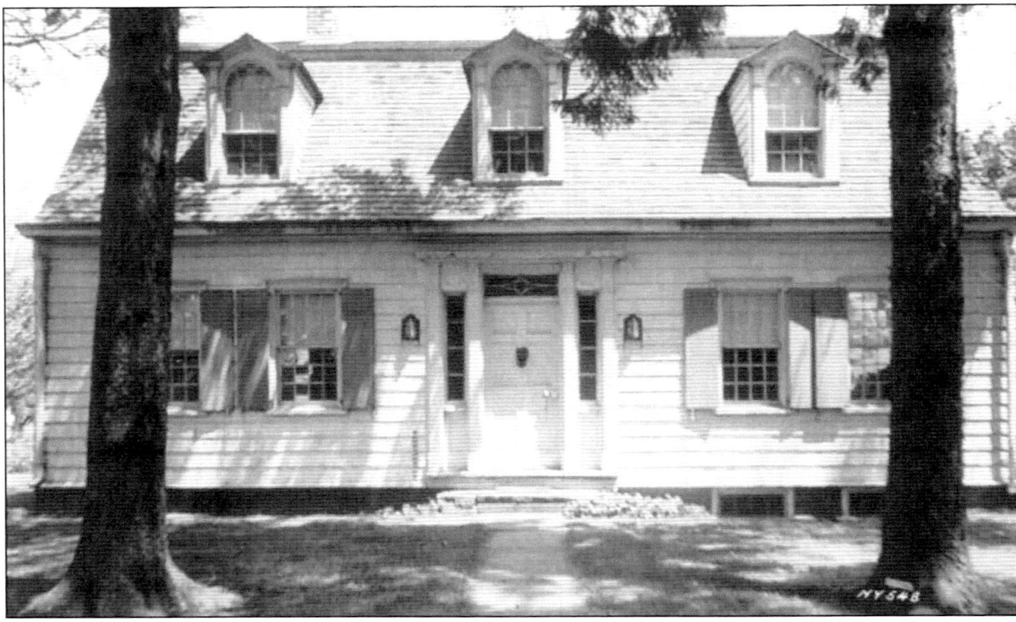

FLEET-GOLDSMITH-KENDRICK HOUSE, 1938. The sophisticated Fleet-Goldsmith-Kendrick House on New Suffolk Road appears stylistically to date from c. 1790, but may be much older, updated in the Federal style. As seen in the above photograph, its elegant center doorway, tall attic dormers, and large 12-over-12 window sashes contrast dramatically with the medieval-style, mid-17th-century Old House nearby. Interior detailing includes refined fireplace mantelpieces with carved fanlike motifs and delicate newel posts and stair railing. The gambrel roof form is typical of Long Island vernacular houses, as is the five-panel door. Both the Fleet and Goldsmith families were among the original Cutchogue settlers, many of whom are now buried in Cutchogue's Old Burying Ground. (Courtesy of Library of Congress, Prints & Photographs Division, HABS, NY-548.)

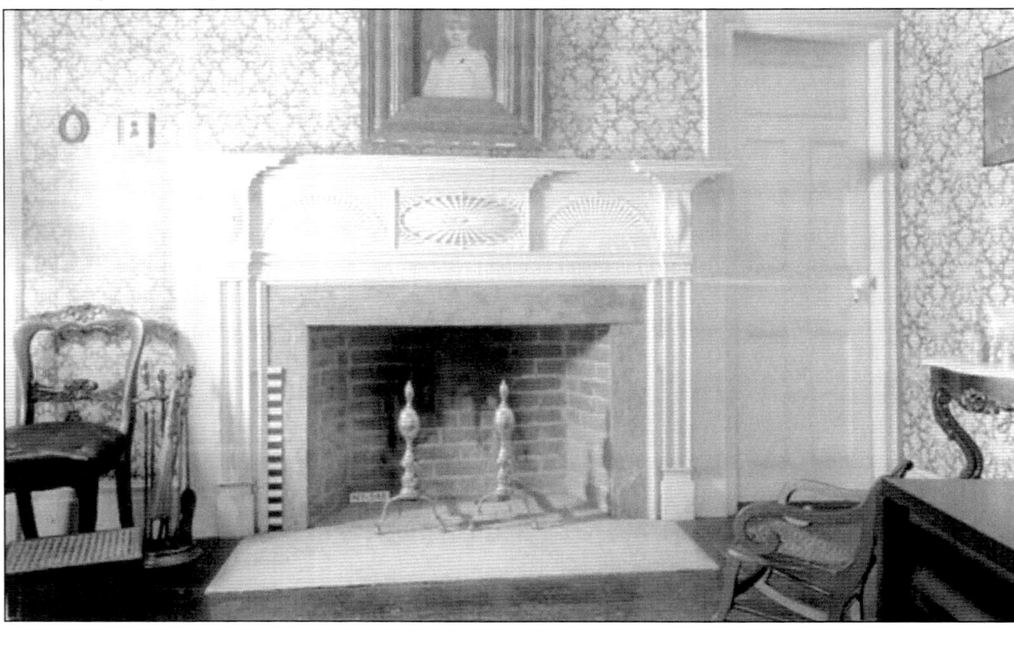

CUTCHOGUE PRESBYTERIAN CHURCH, C. 1900 AND C. 1910. Its steeple soaring high above the Main Road, the Cutchogue Presbyterian Church has been at the heart of village life for centuries. The church was established in 1732, and the present edifice was built and dedicated in 1852. The wood-shingled church is greatly enhanced by its imposing spire (right), which tapers in ever-narrowing stages and incorporates a bronze bell cast at the renowned Meneely Bell Foundry in Troy, New York. The louvered shutters are closed within the windows in this turn-of-the-century view. The interior of the sanctuary (below) boasts a Kilgen pipe organ, first installed in 1905 and replaced in 1948. Stained-glass windows were also installed in 1905, when the nave was enlarged to the north.

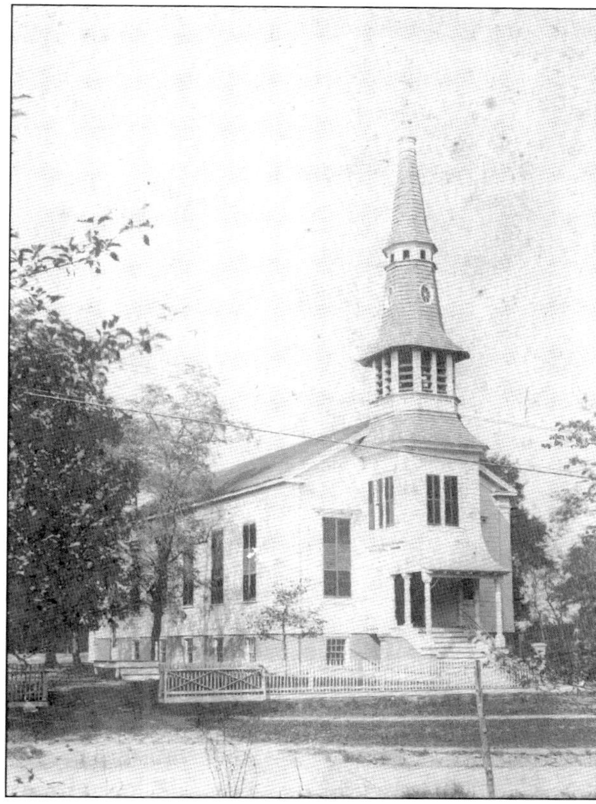

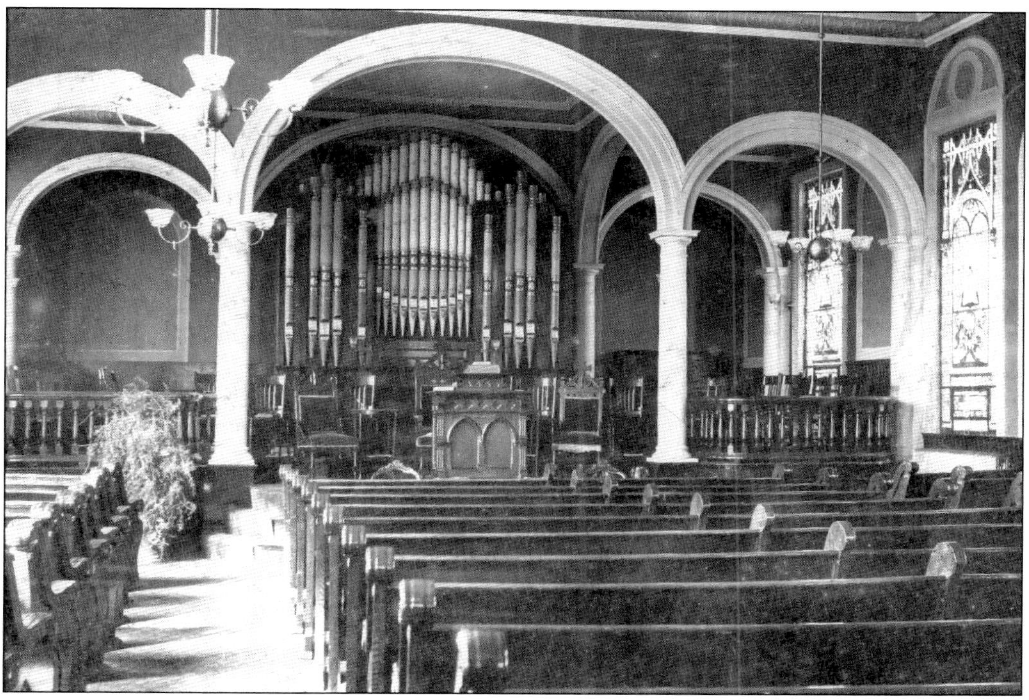

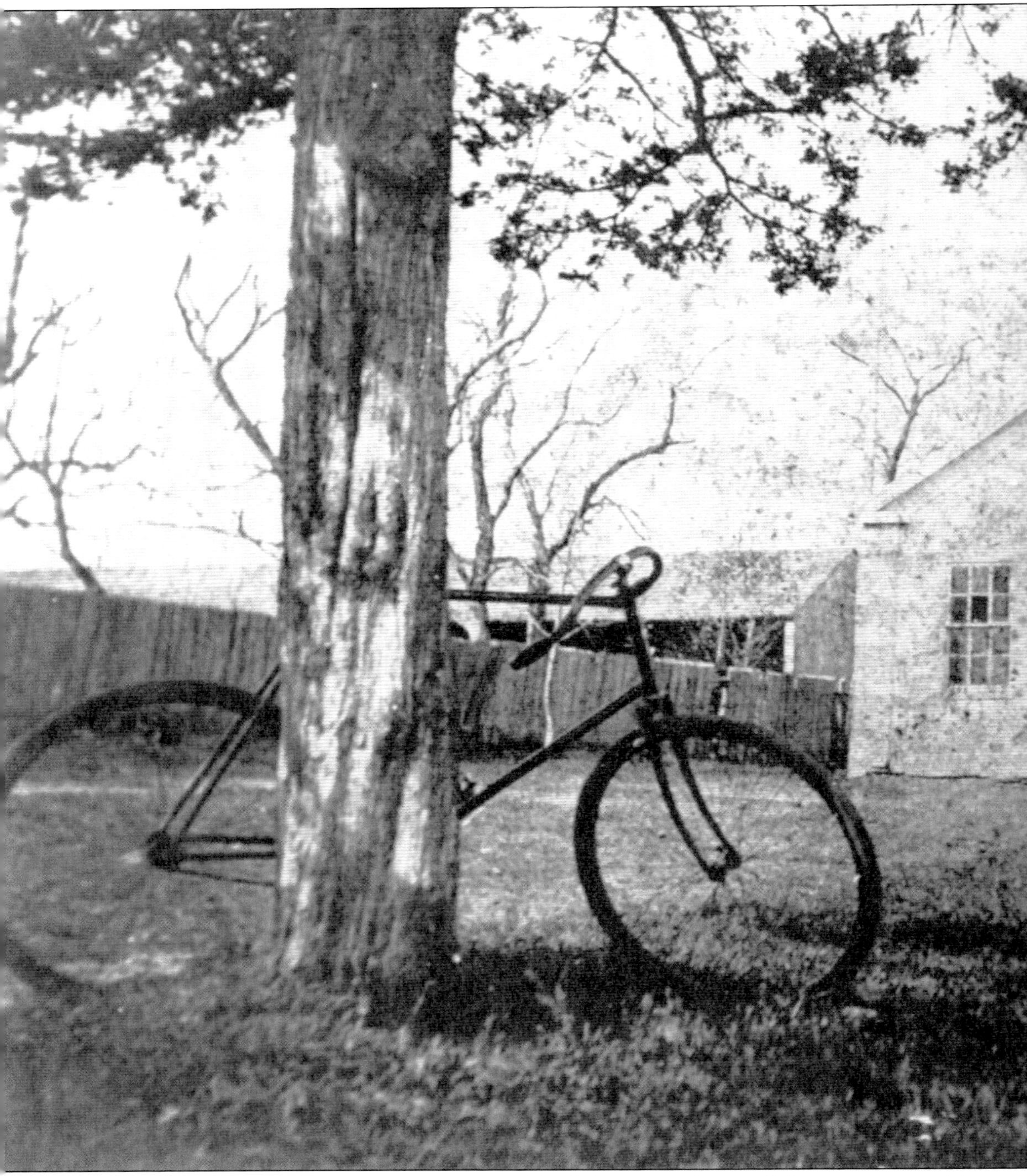

Cutchogue's One-room Schoolhouse, c. 1890. Like many other small farming communities across Long Island, both Cutchogue and New Suffolk were served by one-room schoolhouses in the 19th century, like this one in Cutchogue. The building was located adjacent to the Presbyterian Church on the Main Road. The one-story form, massing, corner pilasters, and entablature above the center doorway indicate a construction date in the Greek Revival period, around 1840. The

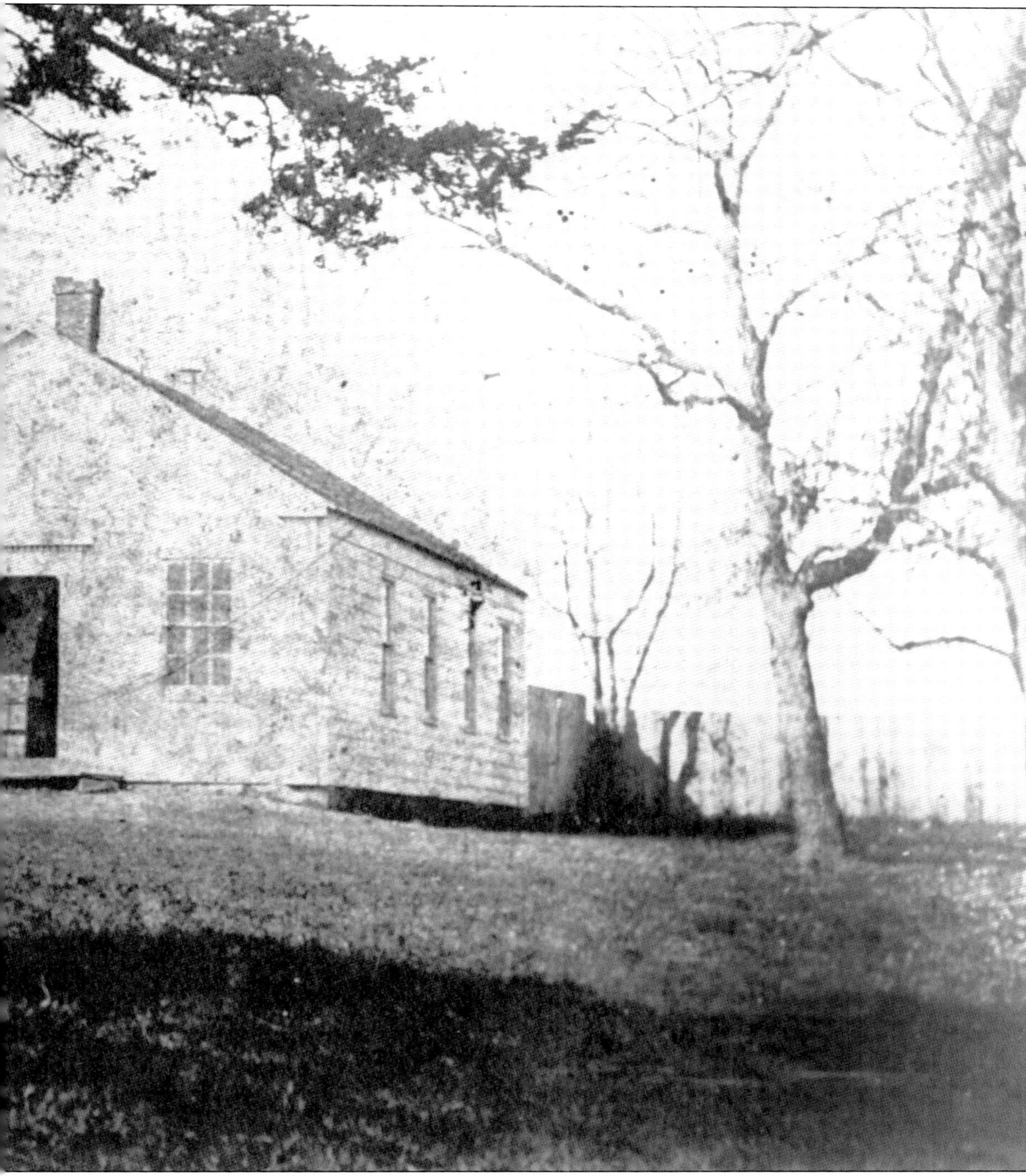

simple rectangular footprint of the building is characteristic of the early schoolhouse form, as are its oversized six-over-six sash windows and tiny brick chimney, which is centered on the ridge. The long wagon shed seen at the rear left behind the fence served the congregants at the adjacent Cutchogue Presbyterian Church. A bicycle, perhaps belonging to the schoolmaster, leans against a tree in the foreground.

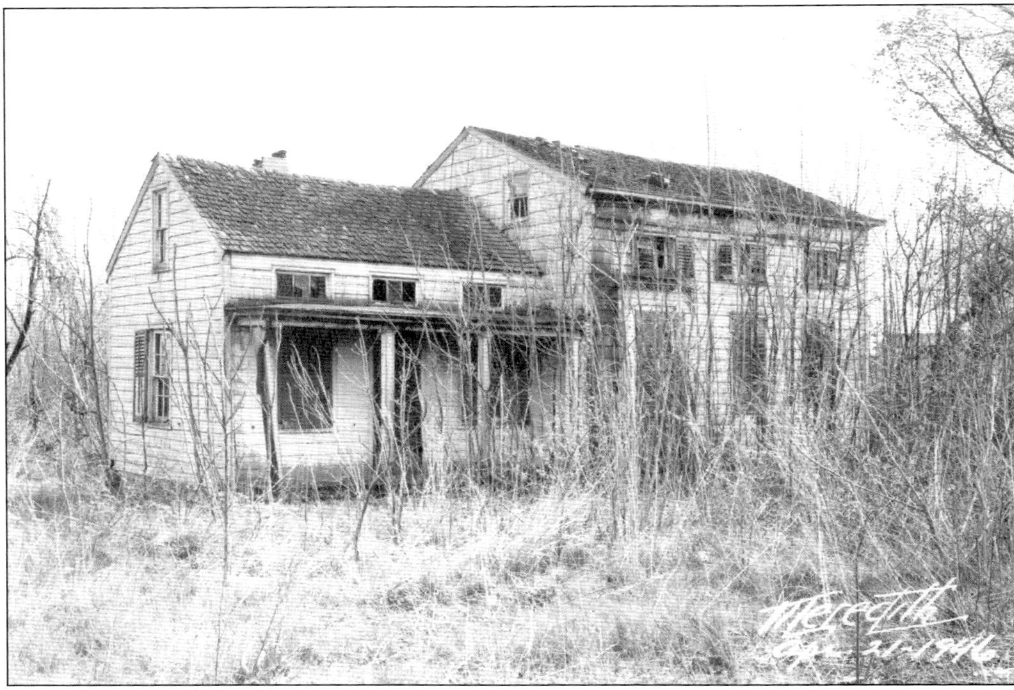

DERELICT HOUSE, CUTCHOGUE VICINITY, APRIL 21, 1946. Charles H. Meredith took this photograph of a deteriorating Greek Revival–era farmhouse in 1946, many years after it began to fall into disrepair. A modest, three-bay "half house" typical of the Long Island farmhouse style, this dwelling was probably built about 1840. By 1946, however, the chimneys had crumbled and it was only a matter of time before the wood frame house would disappear forever.

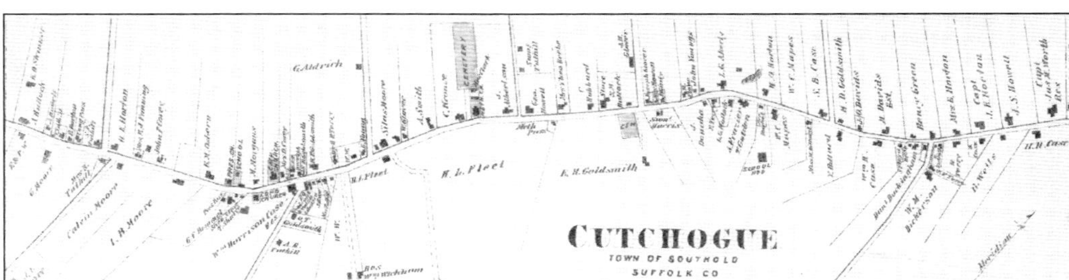

CUTCHOGUE, C. 1873. The linear layout of Cutchogue village was typical of many Long Island farming communities, where the buildings stood on small house lots along main roads close to churches, schoolhouses, and commercial enterprises. In this Beers, Comstock & Cline map detail of 1873, small house lots predominate along the north side of the road, while the larger farms of the wealthier Wickham, Fleet, and Goldsmith families stretch to the south.

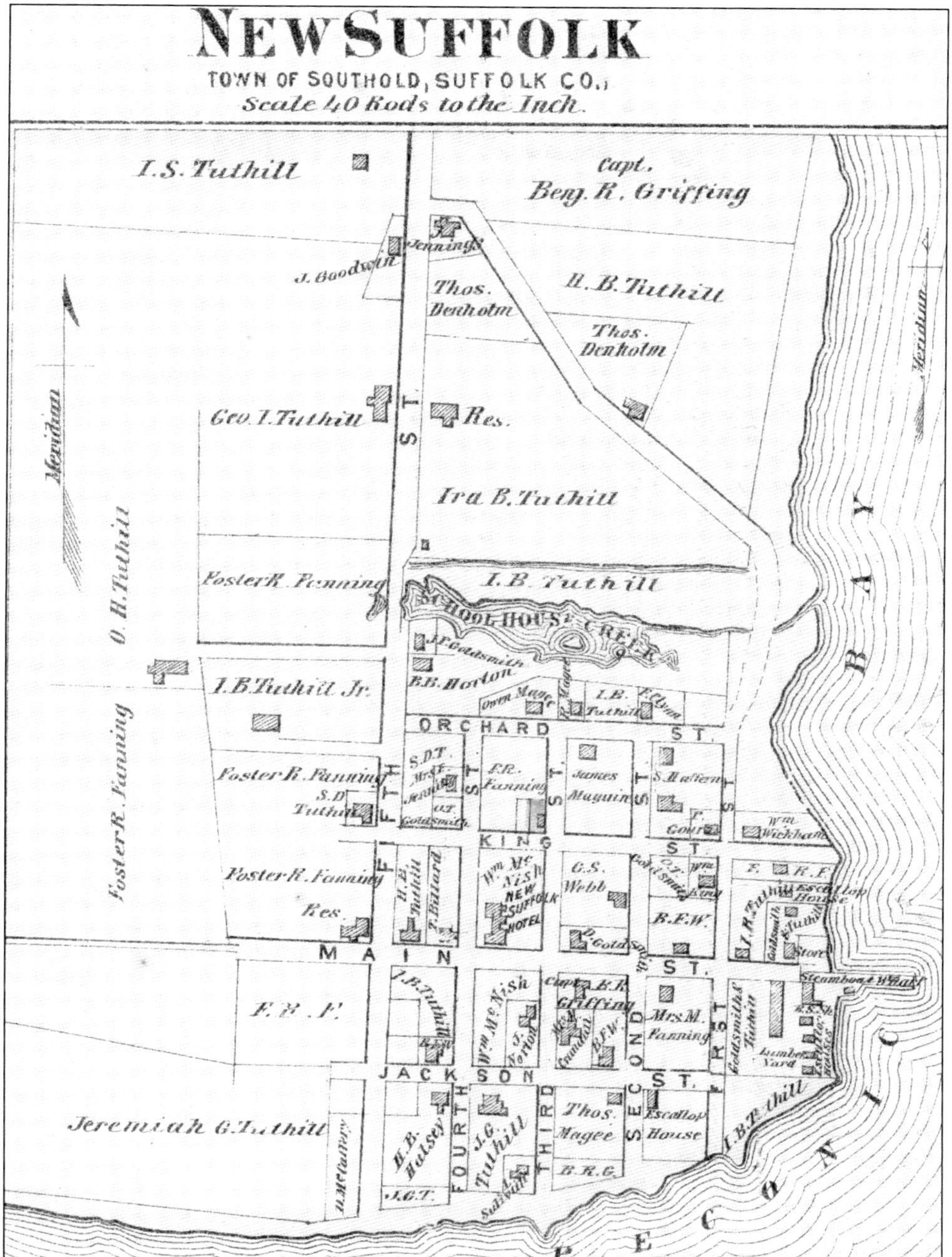

New Suffolk, c. 1873. In contrast to Cutchogue, the neighboring village of New Suffolk, laid out in 1836 by the Reverend Ezra Young and three Tuthill brothers, Abiel, Isaac, and Ira, followed a more regular plan, as seen in this Beers, Comstock & Cline map detail of 1873. Having purchased a large waterfront property from Josiah Albertson, the town planners laid out a new community with parallel, numbered avenues running south to the bay. The perpendicular streets—Jackson (named for Pres. Andrew Jackson), Main, King, and Orchard—formed a regular grid, establishing an unusual but orderly plan for this farming region.

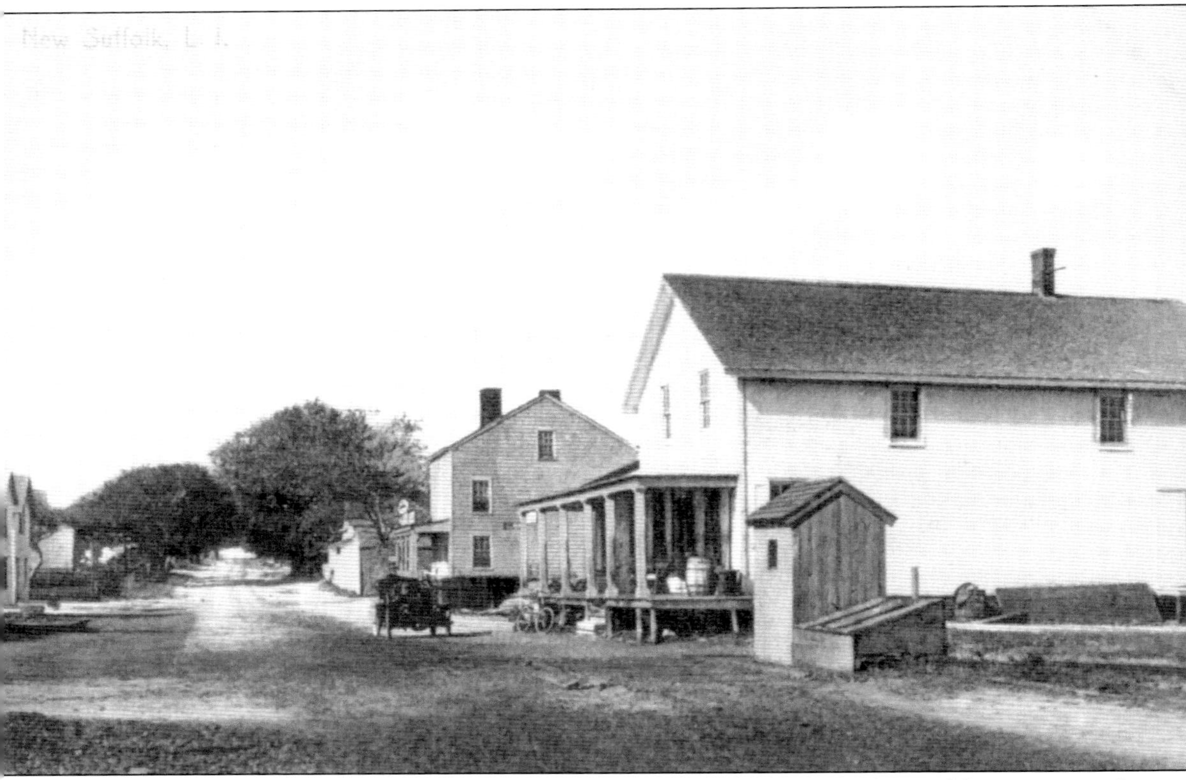

NEW SUFFOLK, C. 1925. As New Suffolk's fortunes and population grew, the need for services, such as a dry-goods store and a post office, became apparent. Ira Tuthill (1803–1898), always a driving force in New Suffolk's growth, built them all. Goldsmith & Tuthill's post office and store on Main Street remain standing in this postcard view from around 1925. Ira Tuthill built his first New Suffolk store and ship chandlery around 1836, and, after a fire destroyed it in 1872, a new one rose from the ashes within the year. Ira's only known disappointment was the grove of mulberry trees that he had introduced to feed silkworms for manufacturing silk. The enterprise did not prove financially feasible and was abandoned. Ira also built a shipyard, which proved more successful. After building whale ships in the 19th century, the shipyard turned to pleasure craft in the 20th century and continued operating into the 1950s.

PUBLIC LIBRARY, C. 1930. The Cutchogue–New Suffolk Free Library is housed in the old Independent Congregational Society church building, constructed in 1862 after the congregants split with the Presbyterian Church across the road. By 1913, the churches reunited and the building was rented out as a library. Ever since, the library has occupied this early example of "adaptive reuse" of a historic structure, a concept that was decades ahead of its time.

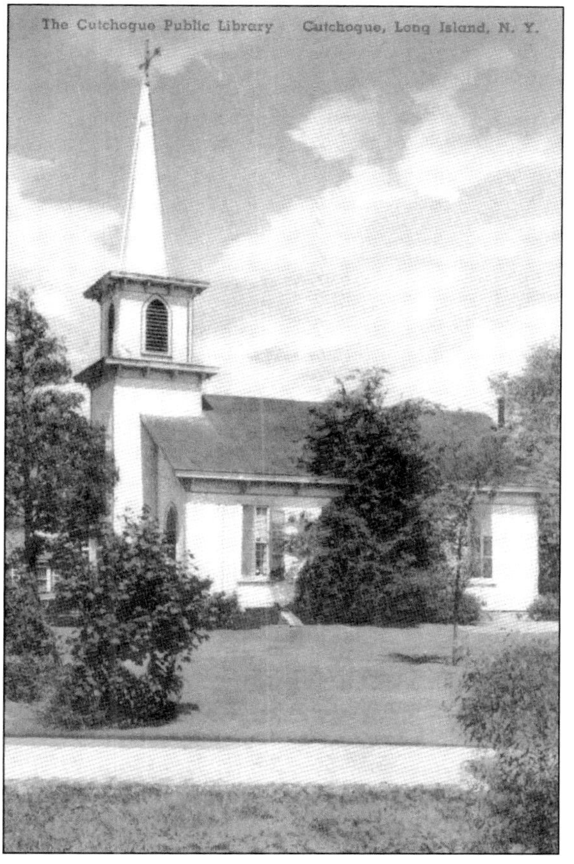

SACRED HEART CHURCH AND RECTORY, C. 1910. Organized as a mission of St. Patrick's Roman Catholic Church in Southold by Rev. John McKenna in 1878, Sacred Heart became an independent parish in 1901 under Rev. James H. Lynch. Father Lynch was also founder and president of the Cutchogue Ice Company. He was succeeded by Rev. John B. Lyle. The wood frame church, with its overhanging eaves, hammer beam detailing, and belfry, remains a Cutchogue landmark.

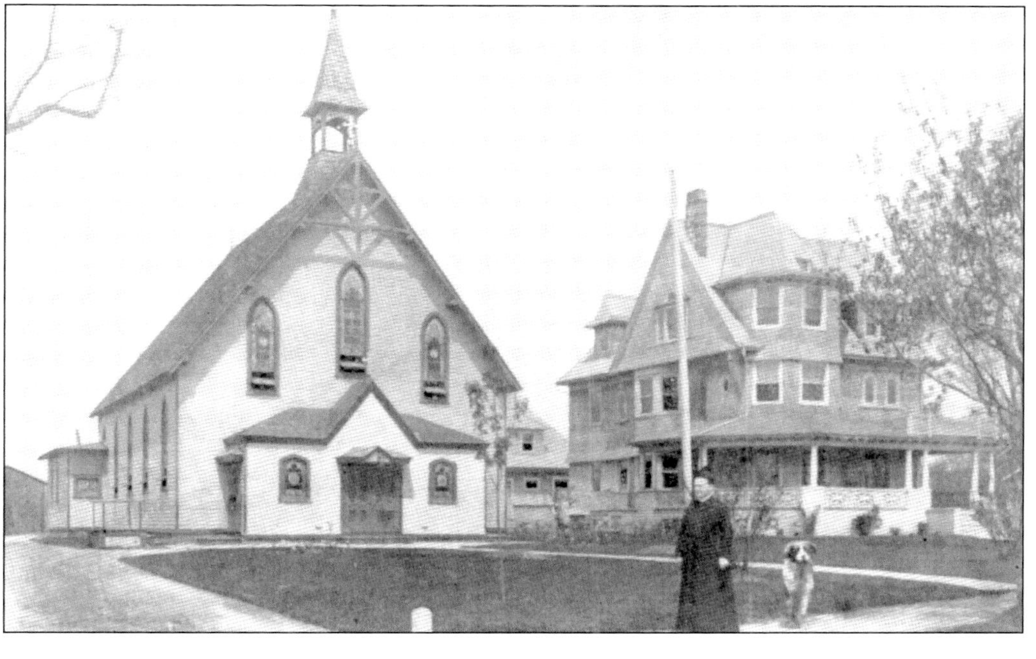

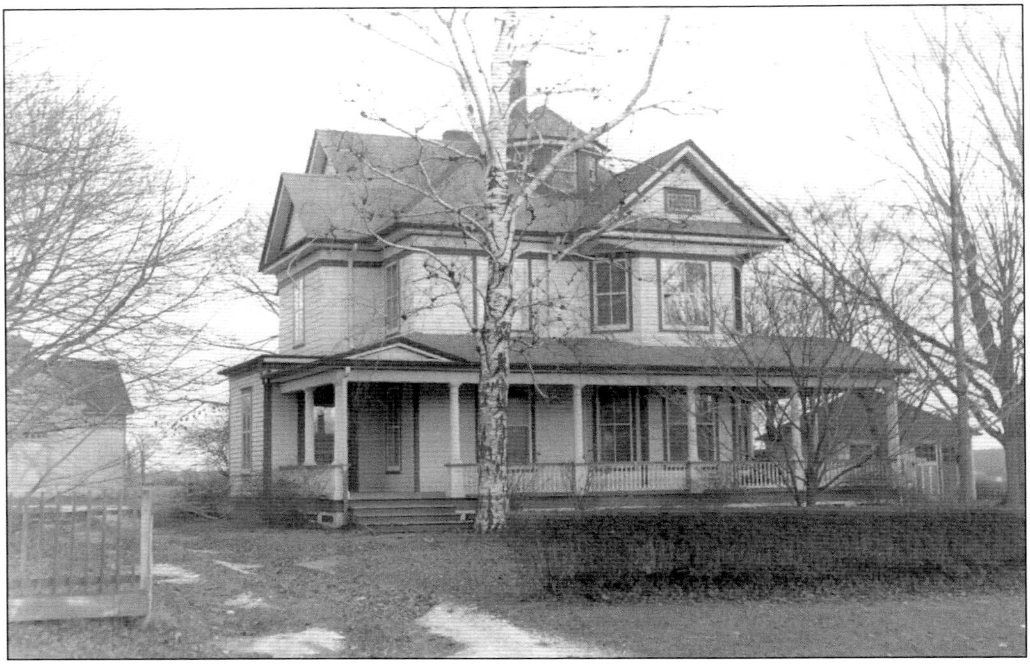

ADULT HOME, CUTCHOGUE, C. 1950. Across the country, large Victorian farmhouses like this one found a new purpose by the middle of the 20th century as "rest homes" or group residences. The house shown here, formerly the Goldsmith-Blashack residence, on New Suffolk Road, retains its Victorian barn. Mrs. Blashack opened the rest home in the 1960s, which is now operated as the Peconic Retreat Home.

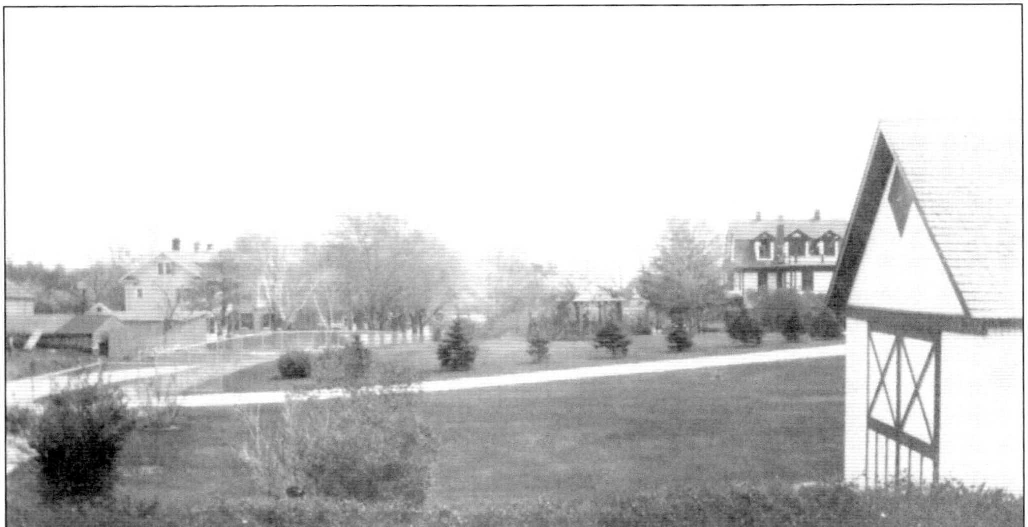

J. BENEDICT ROACHE HOUSE, NEW SUFFOLK, C. 1920. The Victorian-era Roache House (right background) was located at Fifth Avenue and New Suffolk Avenue. It was built as a summer home for J. Benedict Roache and his wife, Laura J., whose father, Hugh McLaughlin, was a Democratic leader in Brooklyn in the late 1800s. Roache was a wealthy shipbuilder from Brooklyn, and his family was active in the Sacred Heart Church of Cutchogue.

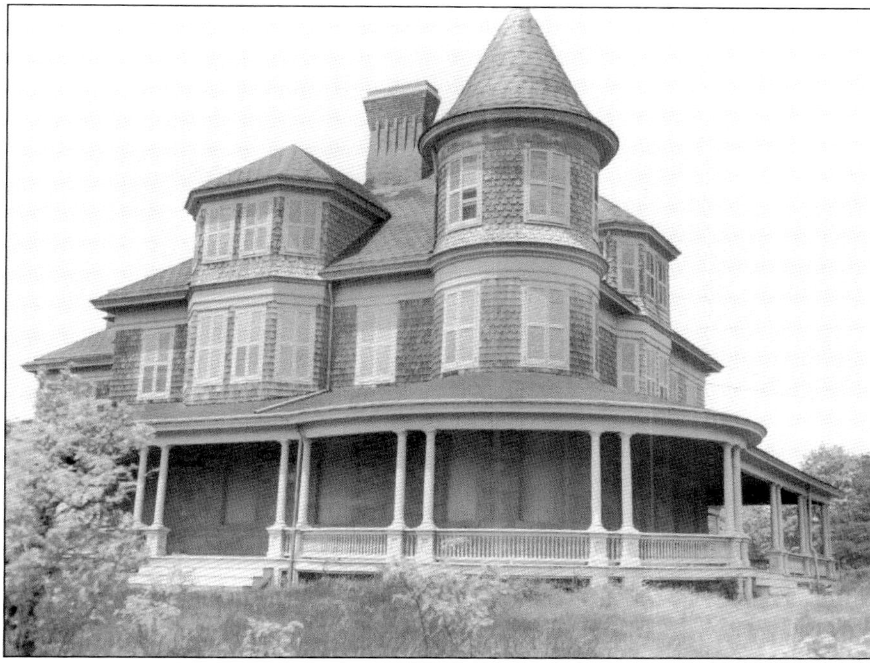

LOEW AND HATHAWAY HOUSES, c. 1945. By the turn of the century, a new generation of affluent homeowners arrived in New Suffolk. These seasonal residents built year-round homes in the late 1800s that boasted towers, turrets, and ample porches to catch the bay breezes. In the above photograph, the Loew House is shown shuttered, its shingled tower and assertive window bays rising above the stone first floor. Judge Loew and his family were wealthy New Yorkers and world travelers, but after the judge's death in 1909, the state of the house declined, and it was demolished in 1972. The sprawling Hathaway House (below) on Old Harbor Lane was built in 1896 overlooking Peconic Bay. Its blend of architectural features disguises the large gambrel-roofed block that harkens back to historic Long Island houses. It was demolished in 1957; all that remains today are the brick icehouse, gateposts, and barn.

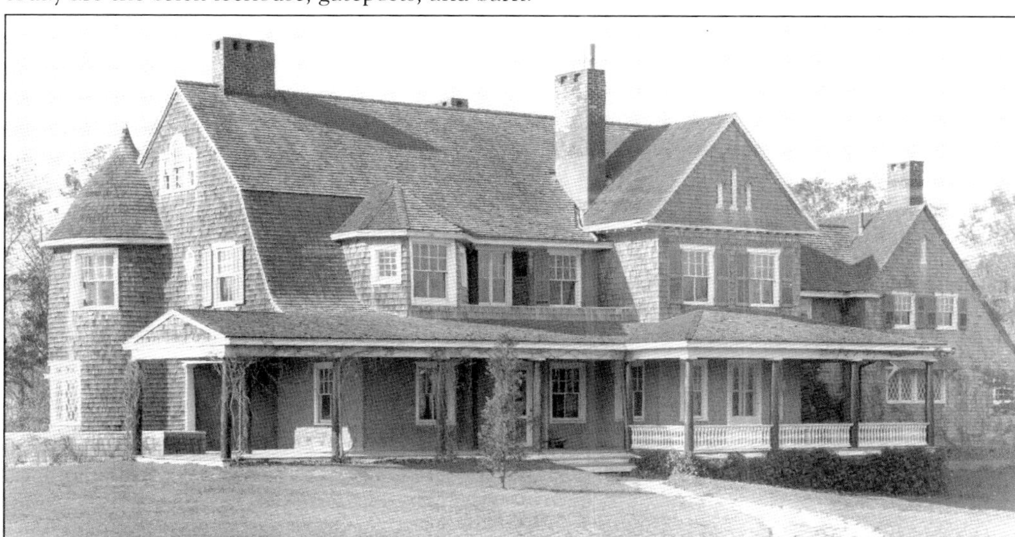

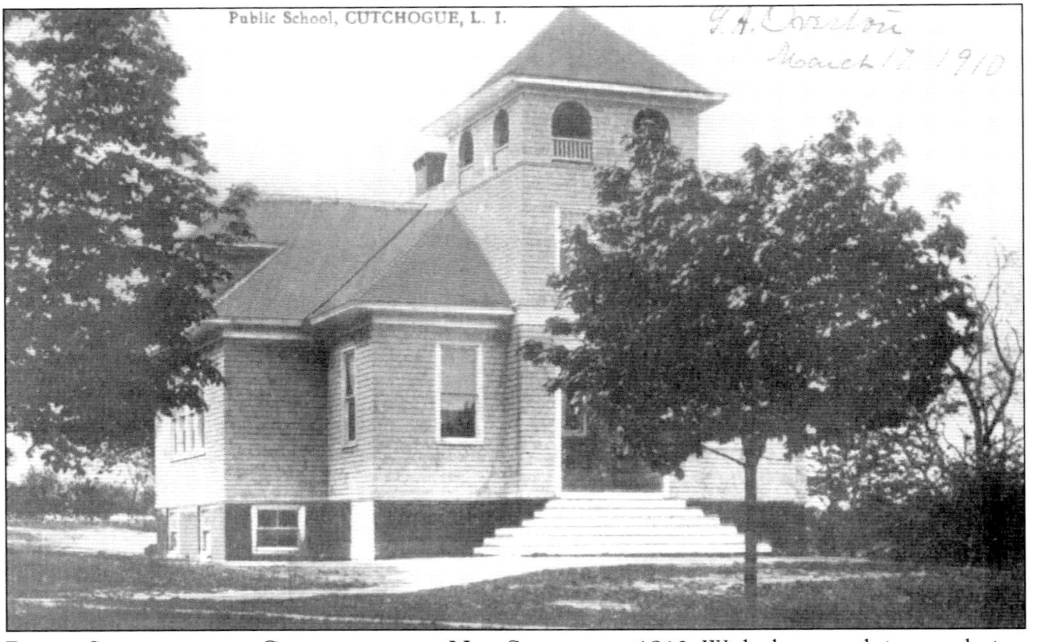

PUBLIC SCHOOLHOUSES, CUTCHOGUE AND NEW SUFFOLK, C. 1910. With the growth in population in the late 19th century came the need to expand public services, including the construction of schoolhouses. The modern, shingle-clad Cutchogue school (above) was built around 1903 on the site of the old one-room schoolhouse and featured an open bell tower and cruciform plan accommodating two large classrooms. The tradition of using oversized windows persisted from the earlier days of schoolhouse construction. More compact than its companion in Cutchogue, the New Suffolk schoolhouse (below) was built in 1907 to replace an earlier one-room schoolhouse. Separate entrances were provided for boys and girls, and its bronze bell could be heard throughout the village. The symmetrical, shingled building with oversized windows was typical of the day's schoolhouse architecture.

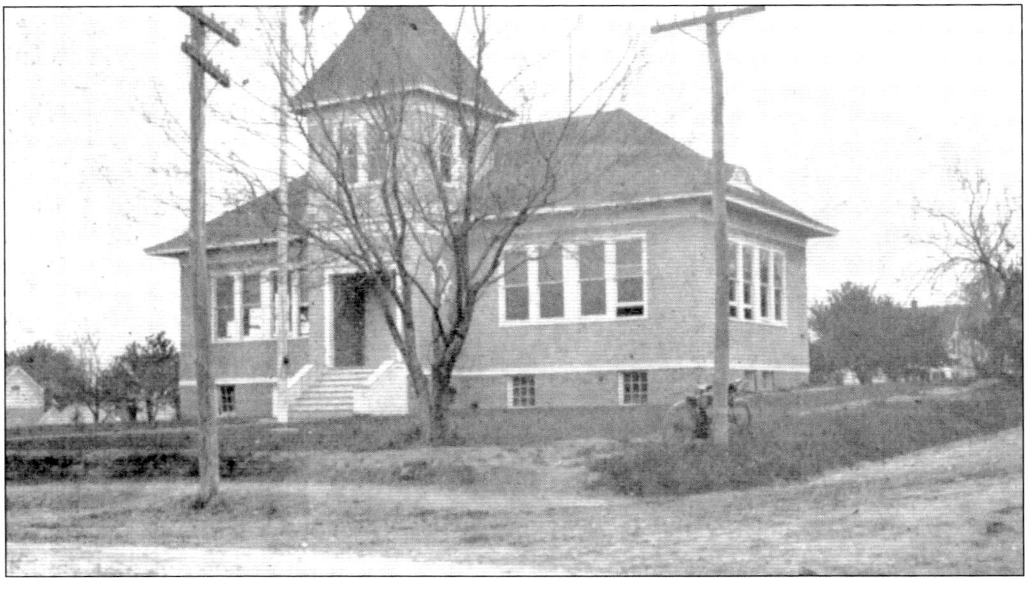

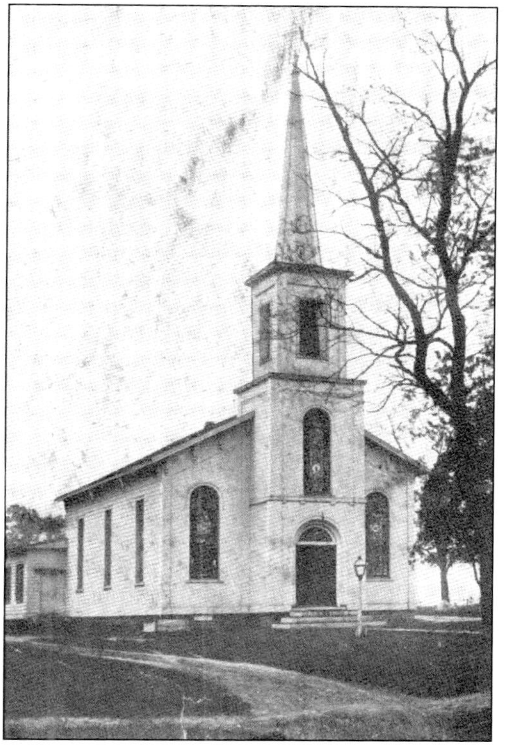

METHODIST EPISCOPAL CHURCH, C. 1910 AND C. 1928. The first Methodist Episcopal Church in Cutchogue was organized in 1829, but the original edifice (right) was consumed by fire in 1928. Traditional in style and boasting an open belfry surmounted by a classically designed front portico, the new First Methodist Church of Cutchogue is shown under construction around 1928 (below). S. Edgar Tuthill, builder (at left), and fellow workman Sherwood Beebe stand on the front steps. After fire destroyed its older sanctuary, the Methodist congregation found temporary quarters by renting the Congregational Society's church building up the road, then in use as the public library. After construction of the new church was completed, the Cutchogue–New Suffolk Free Library resumed its operations, where it remains today, adjacent the Village Green.

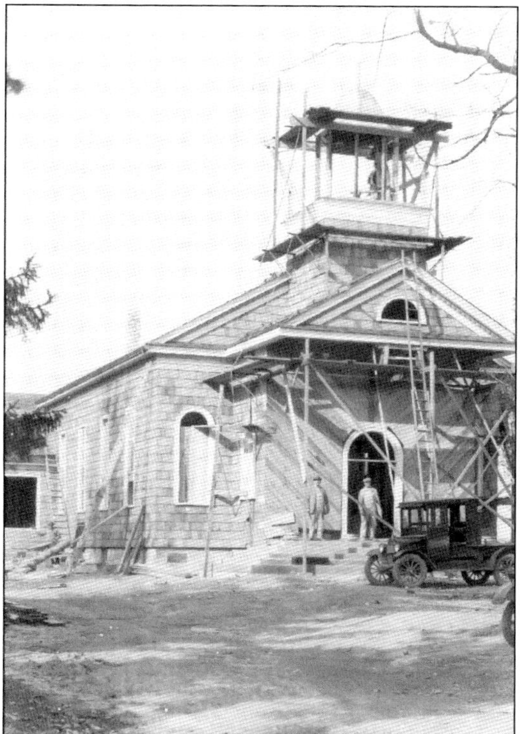

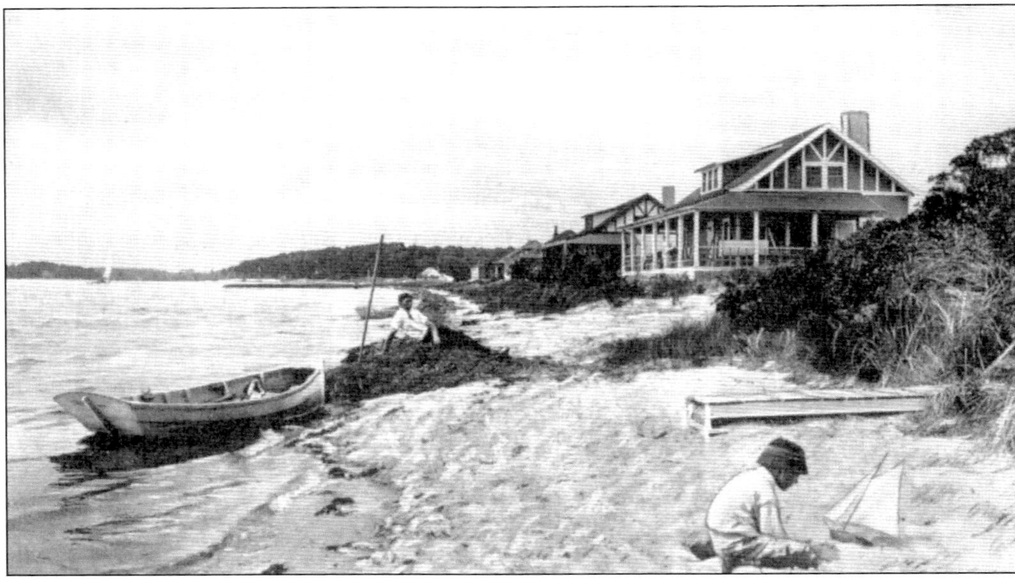

Kimogenor Point Bungalow Colony, Peconic Bay. Clusters or "colonies" of vacation cottages became increasingly popular in the early decades of the 1900s, when city dwellers sought relief from the summer heat. Kimogenor Point was one such vacation destination, the brainchild of Stuart H. Moore and Beverly S. King, who purchased a stretch of beachfront property in New Suffolk in 1900 for the purpose of creating a summer colony. Deriving its name by scrambling the letters of "Moore" and "King," the colony's 11 cottages consisted of six to nine rooms each. By 1920, the Kimogenor Point Company was formed by some of the Brooklyn families who had rented the cottages in previous summers. Despite later additions and improvements, many of the buildings are preserved today and remain in the ownership of the original families.

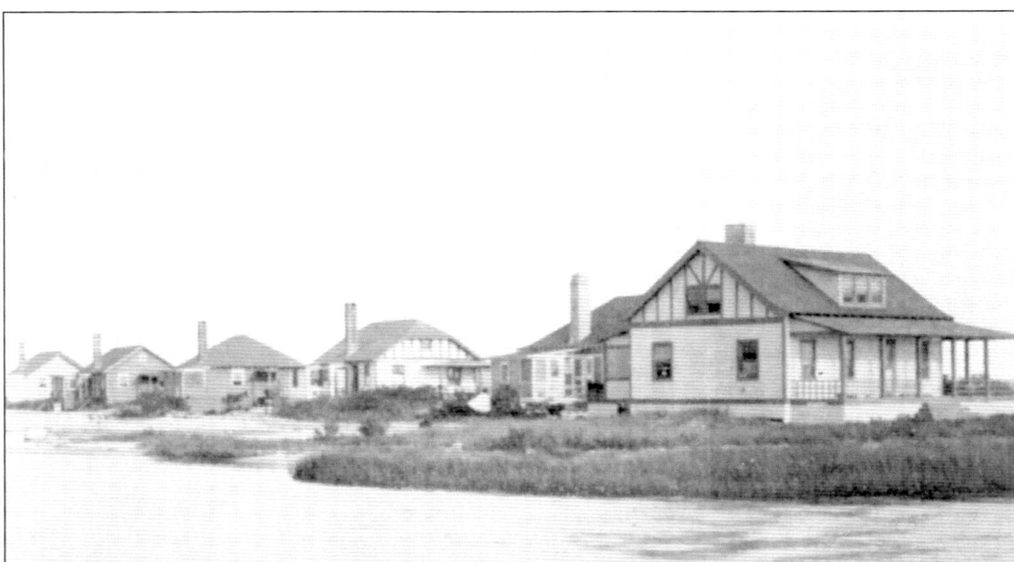

OUR LADY OF OSTRABRAMA CHURCH, C. 1940. Begun in 1909 and dedicated in 1920, Our Lady of Ostrabrama Church (right) is the product of the immigration of Polish farmhands who entered the local workforce at the turn of the 20th century. Venerated as Our Lady of the Gate of Dawn in Vilnius, Lithuania, the popular Renaissance-era image of the Virgin Mary ("Our Lady of Ostrabrama") inspired pilgrimages and parishes of the faithful throughout the world. The Cutchogue church was restored in 1993, and its congregation maintains strong ties with the old country. The interior of the church (below), with its elaborate stained-glass window flanked by frescoes and carved angels in full relief, provides a striking contrast with the austere, stuccoed walls of the exterior. (Courtesy of the Southold Historical Society.)

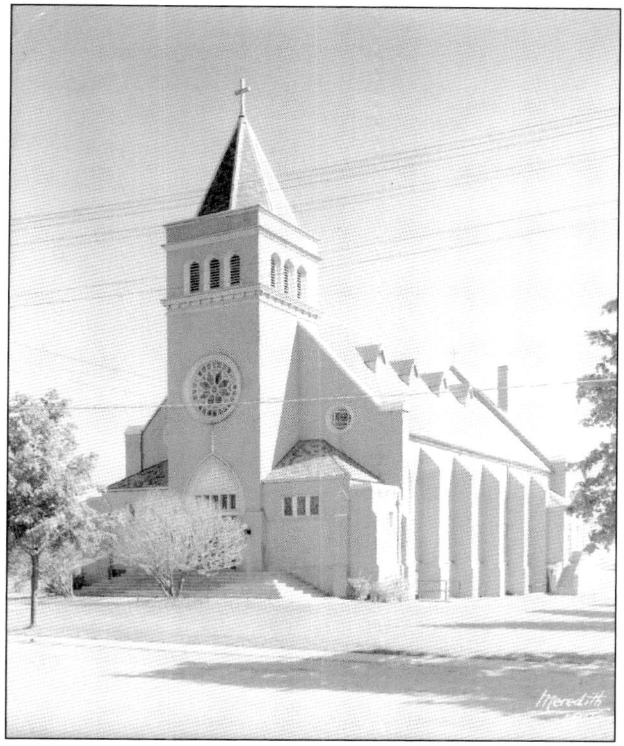

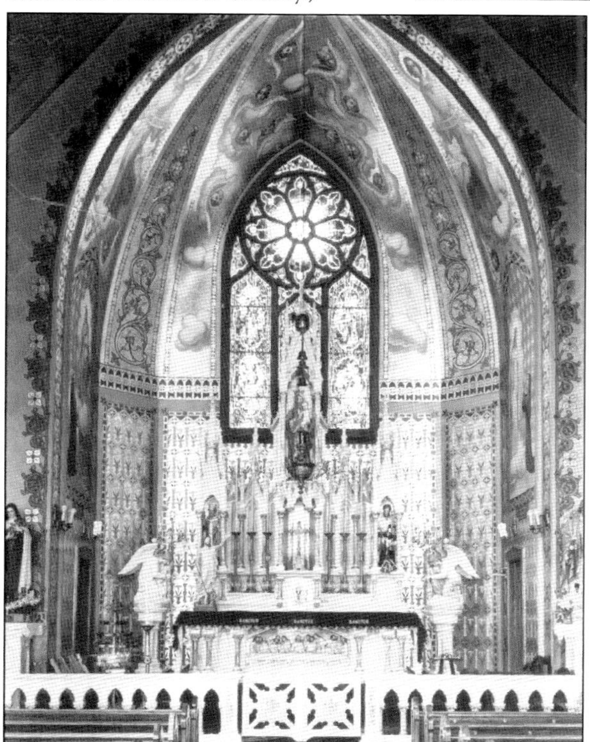

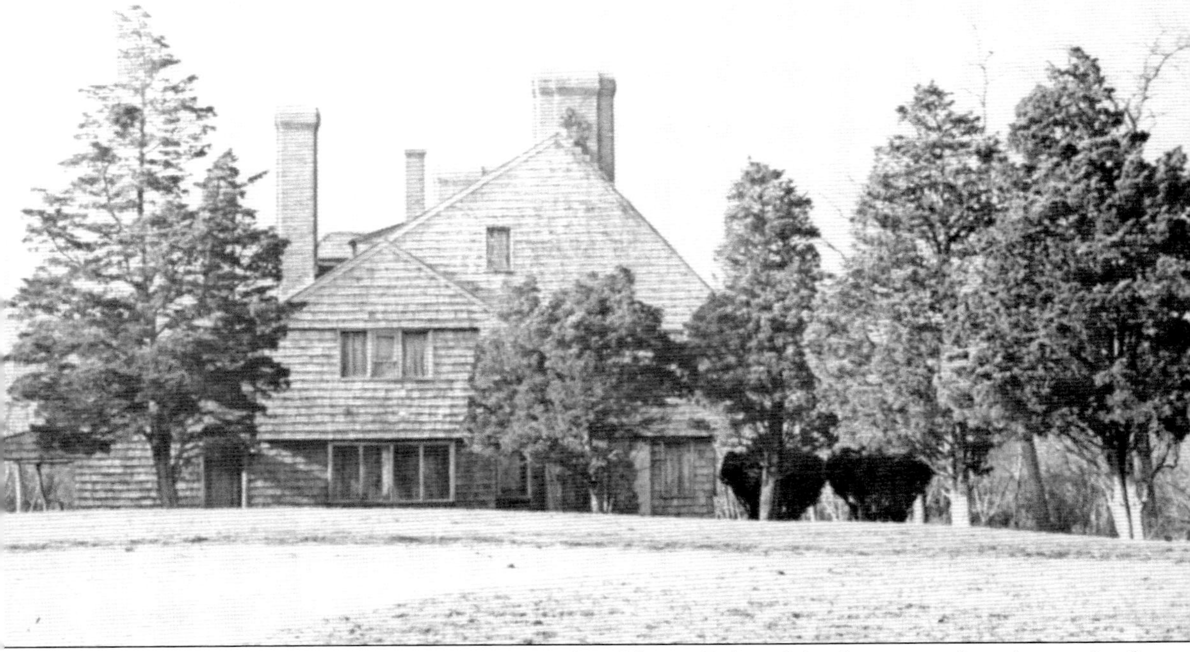

LANE HOUSE, ROBINS ISLAND, C. 1930. The 435-acre Robins Island is situated to the south of New Suffolk in Peconic Bay. It was named in a deed from King Charles I to William Alexander, Earl of Stirling, in 1615. The island was confiscated during the Revolutionary War from loyalist Parker Wickham and was later bought by New Suffolk founder Ira B. Tuthill, who set up a brickyard there. A sportsmen's club was established on the island in the late 19th century, and a large clubhouse was built to accommodate urban patrons. James W. Lane and his wife, Eva Bliss, purchased Robins Island in 1917 and began construction of a summer house there in 1919. Sadly, Eva died soon thereafter, and construction on the house was halted indefinitely.

Two

On Land and Sea

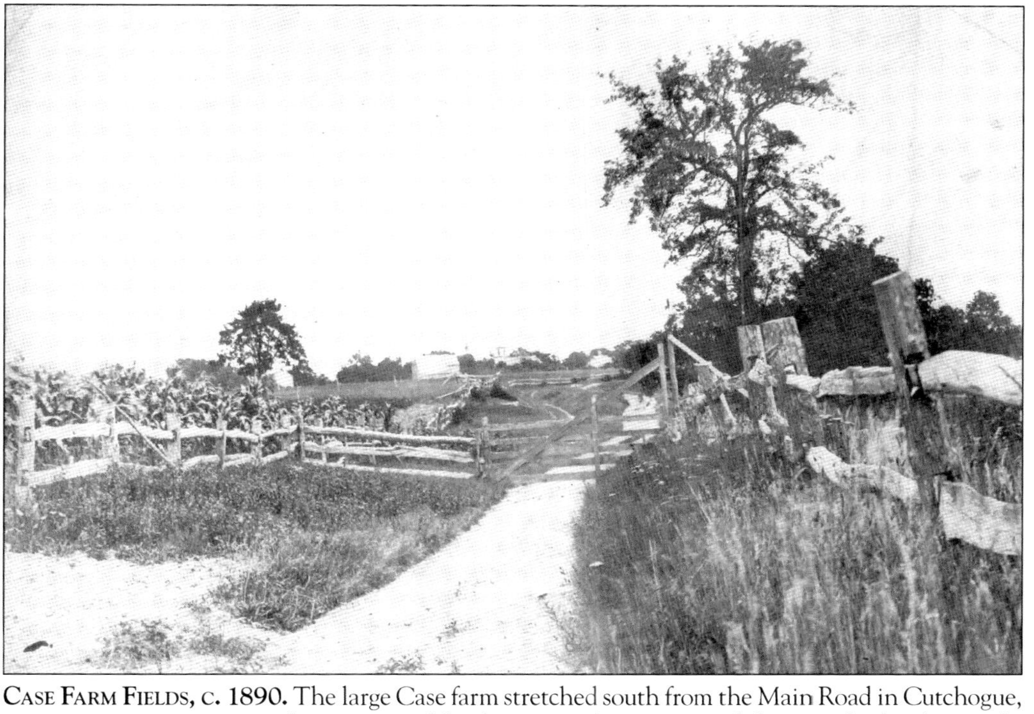

Case Farm Fields, c. 1890. The large Case farm stretched south from the Main Road in Cutchogue, encompassing many acres that supported food crops, such as corn, and sheep and other livestock. This bucolic view looks north along a country lane bordered by fields and split rail fences, toward the Case barn at the center and the spires of Cutchogue's two churches in the distance.

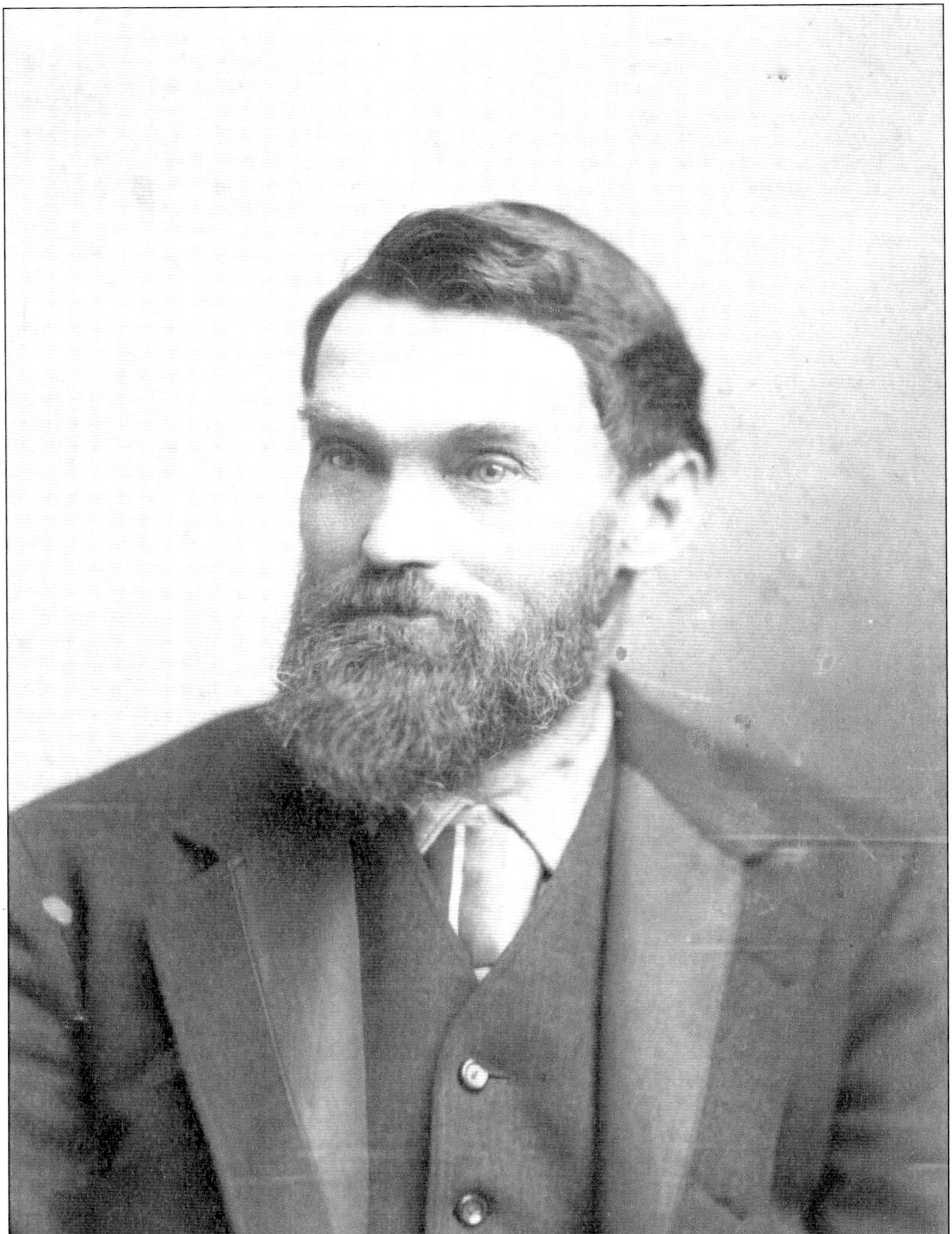

HENRY L. FLEET, C. 1880. By the mid-19th century, an elite group of Cutchogue farmers found a ready market in metropolitan New York that translated into big profits at home. Henry Landon Fleet (1832–1894) was the most celebrated of them all. He descended from William Wells, an early settler, and owned more than 350 acres overlooking Peconic Bay. He and his sons also bred and trained racehorses. (Courtesy of a private collection.)

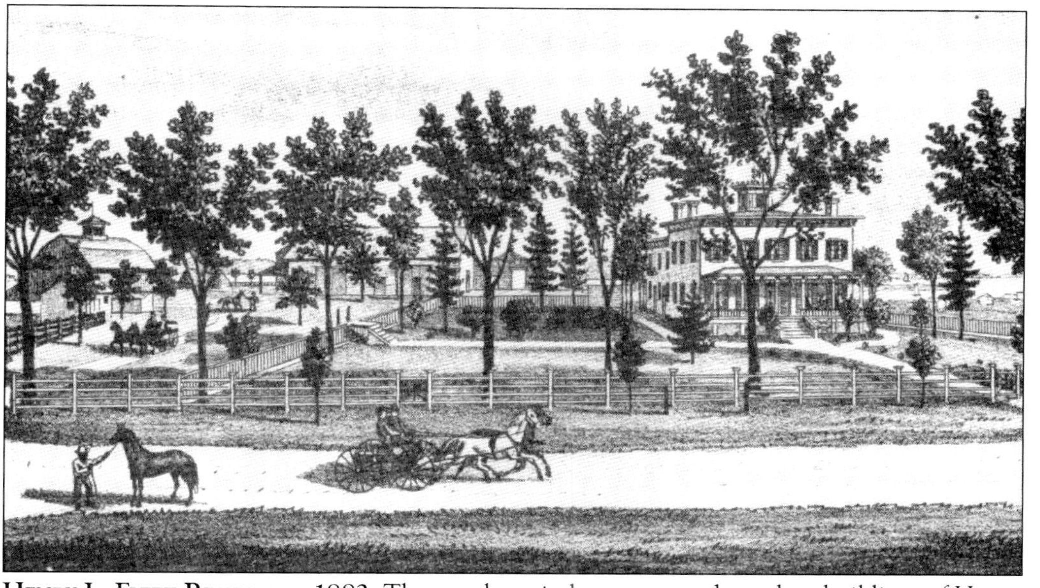

Henry L. Fleet Residence, 1883. The stately main house, grounds, and outbuildings of Henry L. Fleet's country estate were illustrated in W.W. Munsell's *History of Suffolk County, Long Island*, published in New York in 1883 (above). The large residence boasted two pairs of chimneys and a cupola or belvedere centered on the flat, bracketed roof. A broad front porch sits elevated above the lawn, while orderly picket and rail fences surround both the house and adjoining paddocks. Some of Fleet's award-winning trotters are featured in the drawing. While his fine Italianate Revival house (below) was demolished in the mid-20th century, the gambrel-roofed barn remains, along with a portion of Henry L. Fleet's trotting course, which survives today as Track Avenue on Pequash Neck. (Courtesy of a private collection.)

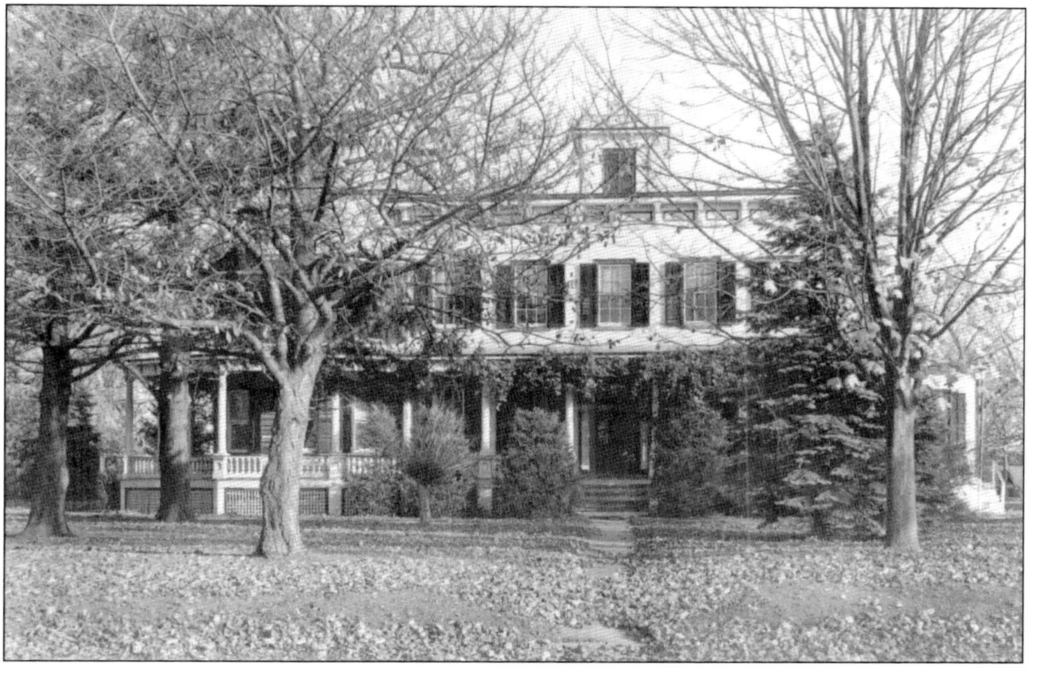

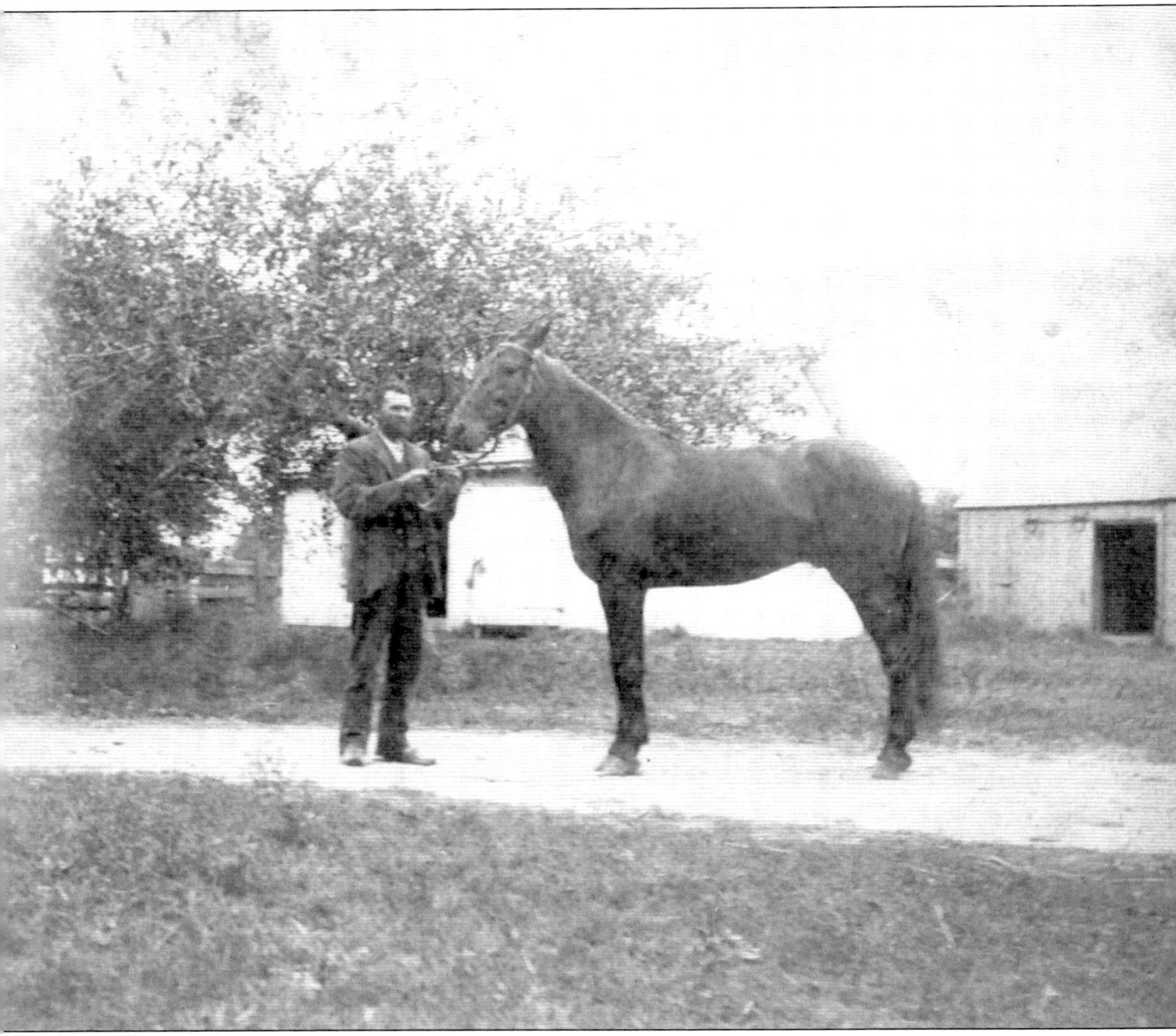

HENRY FLEET AND HORSE, C. 1880. After establishing a profitable farm in the mid-19th century, Fleet turned his attention from growing potatoes, cauliflower, oats, and other traditional crops to pursuing a new career: horse breeding. One of his stallions, Fleet's Hambletonian, was a famous trotter in its day, and Fleet's farm was well known for its superior horse breeding and training. Henry Fleet maintained his own driving course and a stock of superior young horses, and he managed and trained the colts and horses of other owners. He was a lineal descendant of the first William Fleet, one of the most prominent settlers of Southold Town in 1640. His family continued to operate the horse-breeding and training farm until well into the 20th century. (Courtesy of a private collection.)

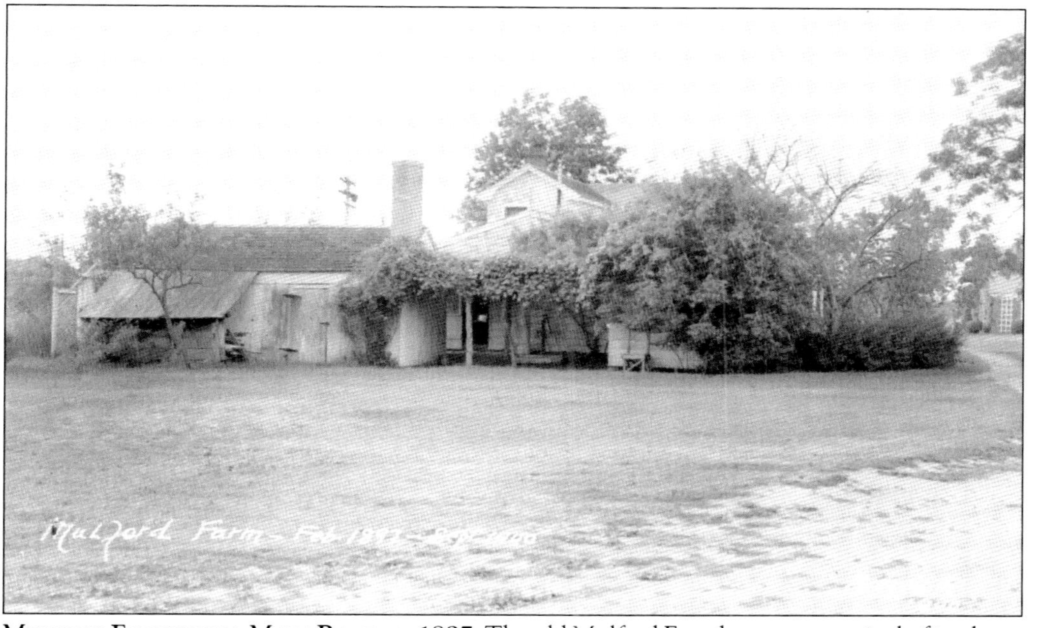

MULFORD FARMHOUSE, MAIN ROAD, C. 1897. The old Mulford Farmhouse was typical of its day, a framed and wood-shingled main house surrounded by later additions and a grape arbor that clung to the back porch. The summer kitchen is seen at the left, with its characteristically over-scaled brick chimney. (Courtesy of James F. Grathwohl.)

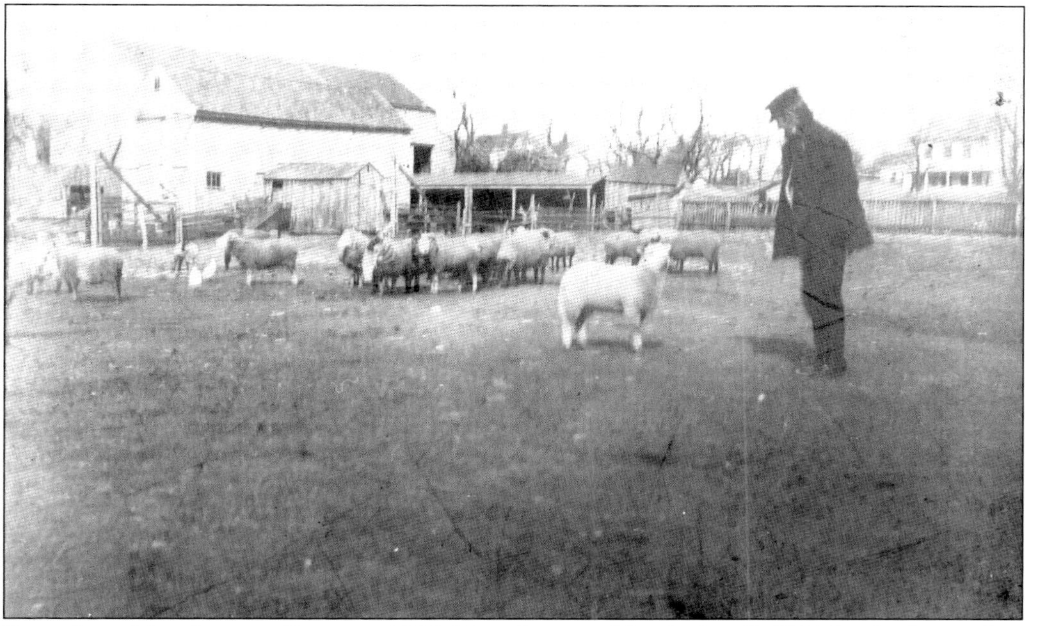

SHEEP LOT, NEW SUFFOLK ROAD, C. 1900. Now the site of the Cedars Golf Club, which stretches from Case's Lane to New Suffolk Road, the "sheep lot" was part of the large Case family farm, where sheep and goats were raised for generations. The old barns, pens, and accessory structures were typical of an agrarian lifestyle that quickly disappeared in the early 1900s with the advent of mechanized farming.

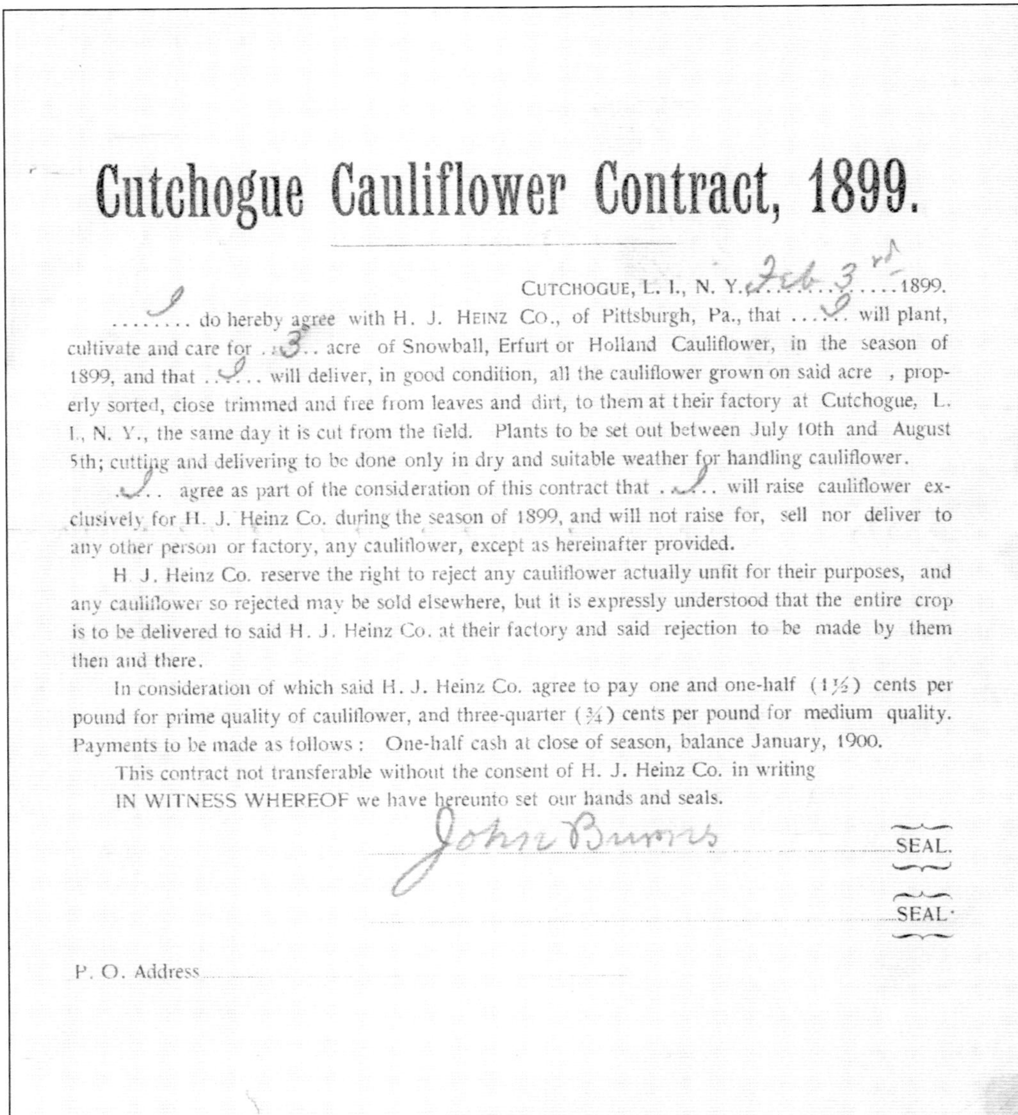

Cutchogue Cauliflower Contract, 1899.

CUTCHOGUE, L. I., N. Y. Feb 3rd 1899.

I do hereby agree with H. J. HEINZ CO., of Pittsburgh, Pa., that I will plant, cultivate and care for 3 acre of Snowball, Erfurt or Holland Cauliflower, in the season of 1899, and that I will deliver, in good condition, all the cauliflower grown on said acre, properly sorted, close trimmed and free from leaves and dirt, to them at their factory at Cutchogue, L. I., N. Y., the same day it is cut from the field. Plants to be set out between July 10th and August 5th; cutting and delivering to be done only in dry and suitable weather for handling cauliflower.

I agree as part of the consideration of this contract that I will raise cauliflower exclusively for H. J. Heinz Co. during the season of 1899, and will not raise for, sell nor deliver to any other person or factory, any cauliflower, except as hereinafter provided.

H. J. Heinz Co. reserve the right to reject any cauliflower actually unfit for their purposes, and any cauliflower so rejected may be sold elsewhere, but it is expressly understood that the entire crop is to be delivered to said H. J. Heinz Co. at their factory and said rejection to be made by them then and there.

In consideration of which said H. J. Heinz Co. agree to pay one and one-half (1½) cents per pound for prime quality of cauliflower, and three-quarter (¾) cents per pound for medium quality. Payments to be made as follows: One-half cash at close of season, balance January, 1900.

This contract not transferable without the consent of H. J. Heinz Co. in writing

IN WITNESS WHEREOF we have hereunto set our hands and seals.

John Burns SEAL.

SEAL.

P. O. Address

CUTCHOGUE CAULIFLOWER CONTRACT, 1899. By the end of the 19th century, Cutchogue's farms were celebrated for their high output, as reflected in this contract between the H.J. Heinz Co. of Pittsburgh, Pennsylvania, and a local farmer, John Burns. The contract obligated the grower to plant three acres of cauliflower (specifically the Snowball, Erfurt, or Holland varieties) and to deliver the produce "properly sorted, close trimmed and free from leaves and dirt" to a processing plant in Cutchogue. Best known for their ketchup and "57 Varieties" slogan, the company began near Sharpsburg, Pennsylvania, in 1869 when Henry John Heinz delivered pickles, sauerkraut, and vinegar to nearby grocers. By the end of the century, the company achieved international stature but relied upon a vast network of small, local growers such as John Burns in Cutchogue. The Long Island Cauliflower Association, a local trade group founded in nearby Riverhead in 1901, remains an active, full-service farm supply company.

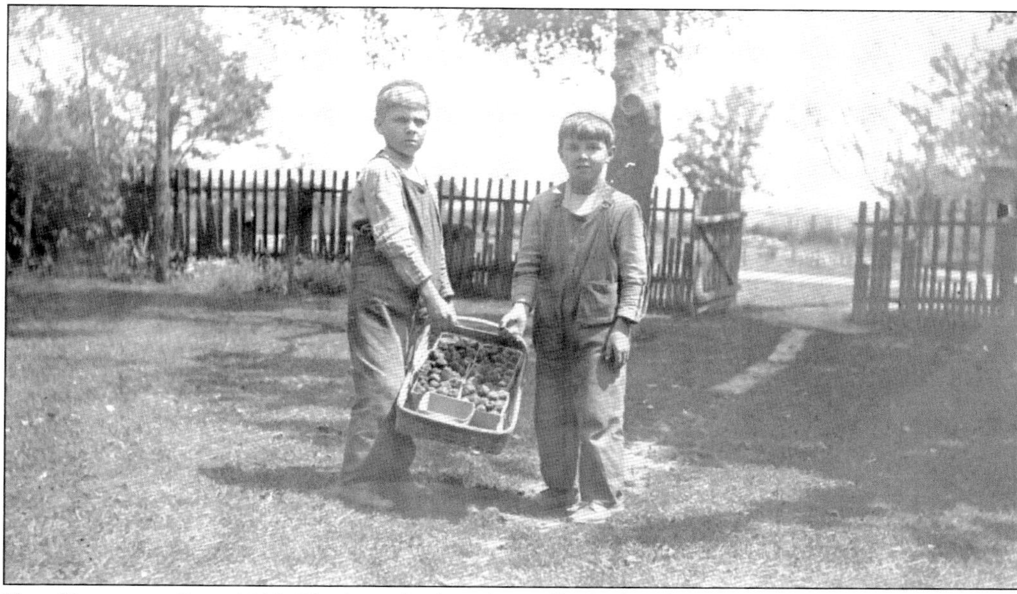

Case Brothers, July 1910. The boys display a large, flat basket that appears to contain strawberries picked on their family farm. Farm children learned early to contribute to the industry of rural life. These boys are dressed simply in denim overalls, which took the place of homemade trousers after Montgomery Ward, Sears Roebuck, and other retailers launched successful mail-order businesses in the late 1800s.

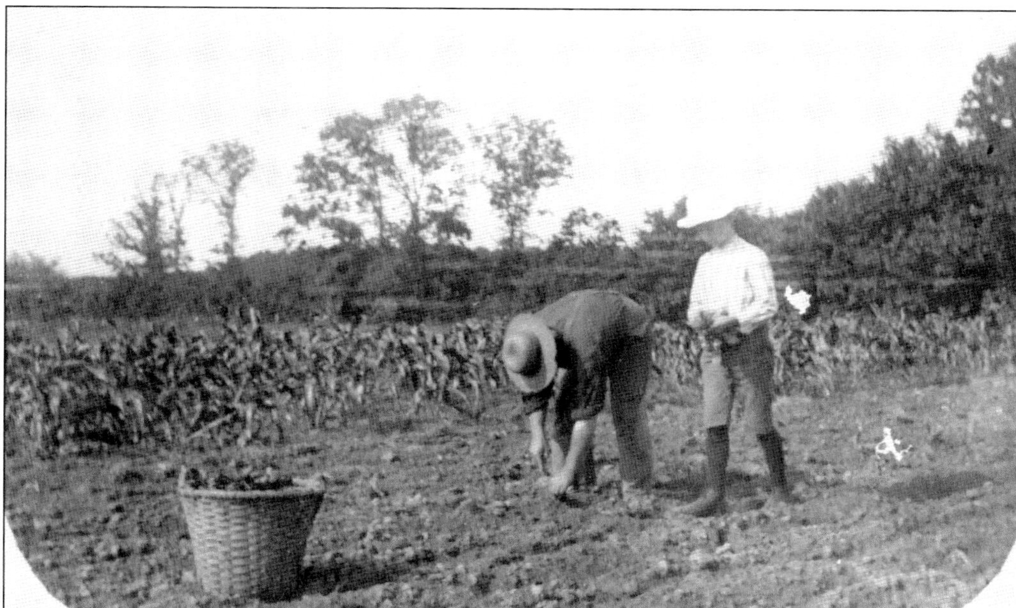

Setting Cauliflower, c. 1920. Stewart Horton (left) and his assistant, young Forest Case, are shaded from the hot sun by broad-brimmed hats as they set cauliflower plants the old-fashioned way. The large woven basket holds the young plants, which were started from seed in early March and planted about six weeks later. Cauliflower, a member of the cabbage family, was a major cash crop for Cutchogue farmers at the turn of the century.

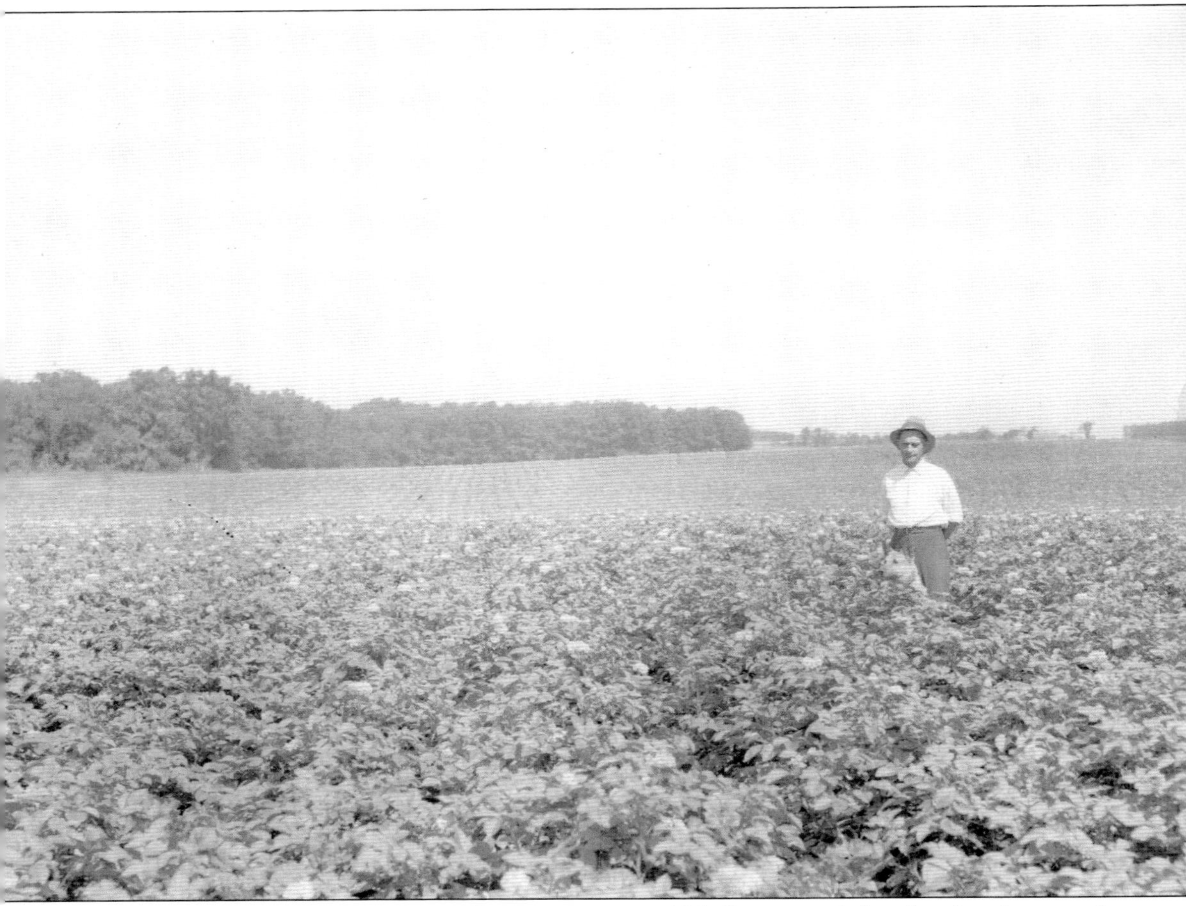

HOWARD ROBINSON AND DOG, CUTCHOGUE, C. 1935. Posing with his dog for photographer Linnaeus Allen in a field of potatoes, Howard Robinson has ample work—and profits—to look forward to. Potatoes would become a major cash crop in the 20th century, but the hand-digging techniques of the previous century prevented the root vegetable from becoming a dominant resource for Long Island farmers. A challenge to small-scale truck farming like that practiced by Robinson had been finding a reliable, seasonal workforce. This problem was alleviated with the advent of the combustion engine in the early 1900s. As a result, water could be mechanically pumped for irrigation, and tractors and trucks took the place of traditional harvesting methods. A lifelong farmer, Howard Burton Robinson (1878–1965) was married to Nancy Wickham Beebe (1885–1942).

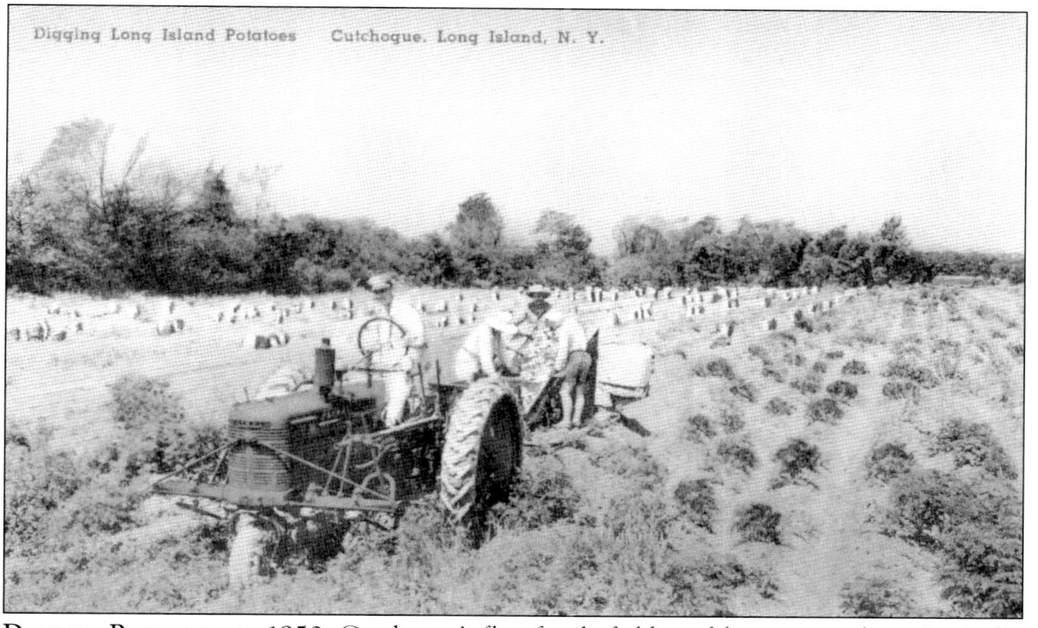

Digging Potatoes, c. 1950. Cutchogue's flat, fertile fields and long sunny days give it the ideal climate for growing potatoes. But potatoes are time-consuming to dig by hand. With the introduction of tractors and mechanized conveyor belts in the early 1900s, the crop became synonymous with Long Island farming. The pickers in this photograph cluster around the conveyor belt, an innovation that greatly increased the speed of harvesting.

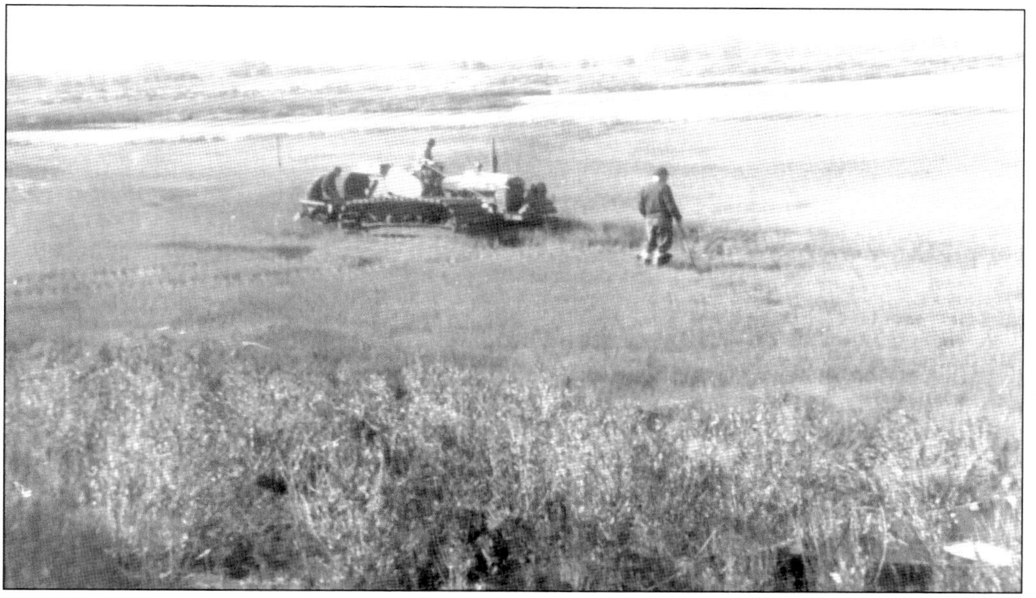

Digging Mosquito Ditches, Fleets Neck, c. 1930. Digging marshes began in Colonial times to encourage the growth of salt hay, which was easier to harvest on well-drained soil. During the early 1900s, marshes were drained to lower the frequency of diseases associated with mosquitoes. The Civilian Conservation Corps (CCC) employed men in the 1930s to dig the ditches. In this photograph, a tractor speeds the process. (Courtesy of a private collection.)

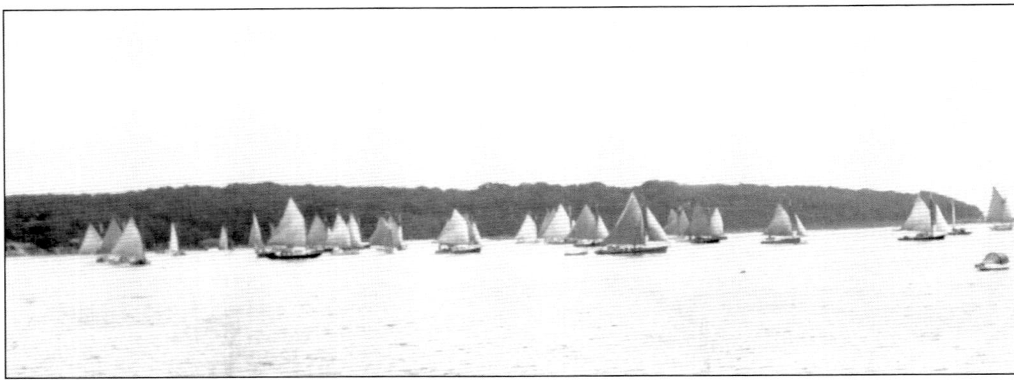

Scallop Fleet, c. 1925. Since the early 1800s, there has been an active commercial fishing economy on Long Island's North Fork. The scallop fleet shown here was anchored off of New Suffolk and plied the Great Peconic Bay and nearby waters in the early to mid-1900s (above). The catch was processed daily in little scallop houses that dotted New Suffolk's shoreline. The method of dredging for scallops and other bottom-dwelling species of seafood, such as oysters, clams, and crabs, had changed little by the early 1900s. An iron frame covered with netting was towed along the sea floor, its open mouth positioned to scoop up the scallops before being winched up to the boat, as shown below. (Below, courtesy of a private collection.)

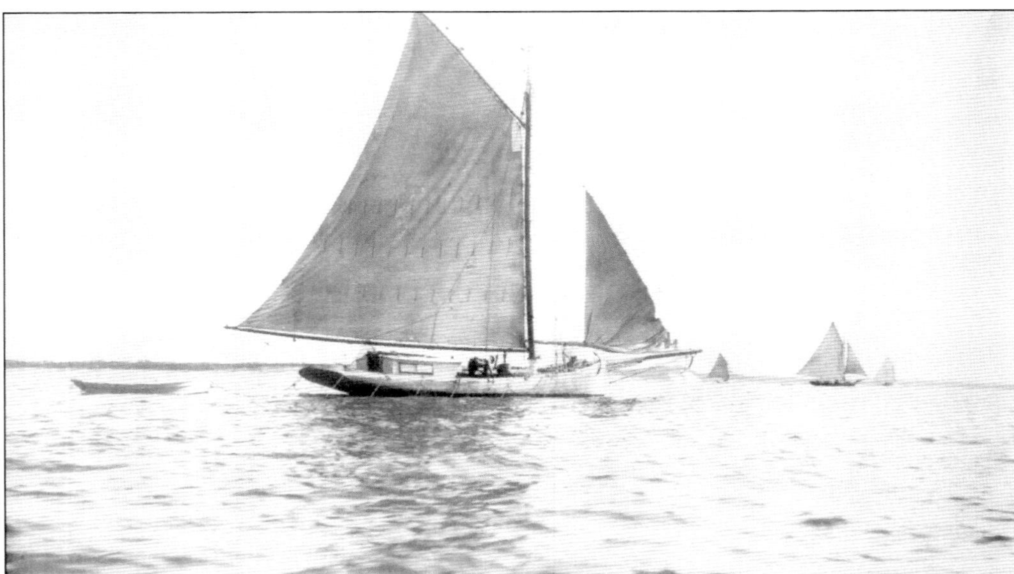

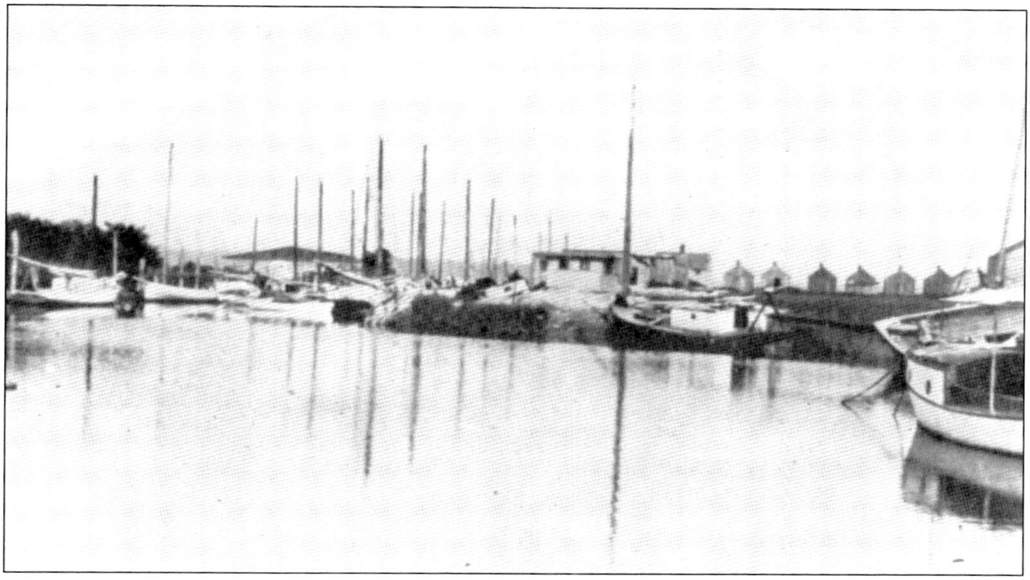

SCALLOP SHACKS, C. 1940. Scallop shacks, synonymous with the New Suffolk waterfront for many decades, dot the horizon at right in the above photograph. Below, shacks front the bay. All 13 have now disappeared, along with the large oyster house seen in the distance at left below. Until it burned down in 1981, the large New Suffolk oyster house stood near the docks, a testament to a once-thriving industry. Over 40 men were employed there at a single time, and at least three work boats were deployed in New Suffolk by the Standard Oyster Company and later by the Radel Oyster Company based in South Norwalk, Connecticut. In addition to the oyster house, where the bivalves were processed, another factory was built on Jackson Avenue for making the barrels that shipped famous Robins Island oysters to New York City restaurants.

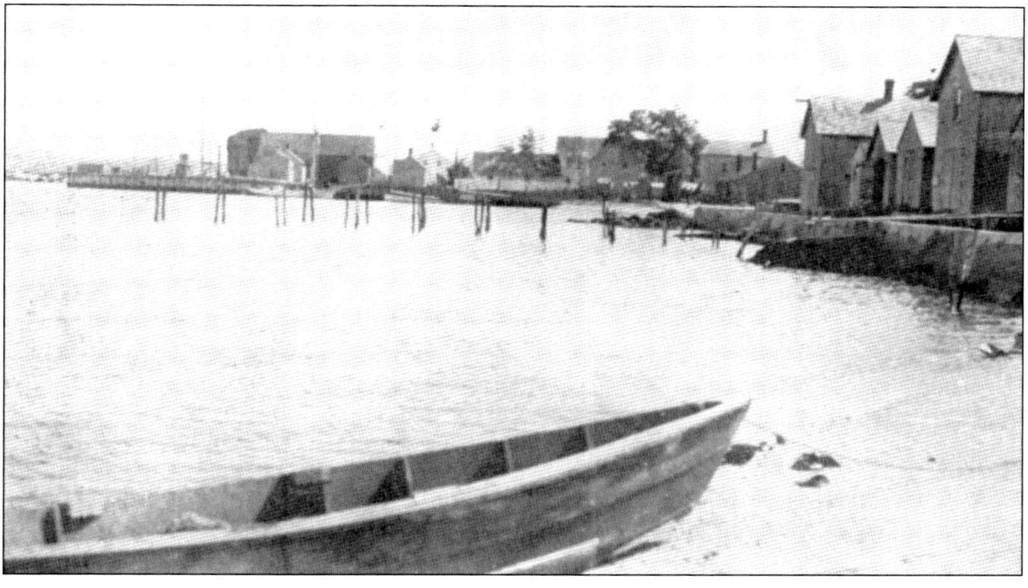

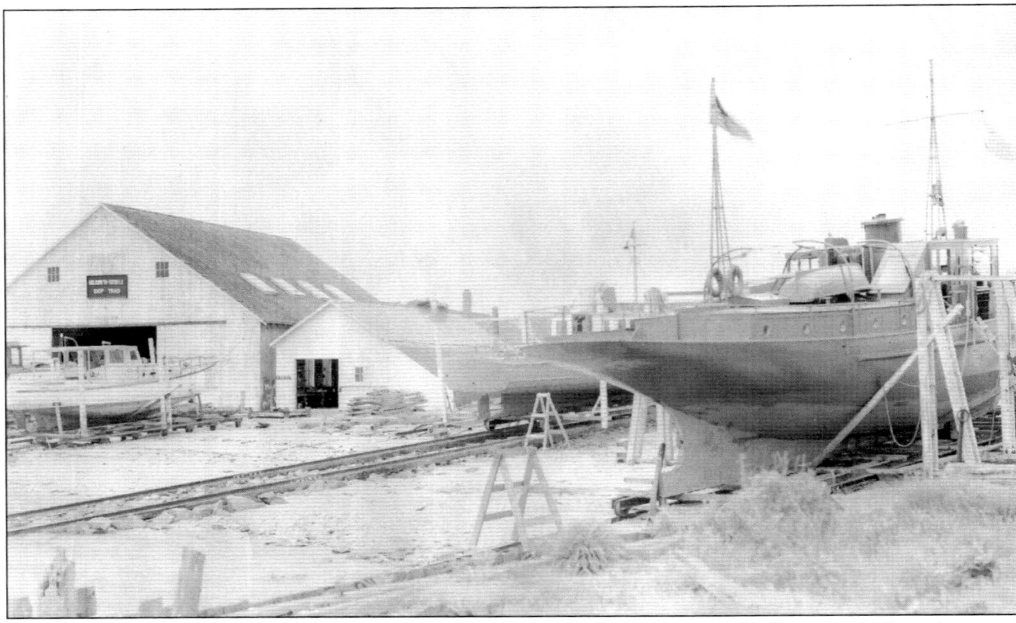

GOLDSMITH & TUTHILL'S BOATYARD, 1949. The yacht *Alma* is ready for launching "on the ways" at Goldsmith & Tuthill's boatyard in an era that began to see more pleasure craft than commercial vessels. With its shipbuilding roots dating to the 18th century, New Suffolk witnessed a surge of activity after Ira Tuthill built his first shipyard in the 1830s.

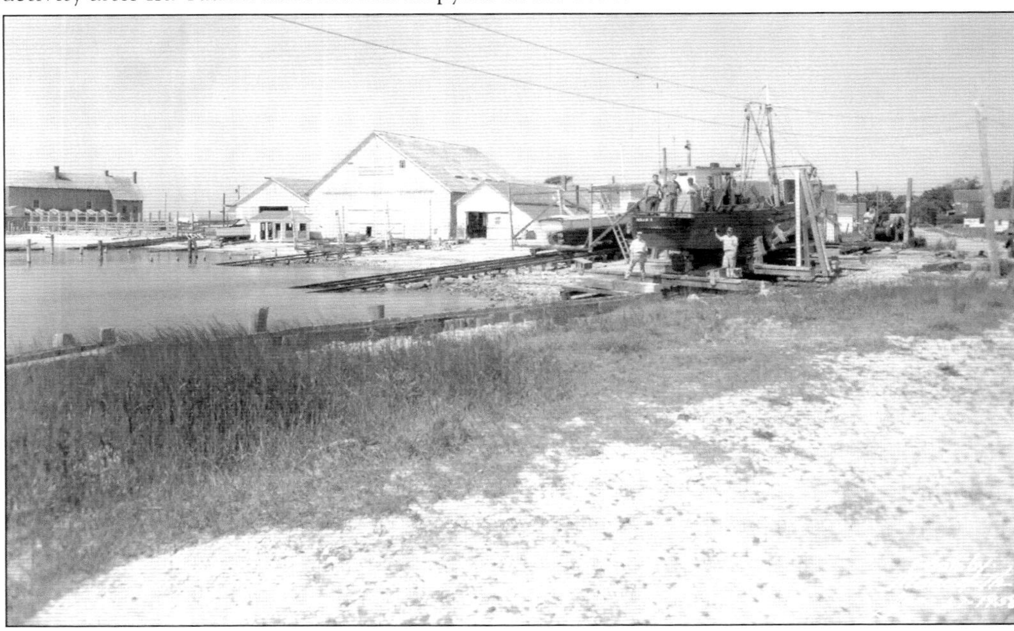

GOLDSMITH & TUTHILL'S BOATYARD, C. 1958. Even after wood masted ships and steam-driven sidewheelers had disappeared, New Suffolk maintained its foothold in commercial and recreational fishing. The boatyard, with its traditional "ways" leading into the water, facilitated launching vessels that were built and serviced on shore. In the distance at left stands New Suffolk's large oyster house, which was destroyed by fire in 1981.

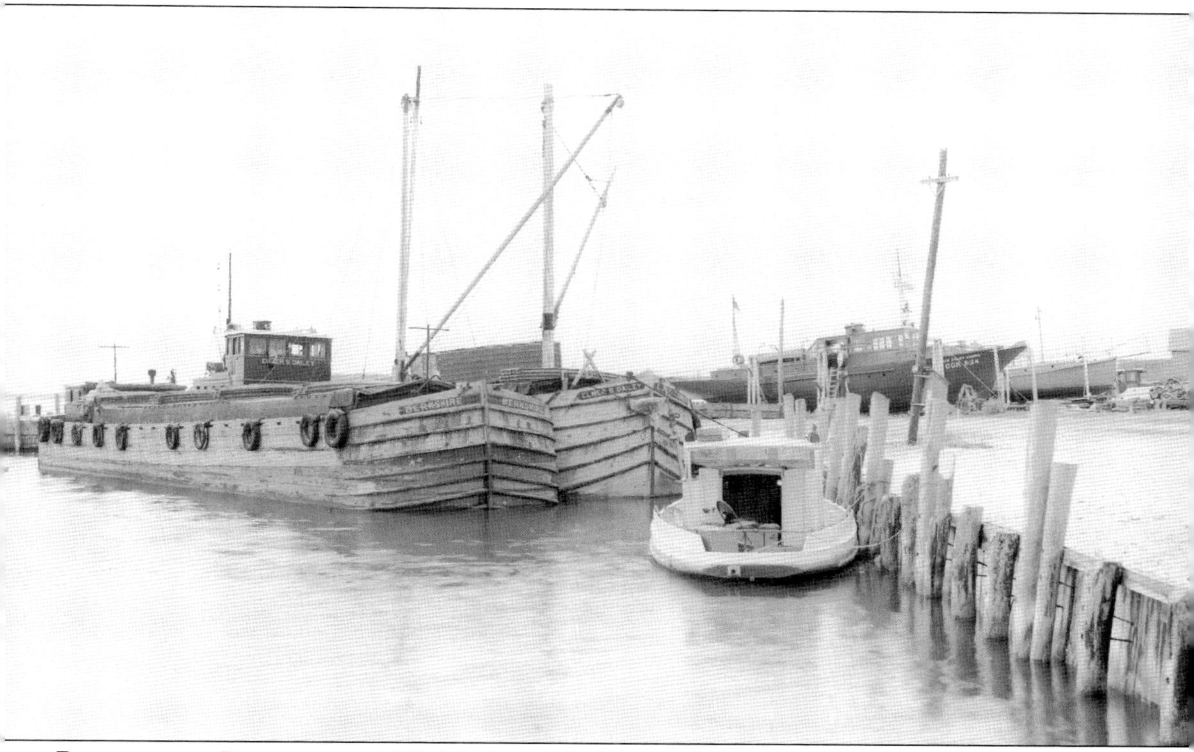

BARGES AT THE BOATYARD, C. 1950. The barges *Berkshire* and *Elmer S. Dailey*, seen here docked at the New Suffolk boatyard, now rest at the bottom of Bridgeport Harbor in Bridgeport, Connecticut. The barges transported fertilizer from Connecticut to Long Island for the S.J. Dailey Company, whose local agent was Joseph Carroll of Southold. The *Elmer S. Dailey* was a wood and steel canal boat built by William H. Folette in 1915 for service on the Erie Canal. Later fitted with diesel power for pushing other barges, it was one of three similar vessels, including the *Berkshire*, that sank at their moorings in Bridgeport Harbor. The *Berkshire* was built in 1935. The *Elmer S. Dailey*, which transported bulk material between New York, New Jersey, and Connecticut, measured 105 feet long and is believed to be the last remaining Erie Canal boat in the country. Both boats were listed in the National Register of Historic Places in 1978. A Coast Guard vessel and two cruisers can be seen in the right background.

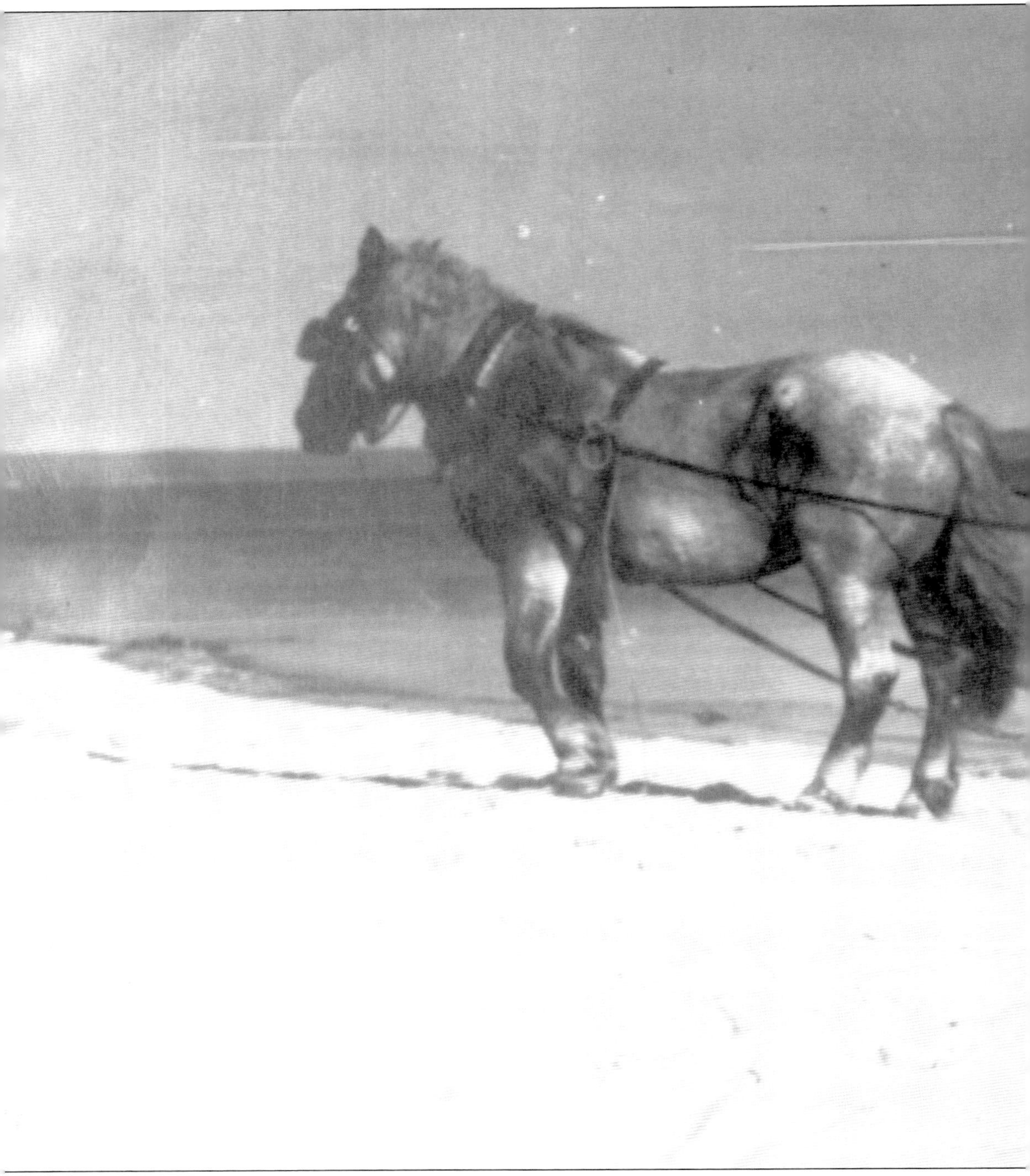

Joe Donnelly and His Horse, c. 1945. Joe Donnelly worked at Johnson & Thorpe's fishing station, one of several such New Suffolk businesses that rented out rowboats to "city people" who came to fish or just enjoy the simple pleasures of rowing on Peconic Bay. The same tranquil waters that provided John P. Holland the perfect setting for testing submarines at the turn of the century were rediscovered by vacationers a half-century later. Joe Donnelly capitalized on this

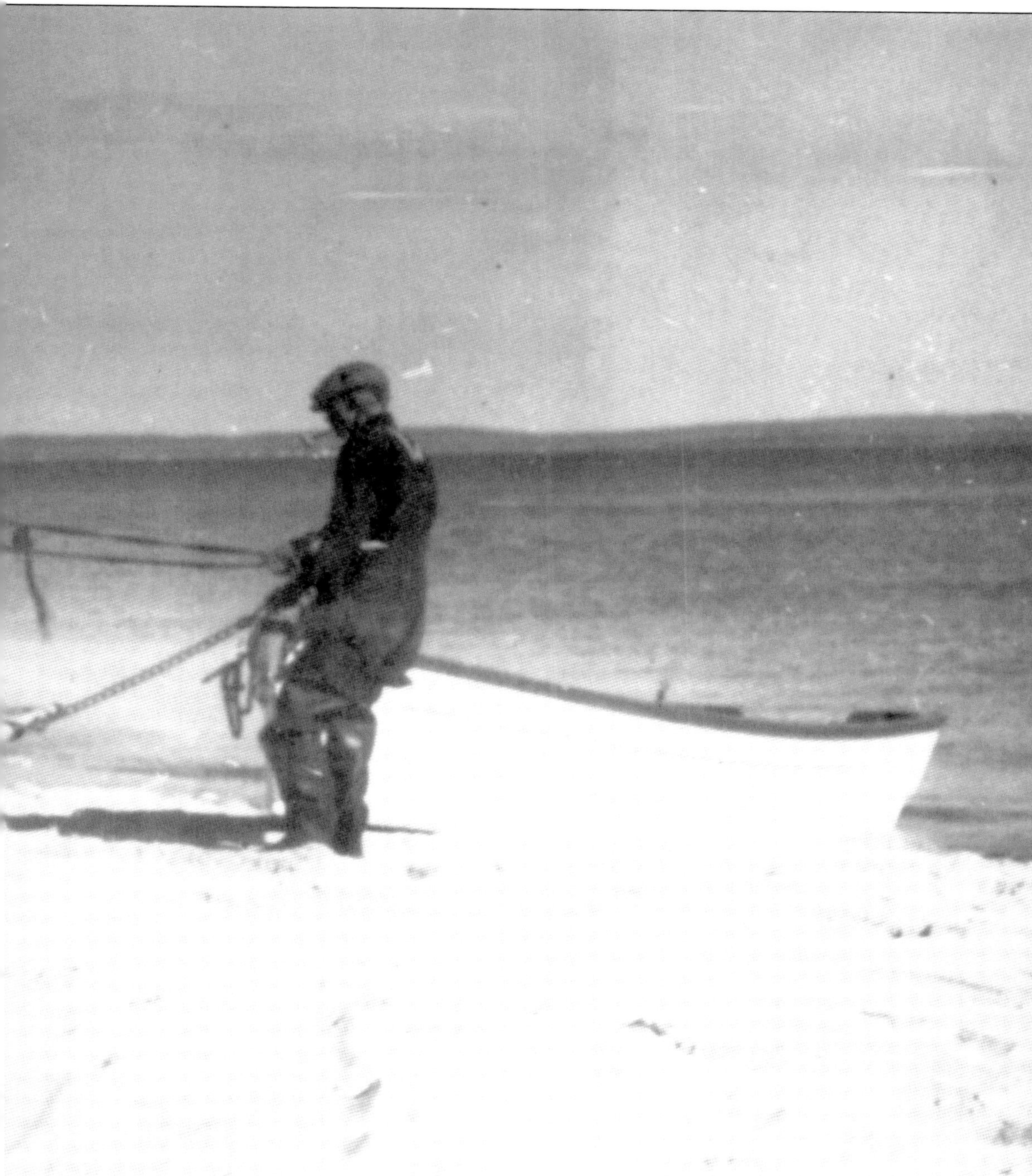

natural resource and was assisted in the work by his faithful horse, who pulled the boats back to shore at the end of each day. Johnson & Thorpe's fishing station was later owned by Anna and Joe Polashock, whose aluminum rowboats were also for hire, replacing the earlier wooden ones (and Joe Donnelly's horse!). (Courtesy of Norman Wamback.)

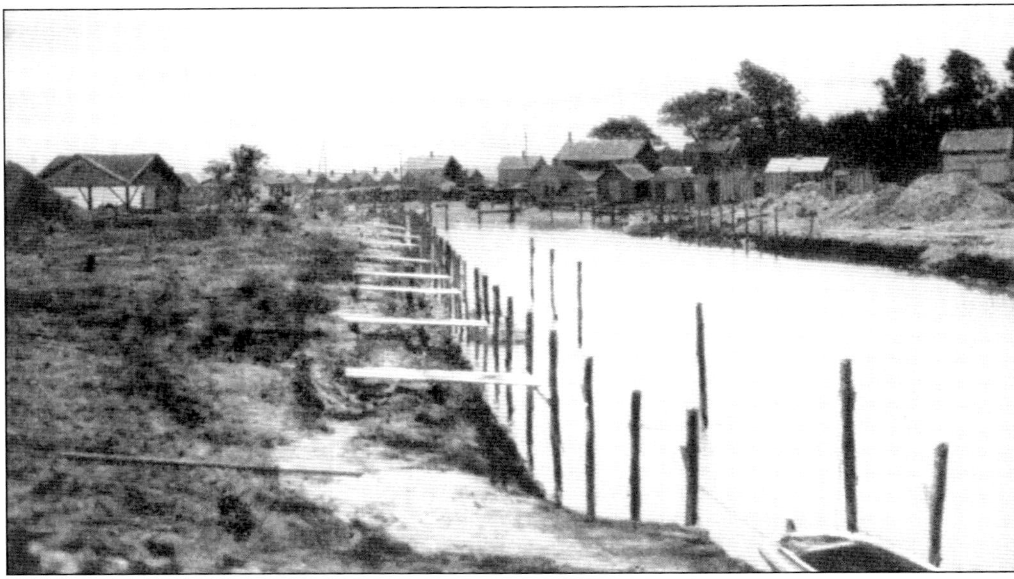

School House Creek, c. 1920 and c. 1940. School House Creek has figured in New Suffolk's history from the start. Early on, the narrow creek only accommodated smaller vessels, requiring a system of posts and planks to enable boaters to reach their vessels from the banks (above). The small scallop shacks that dotted the New Suffolk shoreline are visible in the distance. Later in the century, the creek was dredged and widened, making it more useful for a variety of boaters (below). This picturesque grouping of commercial and recreational craft characterized the vibrant New Suffolk waterfront of the 1940s. School House Creek was named for a nearby one-room schoolhouse that burned in the late 1800s. Classes were then held in a house at King and Third Streets until the new schoolhouse was built.

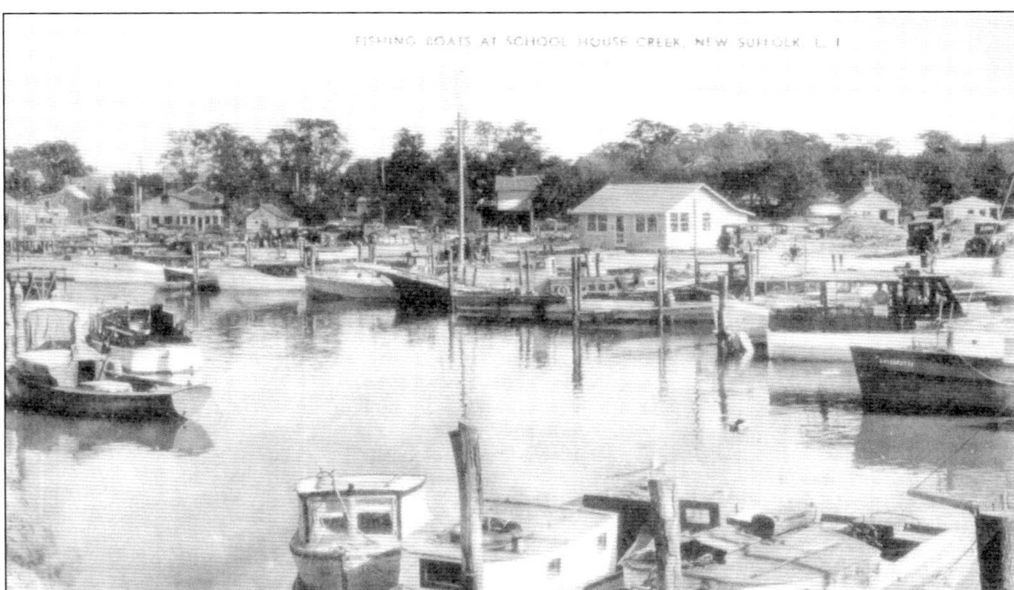

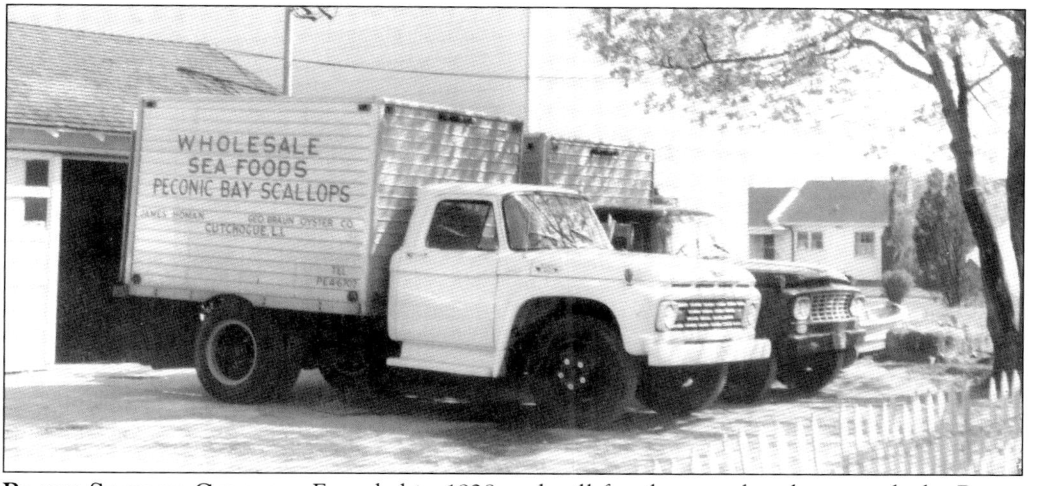

Braun Seafood Company. Founded in 1928 and still family owned and operated, the Braun Seafood Company (formerly George Braun Oyster Co.) is renowned for harvesting fresh seafood from Long Island bays and surrounding waters. Overnight access to the company's New England and Chesapeake Bay fisheries means its fresh seafood is available throughout the year. The company maintains an off-bottom culture permit with New York State in the pristine waters of Cutchogue Harbor (Great Peconic Bay), between Nassau Point and Robins Island. A large fleet of trucks (above) has helped to distribute the wholesale seafood, notably its Peconic Bay scallops and other local specialties, to restaurants across Long Island and in metropolitan New York City. Packing and processing the catch has always been a family affair. (Courtesy of the Braun Seafood Company.)

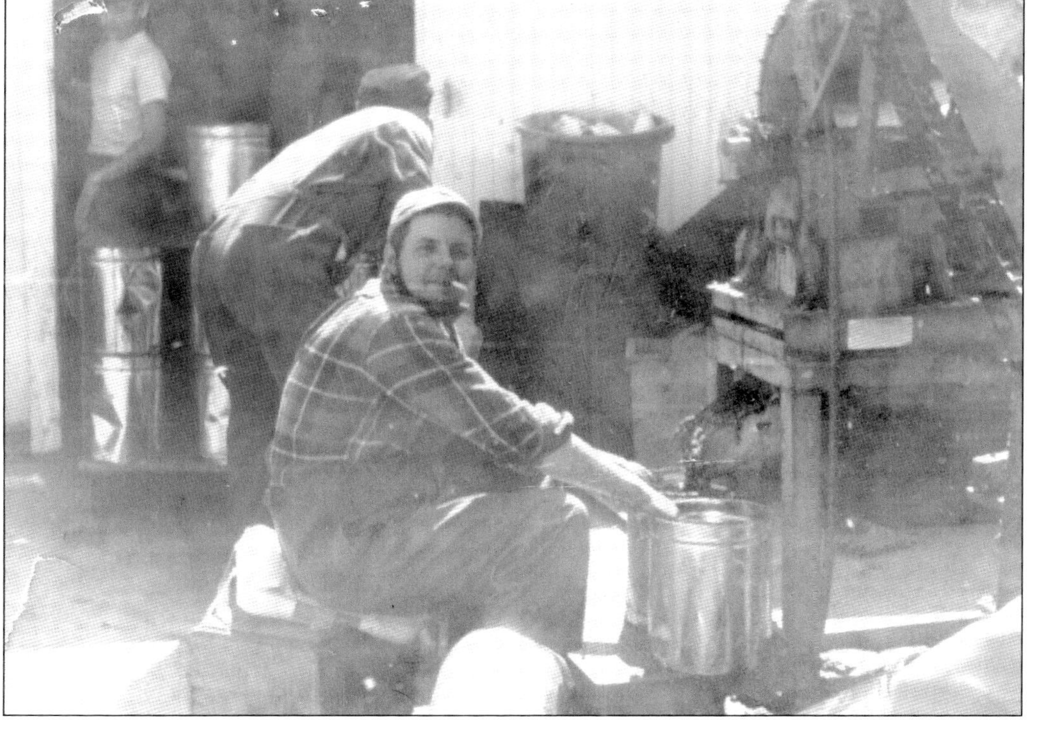

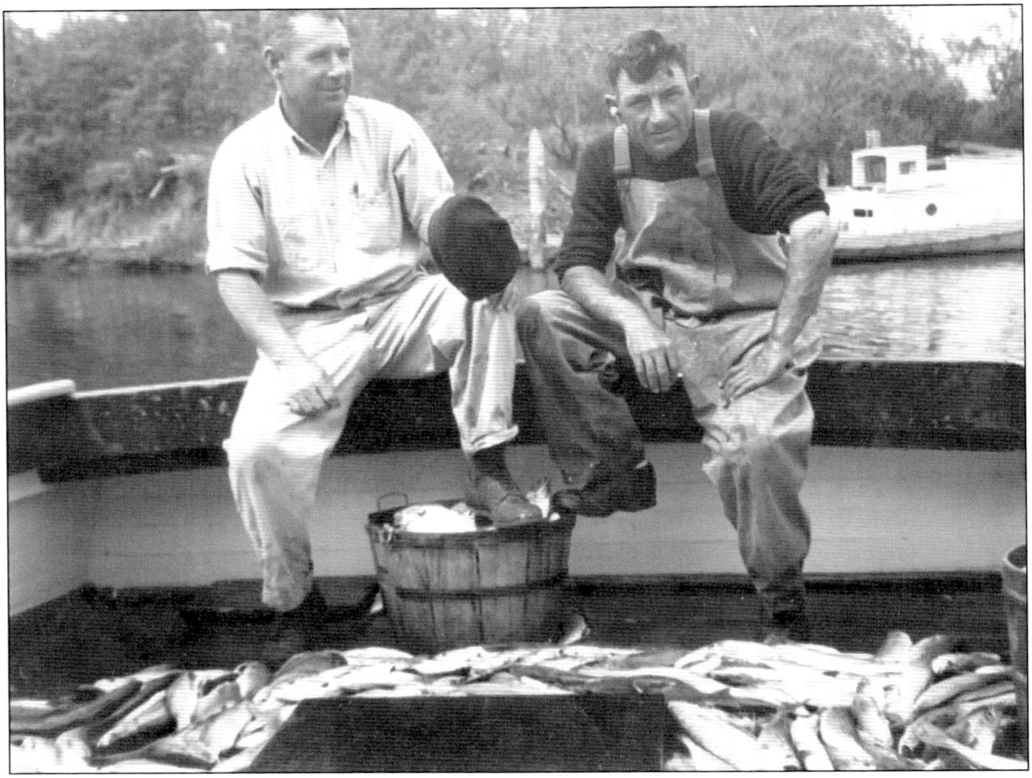

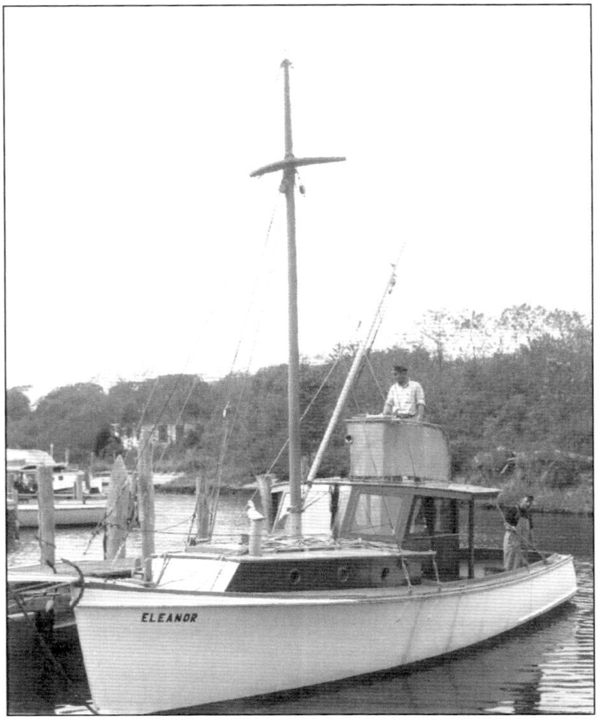

CAPT. TED WAMBACK IN THE *ELEANOR*, C. 1950. Ted Wamback (above, at left) was born in Nova Scotia and went to sea at the age of 13. At 20, he immigrated to City Island in New York City in search of work. After serving as a captain on small yachts, Wamback found his way from Palm Beach, Florida, to New Suffolk on the yacht of Mr. and Mrs. Ambrose Corwin, who summered at Camp Mineola in Mattituck. Captain Wamback met his future wife there and married her in 1935. He designed the *Eleanor* and had it built in Ellsworth, Maine. The *Eleanor*, named for Ted's daughter, was run as a sports fishing boat. During World War II, when fuel was in short supply, he installed the mast (left) and ran the boat under sail whenever possible. (Courtesy of Norman Wamback.)

Three

VILLAGE LIFE

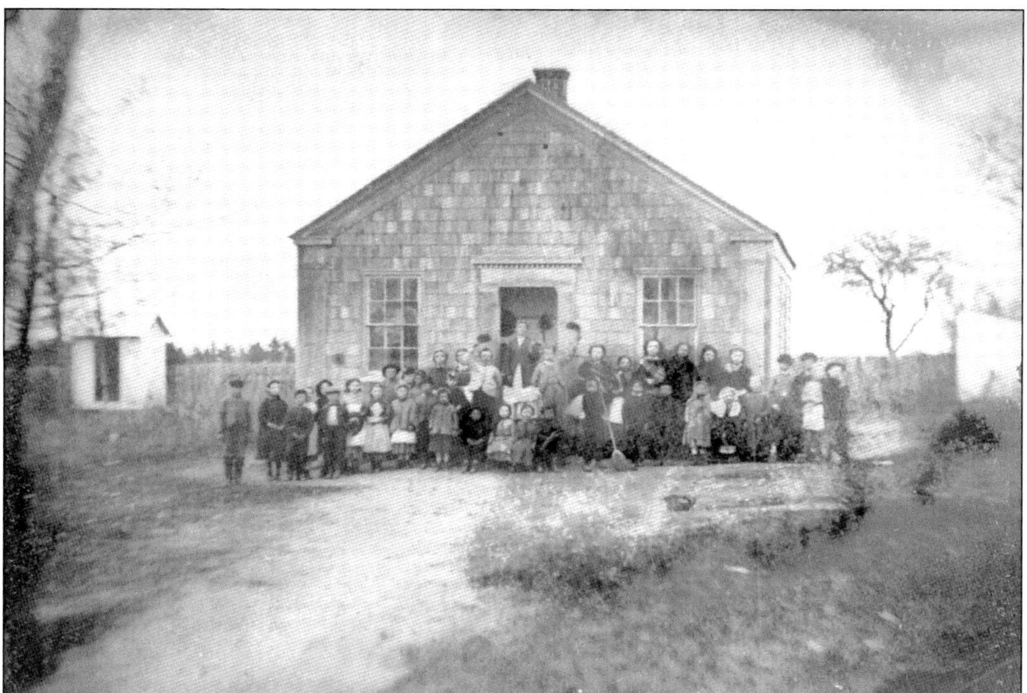

CUTCHOGUE'S ONE-ROOM SCHOOLHOUSE, C. 1890. Students assemble for a formal portrait in front of Cutchogue's original one-room schoolhouse. Their teacher is featured prominently in the open doorway. After a larger public school was built in 1903, the old schoolhouse was moved to a nearby farm field to provide housing for migrant farmers. The schoolhouse was restored on the Village Green in downtown Cutchogue in 1961.

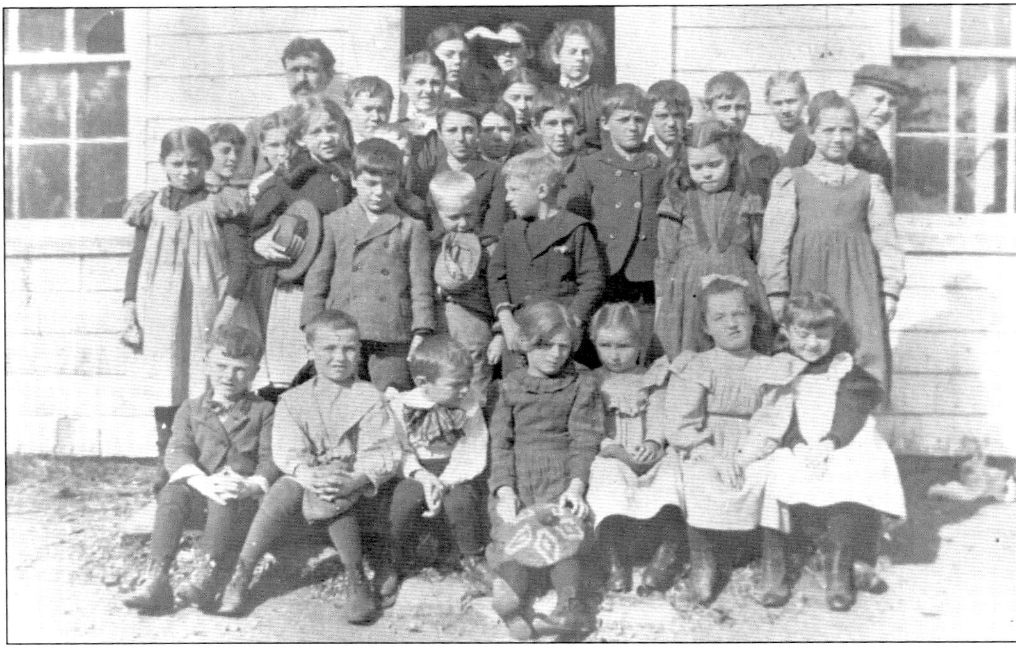

Group Portrait, 1898. The students at Cutchogue's one-room schoolhouse assemble for a group portrait in 1898. This image was copied by Charles H. Meredith in 1961 from an original photograph by M.E. Corey. Dressed in their "Sunday best," the students squint and squirm while waiting for the photographer's camera to capture the moment. The schoolmaster stands at the upper left, identified only as the man with the moustache.

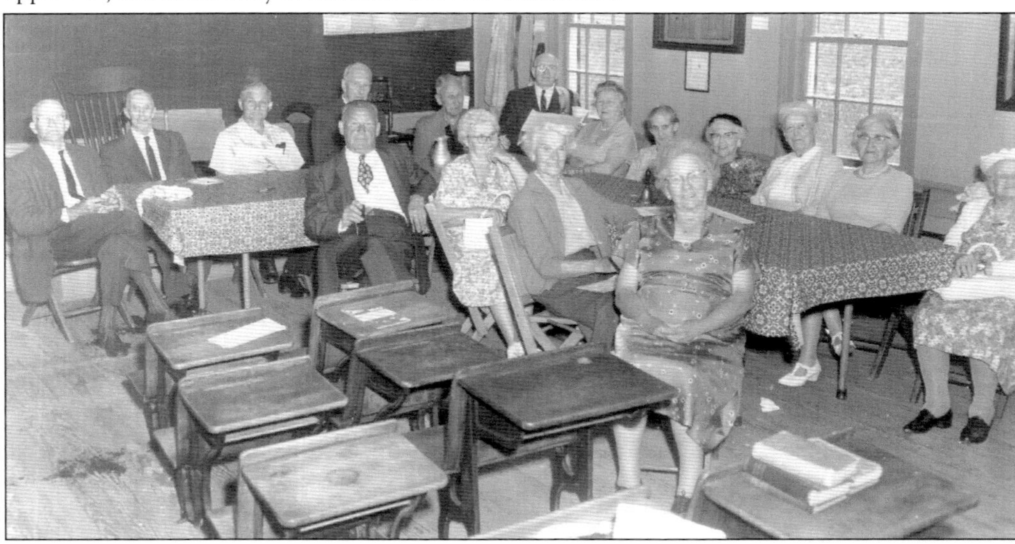

Class Reunion, June 25, 1965. These graduates of the old Cutchogue school assembled for a class reunion after its restoration. Shown here are, from left to right, (in front of table) James A. Hand, Elizabeth Corey, Madolin Fleet Barteau, and Annie Gee Denzler; (behind table) Gerald Fleet, Charles Boutcher, Victor Smolenski, Delancey Pelgrift, Elmer Lennon, Jack Gee, Mary Lennon Shunt, Edna Foster, Ruth Case, Alicia Vail Fanning, Eva Terry, and Lizzie Case Horton. (Courtesy of the Southold Historical Society.)

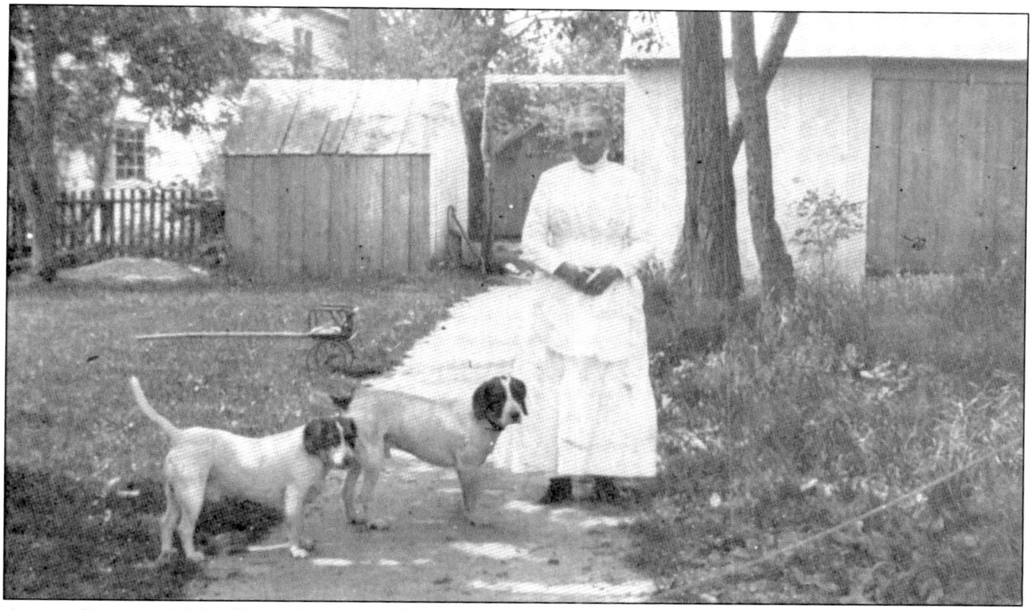

ANNA CASE, C. 1890. Born Anna Sophia Tuthill in 1851, this lifelong Cutchogue resident married George Henry Case in 1870 and lived until 1943. George H. (1849–1932) was the son of William Harrison Case, a Southold native whose large farmhouse was located at the corner of Main and New Suffolk Roads and later served as Bett's Hotel. Many members of the family are buried in Cutchogue's Old Burying Ground.

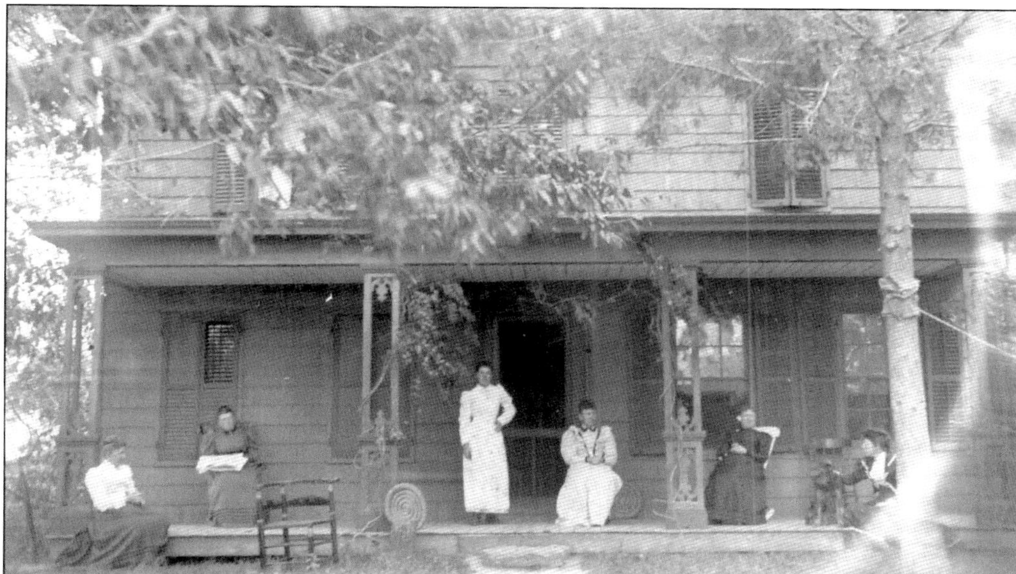

WICKHAM LADIES, CUTCHOGUE, C. 1890. Frances Wickham (second from right in dark dress) poses with other village ladies on a summer afternoon. The house, at the corner of Main Road and Alvah's Lane, was built in 1820 by Frances's father, Henry Wickham of Southold. It was later owned by Corwin C. and Ruth Grathwohl. Corwin's carpentry shop was located in the house for many years. (Courtesy of James F. Grathwohl.)

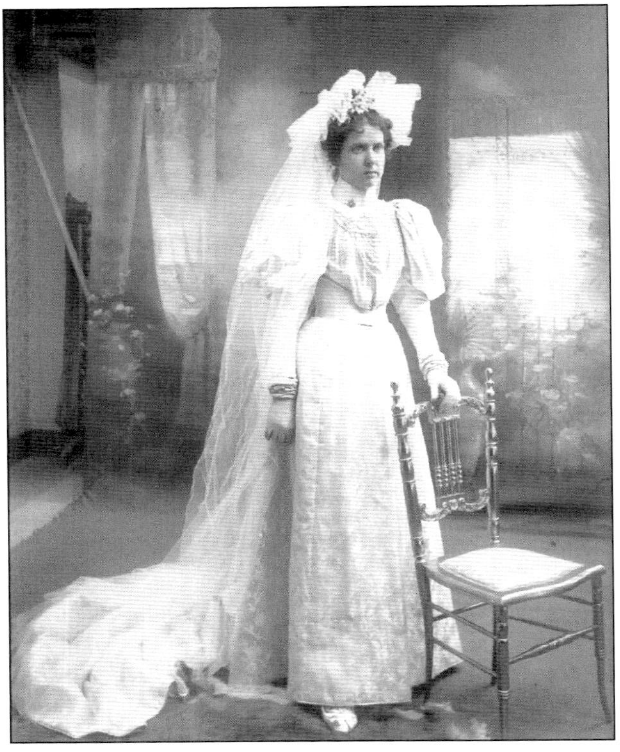

Ida Randolph Cooper and Ring Bearer, 1895. Ida Randolph Cooper (left), posing in her elaborate silk wedding dress, married Henry Lewis Fleet on November 27, 1895, at the Presbyterian Church in Mattituck. The bride's father, G. Clarence Cooper, was a prosperous Mattituck farmer and life member of the Suffolk County Agricultural Society. The groom was a member of the prominent Fleet family of Cutchogue, whose large, productive farm and breeding stables were renowned throughout Long Island. The young ring bearer (below), who was dressed for the occasion in silk and lace to match the bride, was also a member of the Fleet family and joined the wedding party for the post-ceremony festivities at the Mattituck Hotel.

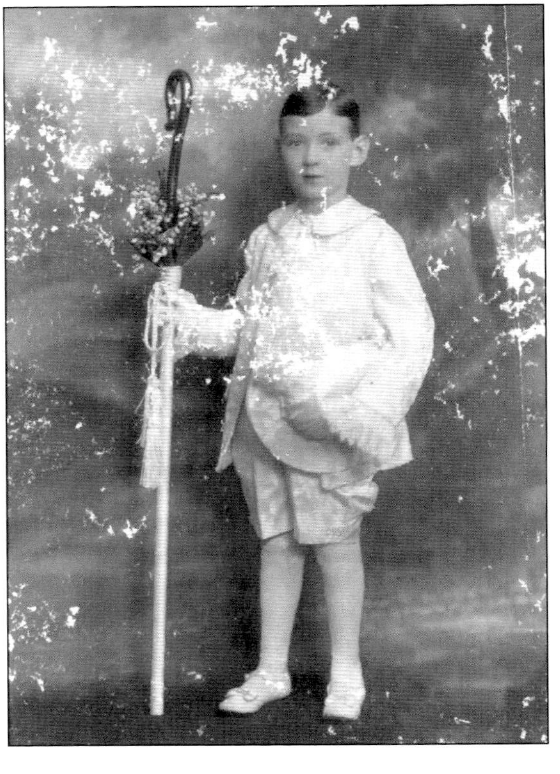

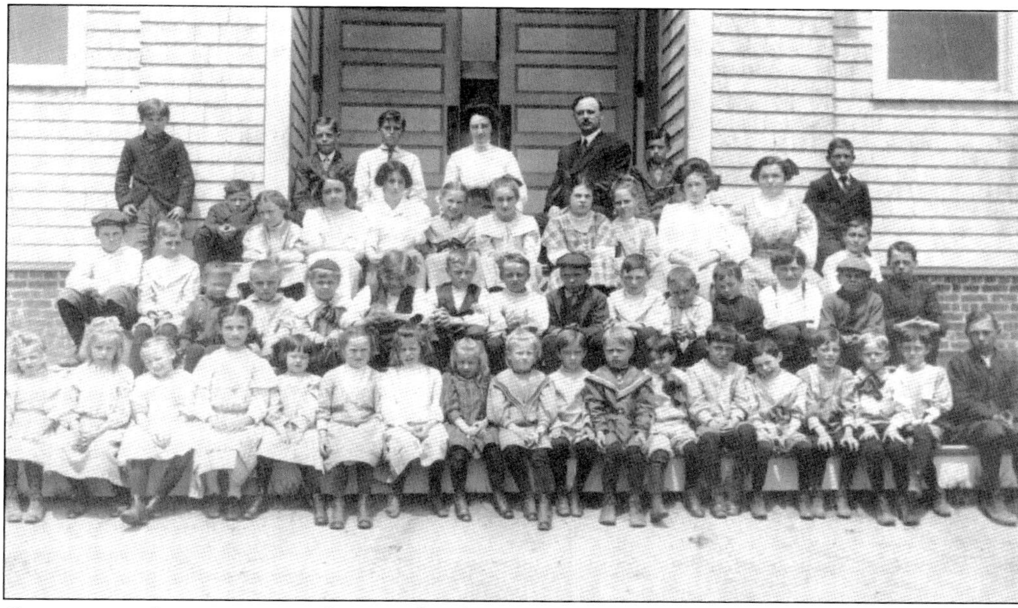

CUTCHOGUE SCHOOL, 1908. Boys and girls were separated and arranged by age for this class photograph. Principal Sprague and his assistant, Miss Babcock, stand in the top row and appear to be in control of the school body, with help from two other female instructors (third row, second and third from right). The Cutchogue School functioned in this building from 1903 until the 1930s, when a new school was built on Depot Lane. In 1973, Cutchogue merged with Mattituck to form the Mattituck-Cutchogue Union Free School District.

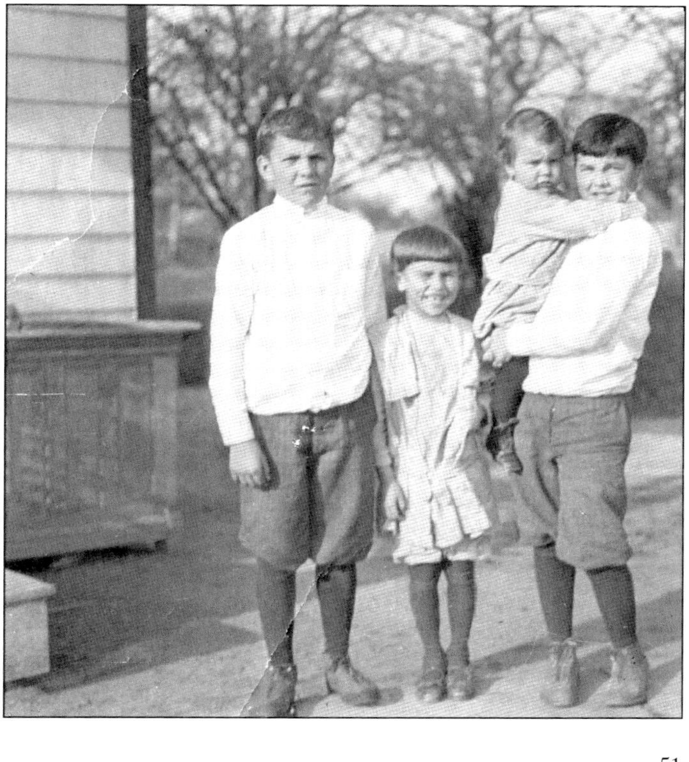

CASE BROTHERS, C. 1914. The four Case brothers—William Harrison, Russell B., Ralph H., and Henry E.—pose patiently for the camera at their home on New Suffolk Road in Cutchogue. Their parents, Frank Hoyt and Jennie Bond Case, had a large sheep farm that later became the Cedars Golf Club. An ice box is stationed prominently by the back porch.

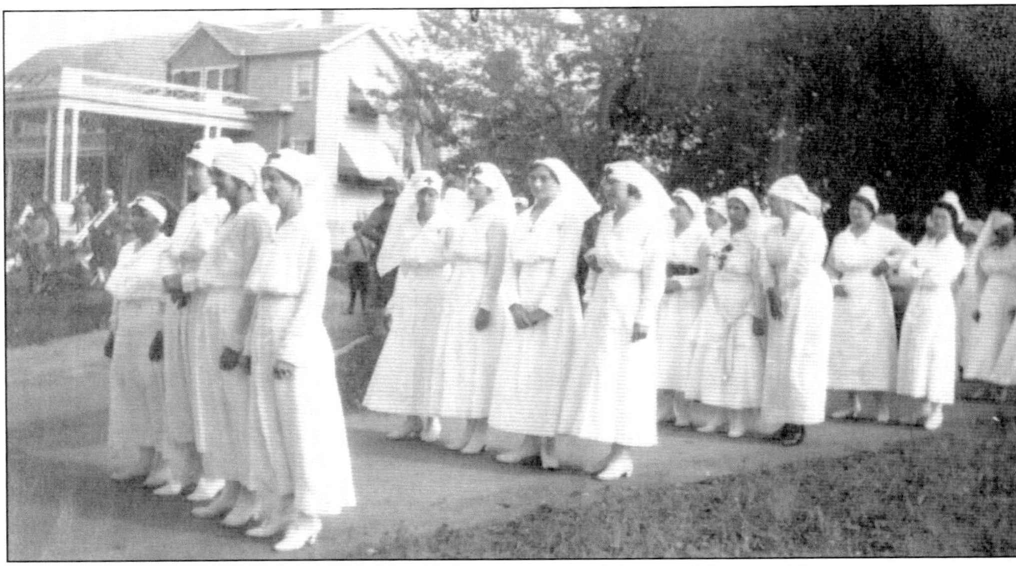

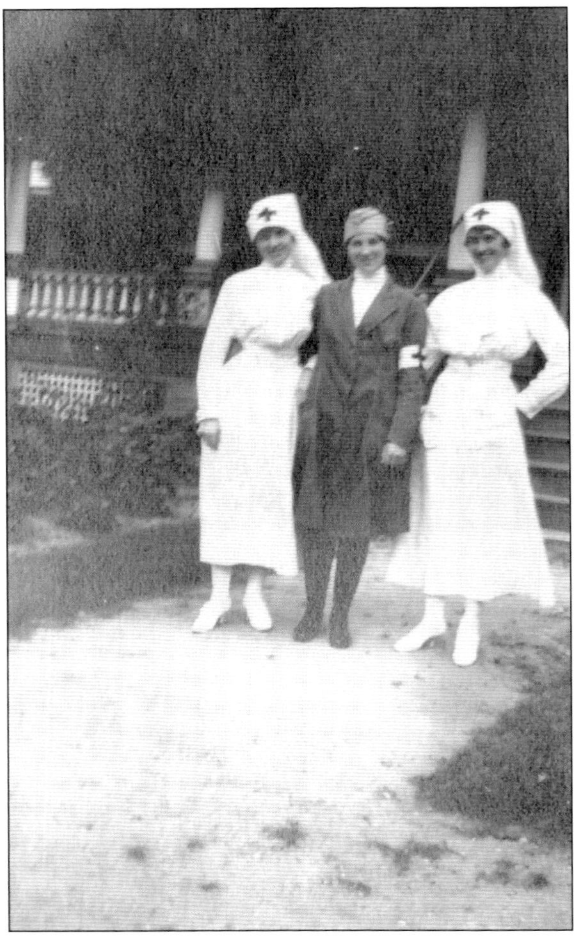

Nurses March, Cutchogue, c. 1918. In the above photograph, Red Cross nurses parade in front of the newly completed North Fork Country Club, showing support for American troops entering World War I. Such solidarity was heightened in Suffolk County, Long Island, because of recent memories of Camp Wikoff in Montauk and Camp Upton in Yaphank. The 1898 Camp Wikoff received troops returning from the Spanish-American War and grew to encompass 21,000 men, with camp hospitals staffed with 300 nurses. Camp Upton was built in 1917 as a World War I training camp. Many of these nurses likely saw service at both camps. At left, the three Fleet sisters—Elizabeth (left), Kathryn (center), and Madolin, daughters of George Henry Fleet—pose in their nurse's uniforms. (Courtesy of a private collection.)

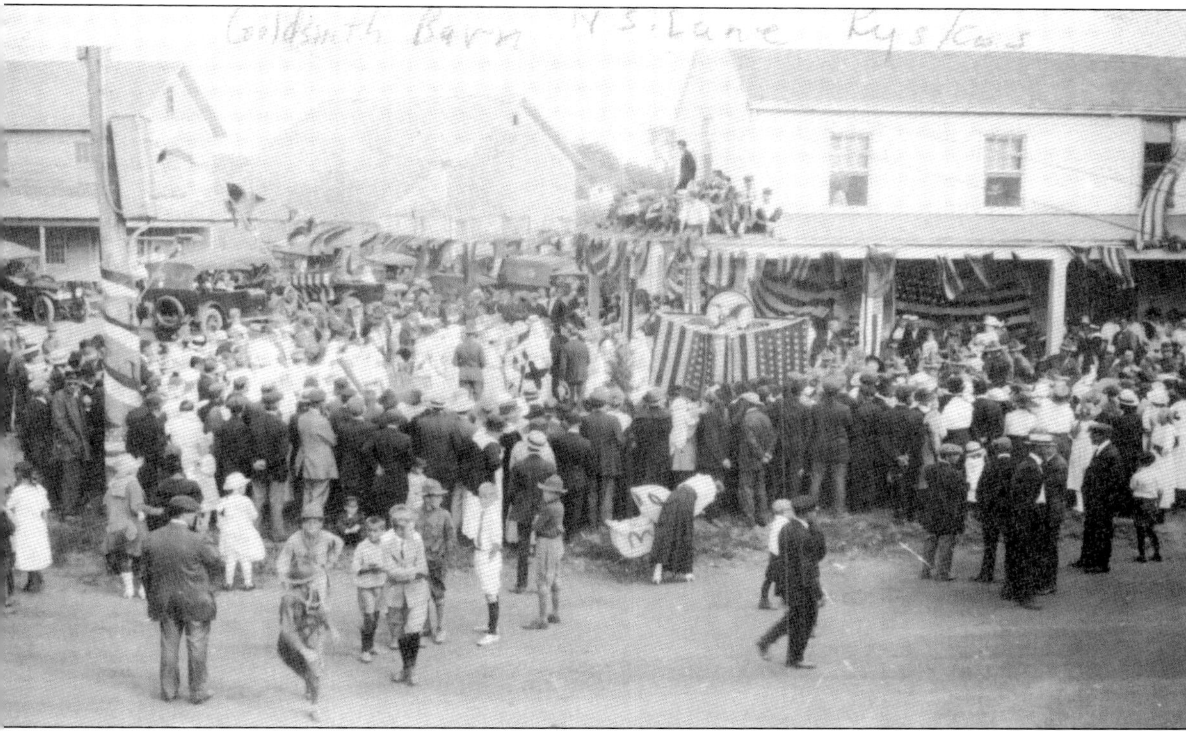

Reading of the Honor Roll, 1918. The end of World War I was a cause for great celebration in Cutchogue, as illustrated in this photograph, taken at the reading of the Honor Roll of those who had served. A sense of relief was felt by those in attendance, all of whom had been touched by the war. Local dignitaries took their turns speaking. The festive crowd turned out to view the flags and bunting, which decorated the intersection of the Main Road and New Suffolk Road. Some spectators took to the roof of Bett's Hotel to catch a better view of the proceedings. The Goldsmith barn is seen at center. In the foreground, several young boys are dressed in Army uniforms to take part in the celebrations. (Courtesy of a private collection.)

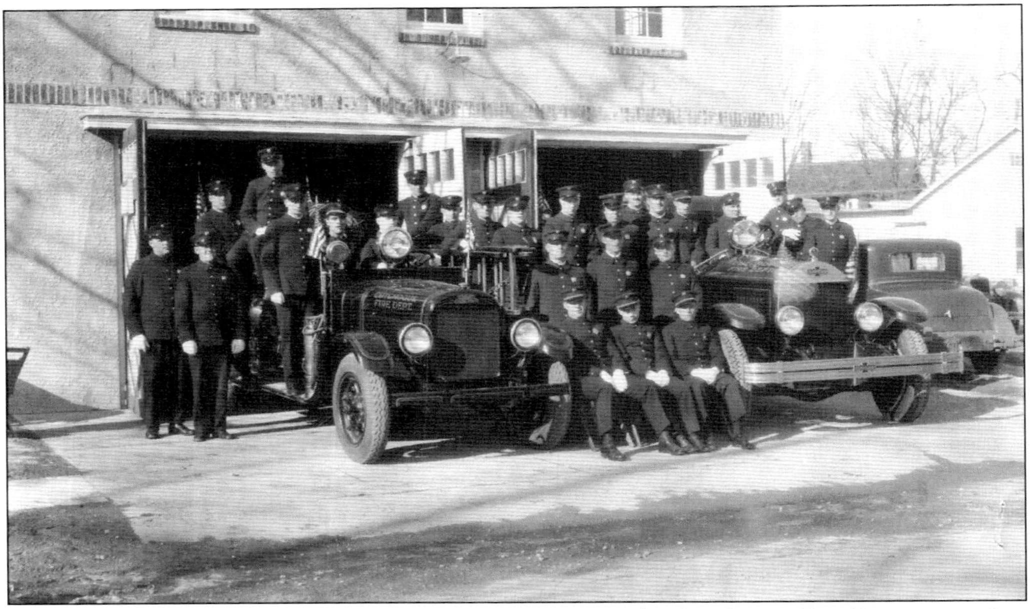

CUTCHOGUE FIRE DEPARTMENT, C. 1930 AND C. 1950. The Cutchogue Fire Department has been a volunteer service since its founding as the United Chemical Company No. 1 in 1927. It was reorganized in 1930 (above) as the United Fire Company No. 1, with 54 charter members. Sherwood Beebe served as chief, and the officers were: Charles P. Hawkins, captain; Howard Robinson, lieutenant; Ernest Morrell, secretary and chief driver; Goldsmith Horton, treasurer; and Oliver W. Case, Michael S. Hand, and Burnett Tuthill, trustees. The vehicles in the above photograph are the original American Lafrance "chemical truck" dating from 1928 (left) and the larger American Lafrance 500-gallon pumper, acquired in 1930 (right). An addition, seen below, was later erected beside the original firehouse to provide space for new firefighting equipment as the department grew to serve a growing population. (Courtesy of Cutchogue Fire Department.)

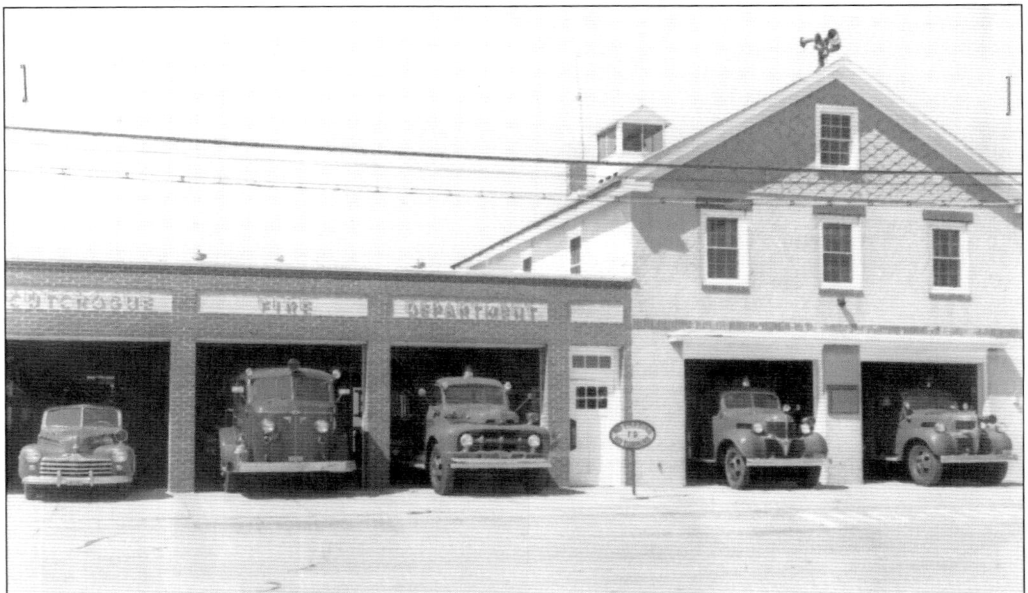

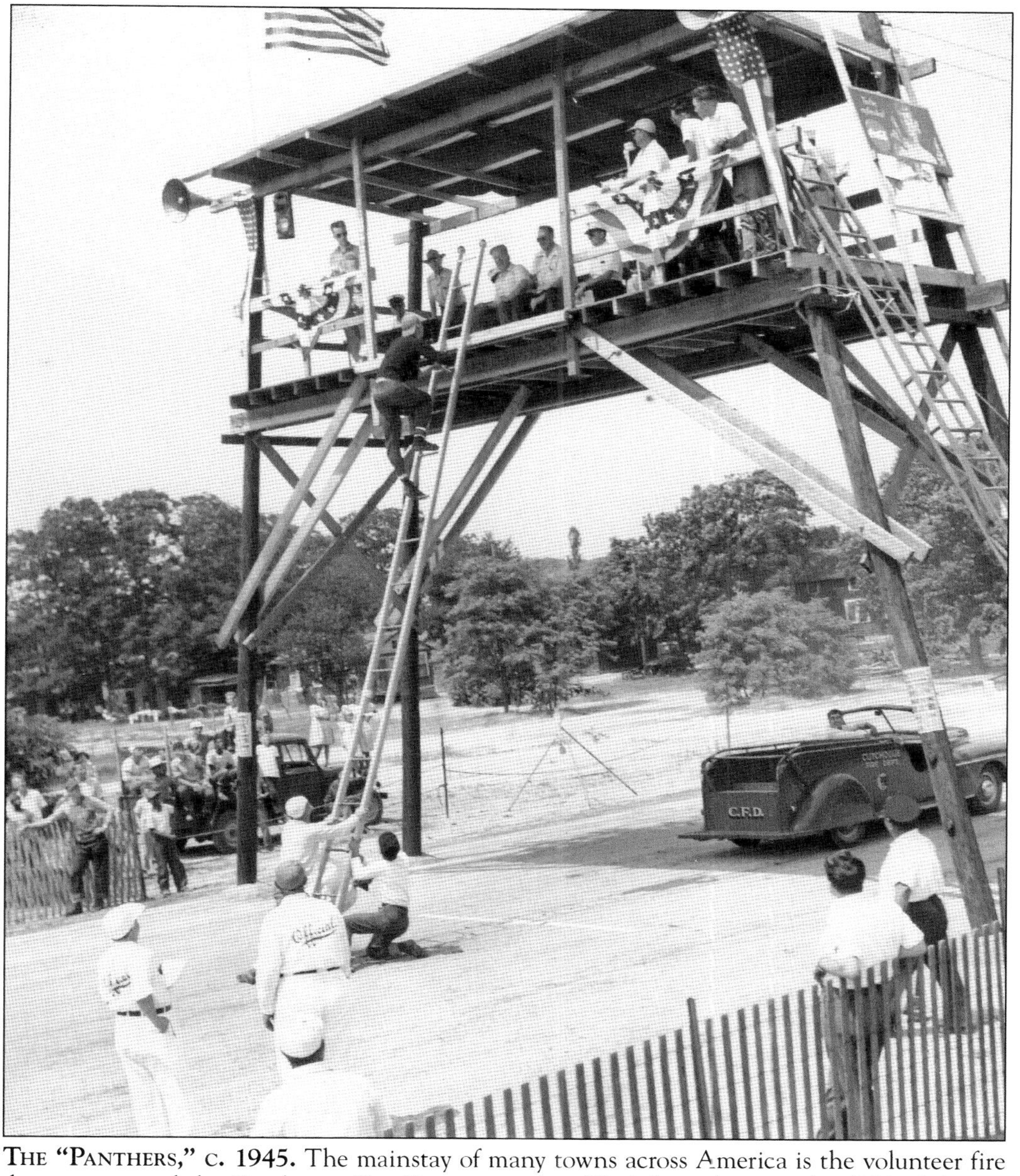

The "Panthers," c. 1945. The mainstay of many towns across America is the volunteer fire department, and the Cutchogue Fire Department has filled this role since the 1920s. It began competing in tournaments with other departments with equipment borrowed from nearby Greenport. But in 1932, when motorized equipment was needed, the firemen raised funds to buy a used Pierce Arrow, which they converted into a hose car. After World War II, the department saw renewed interest in participating in competitive tournaments with other fire companies, and a new drill team, the "Panthers," was born in 1946. The team set a state record in the bucket brigade contest in Rome, New York, in 1948, but it lasted only 10 minutes. The next competitors broke the record again! One of the Panthers' biggest accomplishments was winning the 1985 Suffolk County Championship in Patchogue. The Panthers remain an active component of the Cutchogue Fire Department and participate in many local, regional, and state contests. (Courtesy of Cutchogue Fire Department.)

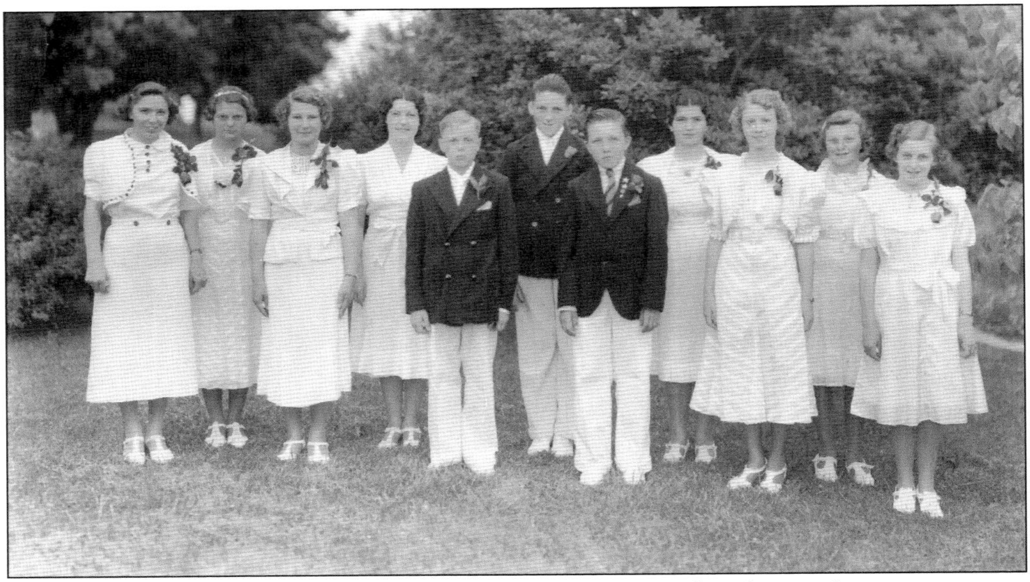

NEW SUFFOLK SCHOOL, CLASS OF 1938. The boys were outnumbered more than two-to-one at their eighth grade graduation from New Suffolk School in 1938. Uniforms were the order of the day, with the girls in white dresses with jackets and open shoes, and the boys in blazers and white trousers. Each student sports a corsage, and by the looks on their faces, refreshments await them on the lawn!

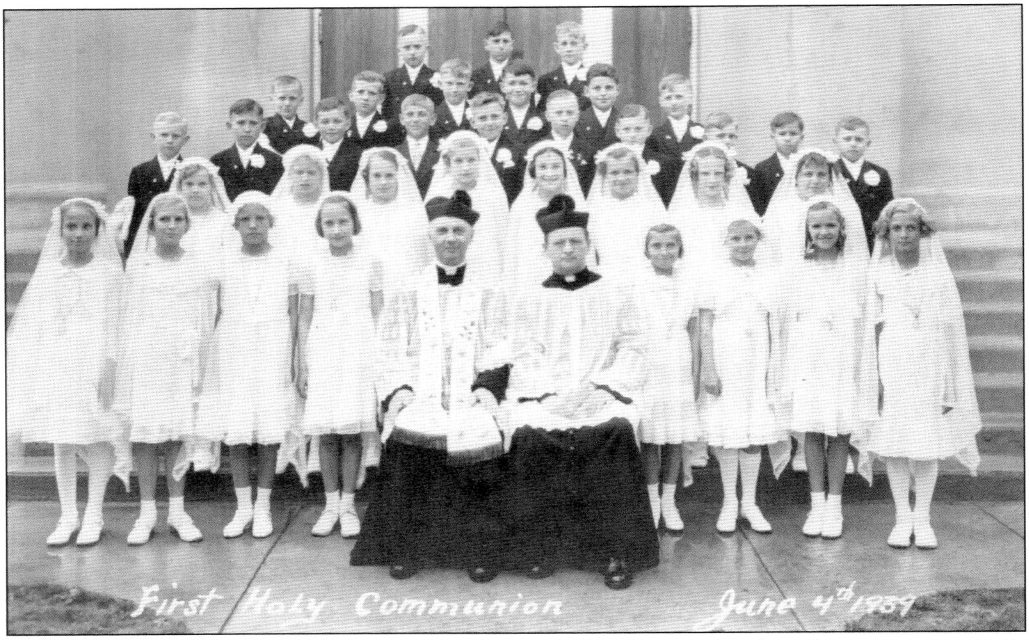

OUR LADY OF OSTRABRAMA CHURCH, JUNE 4, 1939. The boys and girls making their first Holy Communion were sons and daughters of Polish immigrants drawn to Cutchogue's farms at the turn of the century. Many prospered and acquired their own farms, while others joined the larger workforce. Our Lady of Ostrabrama Church remains at the center of Polish social life today. (Courtesy of the Southold Historical Society.)

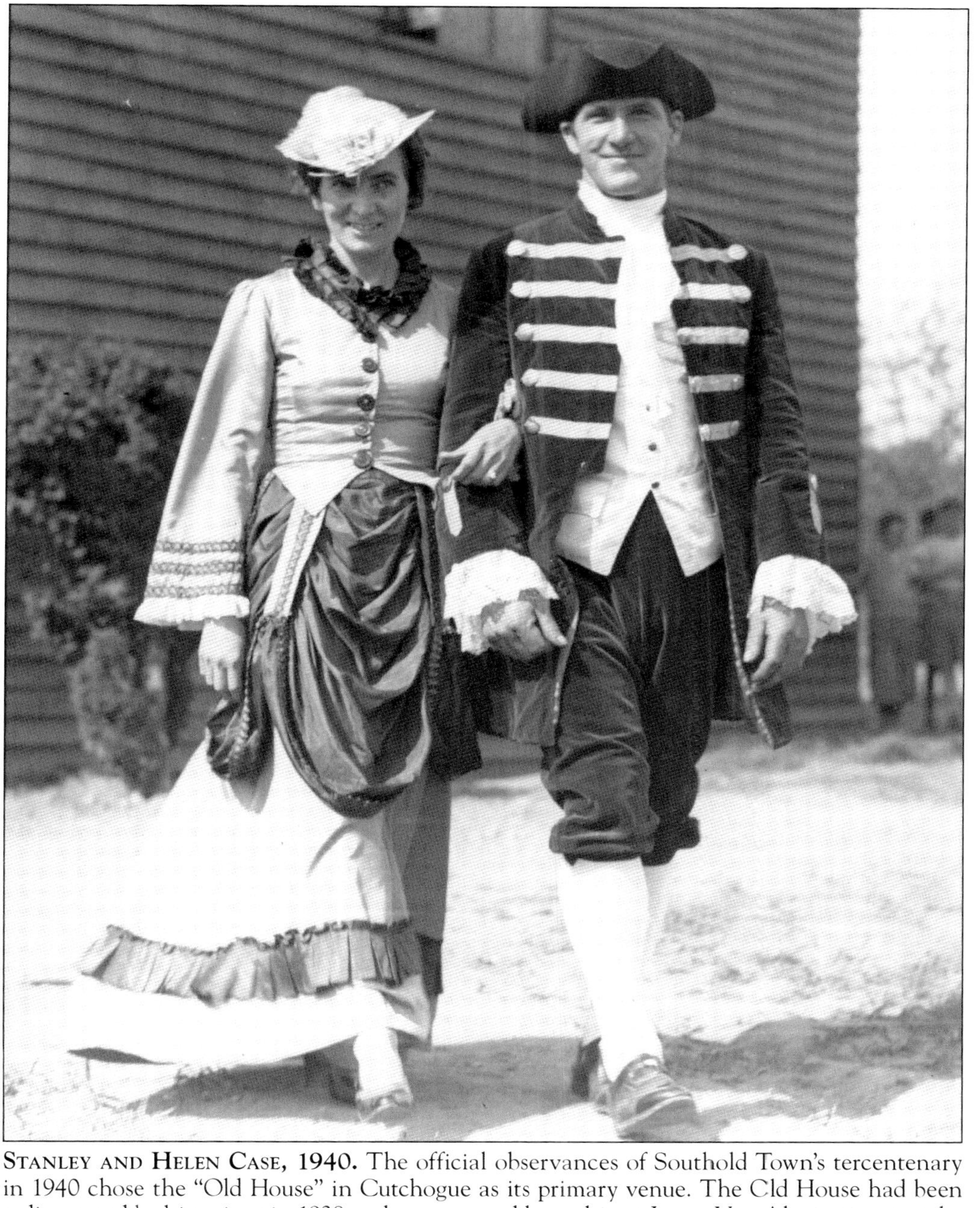

STANLEY AND HELEN CASE, 1940. The official observances of Southold Town's tercentenary in 1940 chose the "Old House" in Cutchogue as its primary venue. The Old House had been rediscovered by historians in 1938 and was restored by architect James Van Alst in time to take center stage in the festivities. Stanley G. Case (1905–1976) and his wife, Helen Boisseau Case (1908–2001), both descendants of the Case family that had owned the house in the early 1900s, dressed in period costume for the occasion. The historic house was built by John Budd in Southold around 1649, but was relocated to Cutchogue in 1660 and descended in the Horton, Wickham, Landon, and Case families before becoming a museum site in 1940. The Old House is now maintained and interpreted for public tours during the summer months by the Cutchogue–New Suffolk Historical Council.

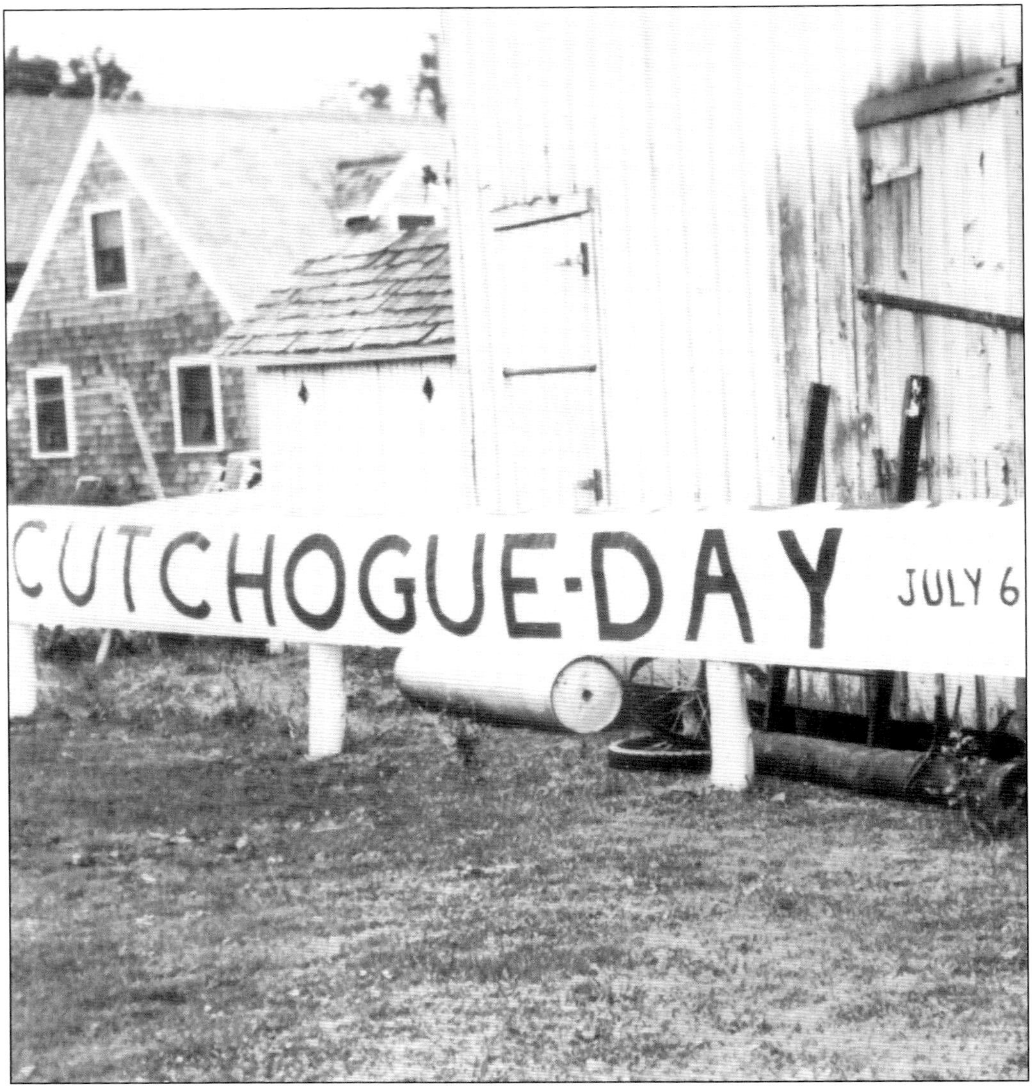

CUTCHOGUE DAY, JULY 6, 1941. "Cutchogue Day" was initiated by the Cutchogue Fire Department as a way to sponsor a community flag and flagpole, and the idea grew to encompass a parade in which many civic organizations, church leaders, and politicians took part. The dedication was planned for the Sunday following July 4, 1941, and Maj. Louis W. Bleser accepted the flag from the Knights of Columbus and gave it to fire department officers on behalf of the commanding officer of Camp Upton, Col. C.W. Baird. Camp Upton had been created in Yaphank, Long Island, in 1917 to train and mobilize soldiers for World War I. Closed in 1921, the camp was reactivated in 1940 prior to US entry into World War II, and it was undoubtedly the patriotism that Cutchogue's citizens felt that prompted the creation of "Cutchogue Day" in 1941. (Courtesy of Cutchogue Fire Department.)

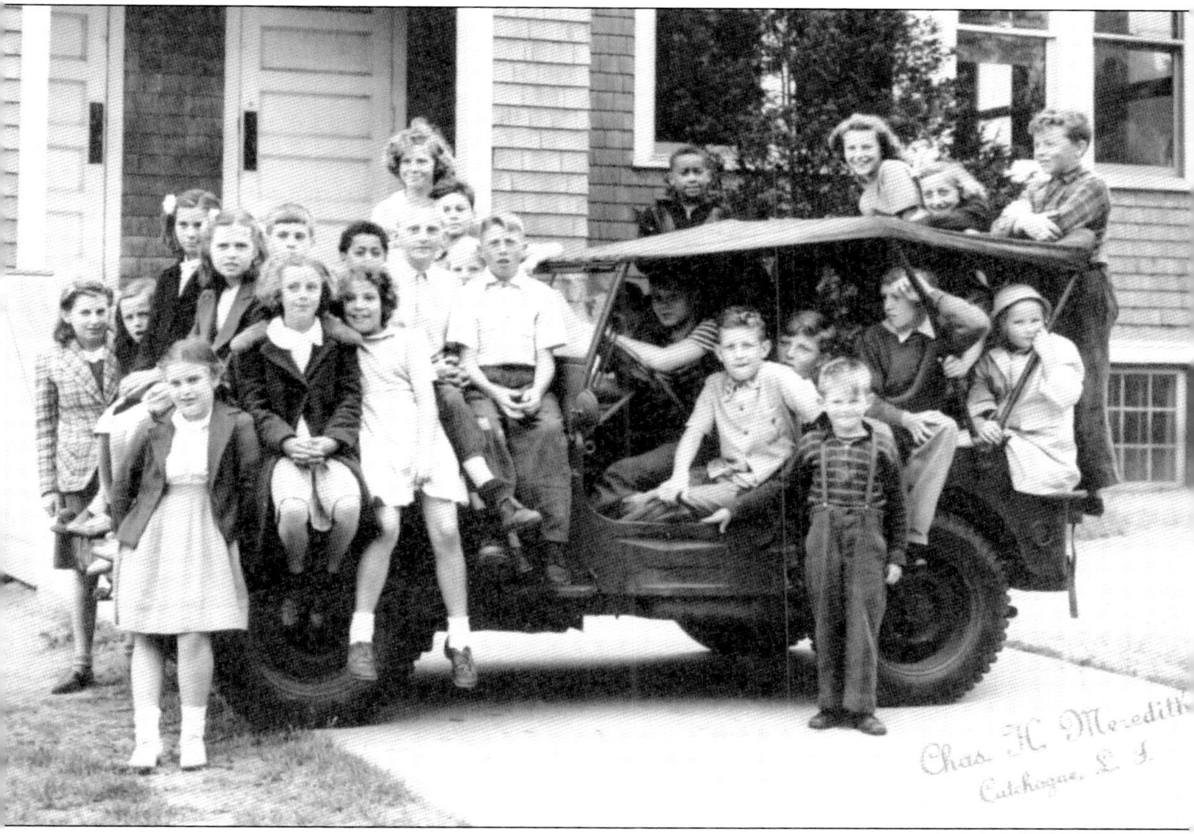

New Suffolk School Students, 1944. Glee and a little mischief can be detected in this class portrait, which was taken by local photographer Charles H. Meredith. The New Suffolk elementary school students are clamoring over a Jeep, which they had raised funds to acquire and contribute to the war effort. The Willys World War II Army Jeep was manufactured between 1941 and 1945 and became emblematic of the war. The name is thought to derive from a popular cartoon character of the day, "Eugene the Jeep," who appeared in Popeye's cartoons as a small and nimble jungle pet, capable of solving difficult problems. The grade-school students shown here would have known about Eugene the Jeep, and some of their family members were undoubtedly swept up in the conflict. Their generous fundraising effort exemplified the commitment felt among all age groups during the war.

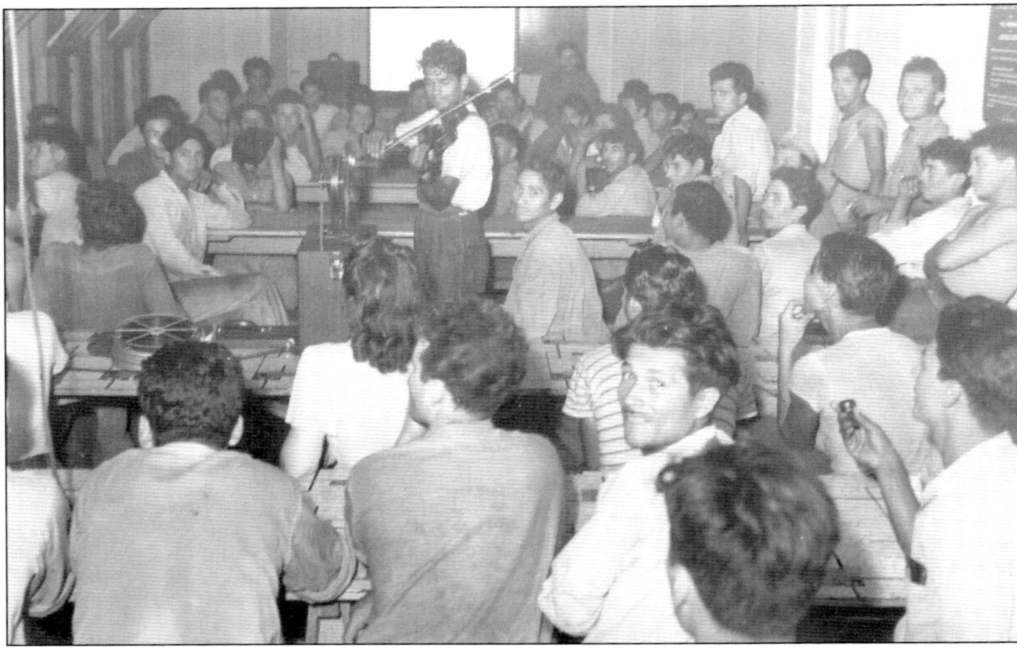

MIGRANT LABOR CAMPS, 1947. Responding to labor shortages brought on by World War II, Cutchogue farmers sought permission from Southold Town to bring in Jamaican workers when students proved inadequate for harvesting crops. By 1943, a labor camp was established for migrant workers at Lake Lodge in Peconic. As seen above, even after a ten-hour day in the fields, there was time for recreation. After the war, the shortage of farmhands persisted, and the Eastern Suffolk Farm Cooperative was formed to attract African American migrant workers from the South. The cooperative bought land on Cox's Lane and set up barracks and platform tents capable of housing 400 men, women, and children (below). In 1949, a classroom was established for the children, and more were added in the 1950s. (Courtesy of the Southold Historical Society.)

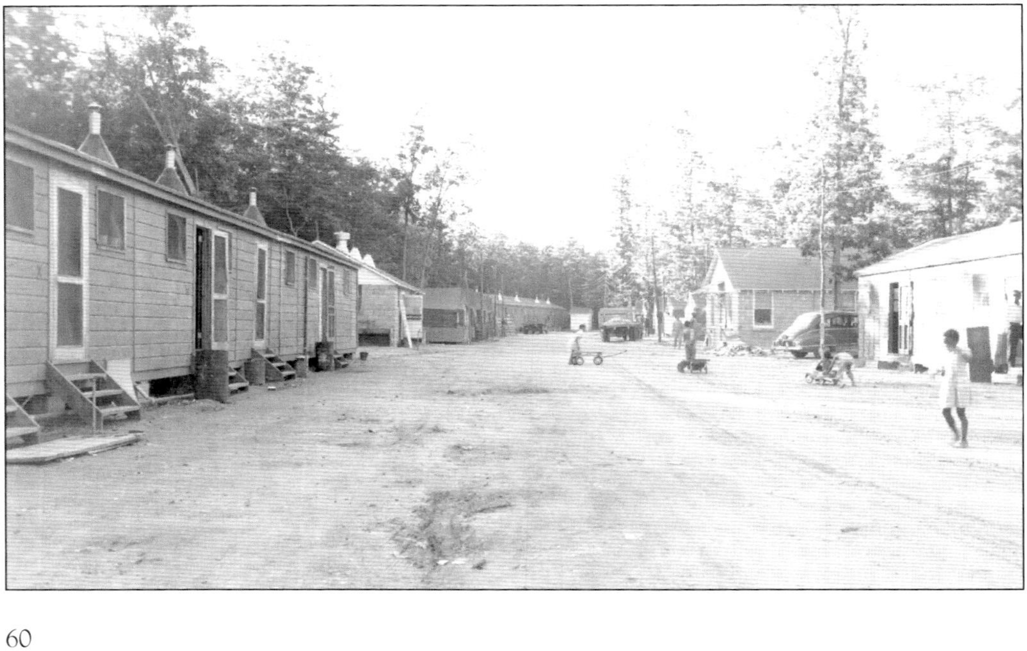

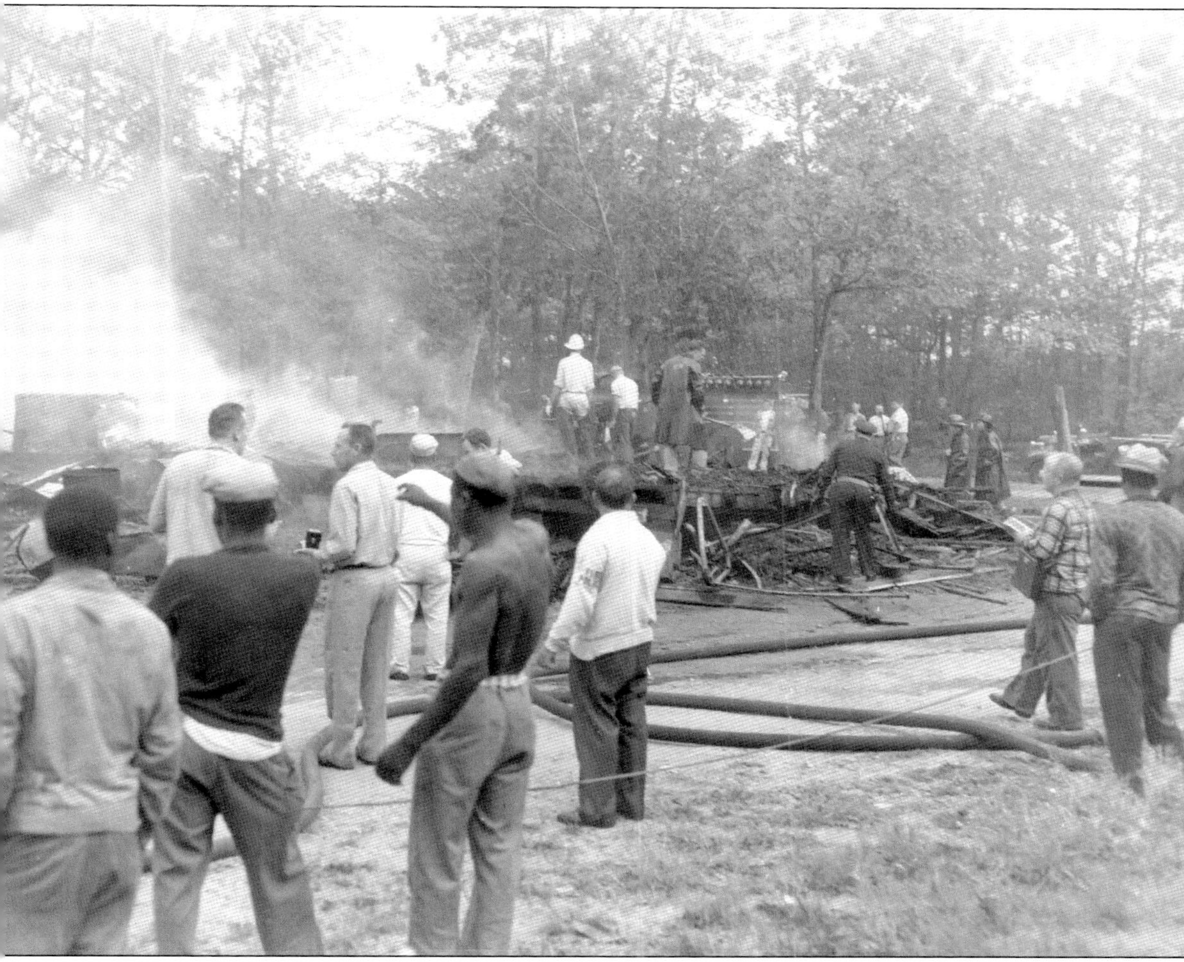

Labor Camp Fire, 1961. Disaster struck Cutchogue's migrant labor camp in October 1961 when a fire broke out in one of the barracks. Tragically, four men perished in the blaze, one from each of four states represented in the camp: North Carolina, Ohio, Maryland, and Mississippi. Conditions were then improved in the camp, due in large part to the intervention of Suffolk county executive H. Lee Dennison. A county-funded Migrant Health Program was set up in the 1970s, and nurses and translators were hired to deal with a new generation of migrant farmers, including not only African Americans from southern states but also Hispanic workers from Puerto Rico, Mexico, and other Spanish-speaking countries. (Courtesy of the Southold Historical Society.)

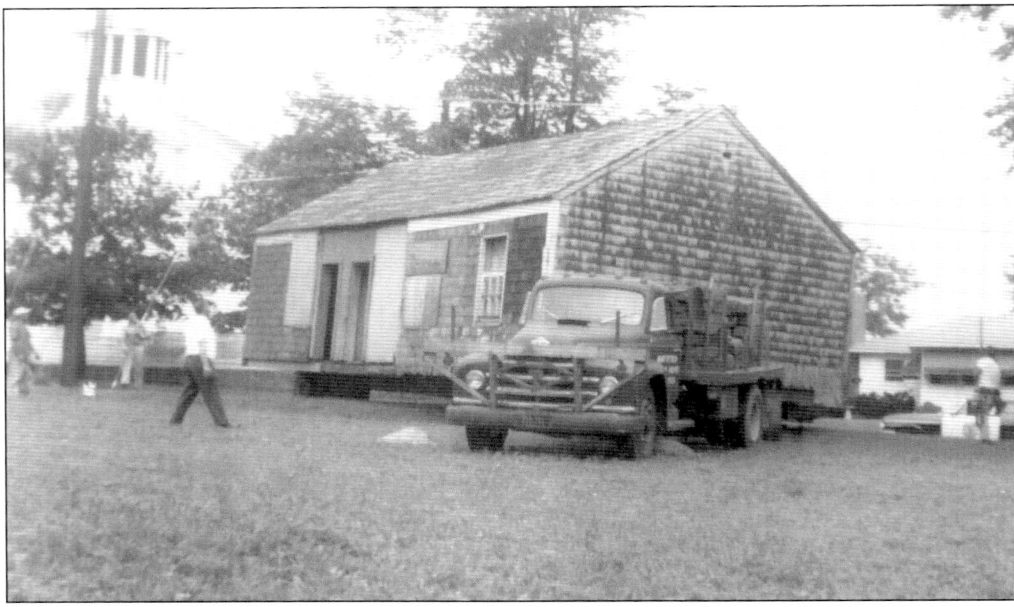

Schoolhouse Relocation, 1961. The one-room Cutchogue schoolhouse, which had been moved from its original location to a field behind the Presbyterian Church, found its way to the Village Green in 1961 to be preserved and to start life anew. The little building is still on skids in this photograph, awaiting restoration on a new foundation. The church can be seen on the left.

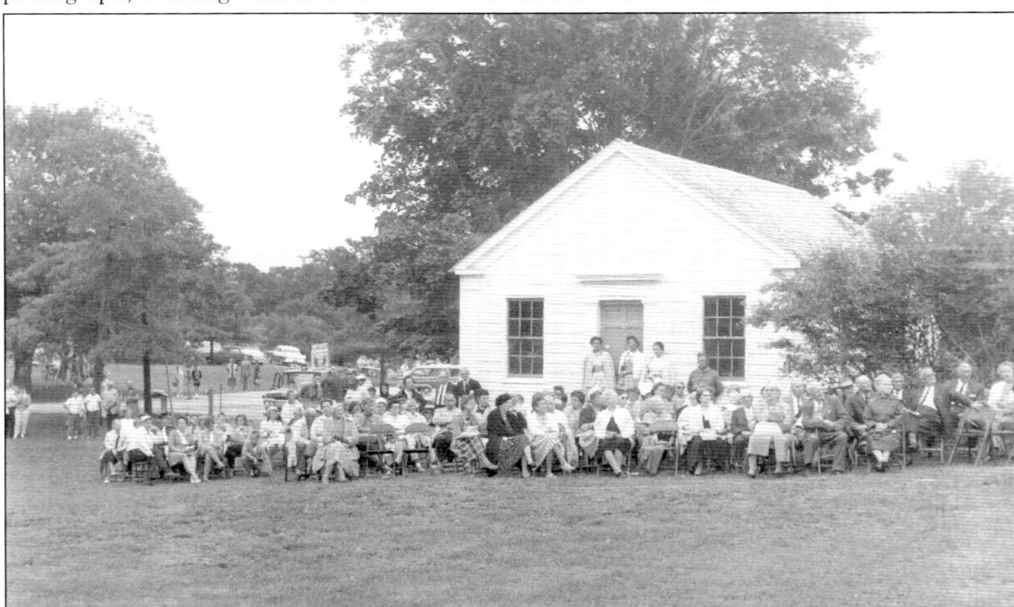

Cutchogue Schoolhouse Dedication, c. 1962. Local Cutchogue residents, many of them graduates of the old one-room schoolhouse, gathered on the Village Green to celebrate the preservation and restoration of this local landmark by the Cutchogue–New Suffolk Historical Council. The schoolhouse was the first of several historic buildings preserved by the organization for public enjoyment on the green. (Courtesy of the Southold Historical Society.)

Four

Doing Business

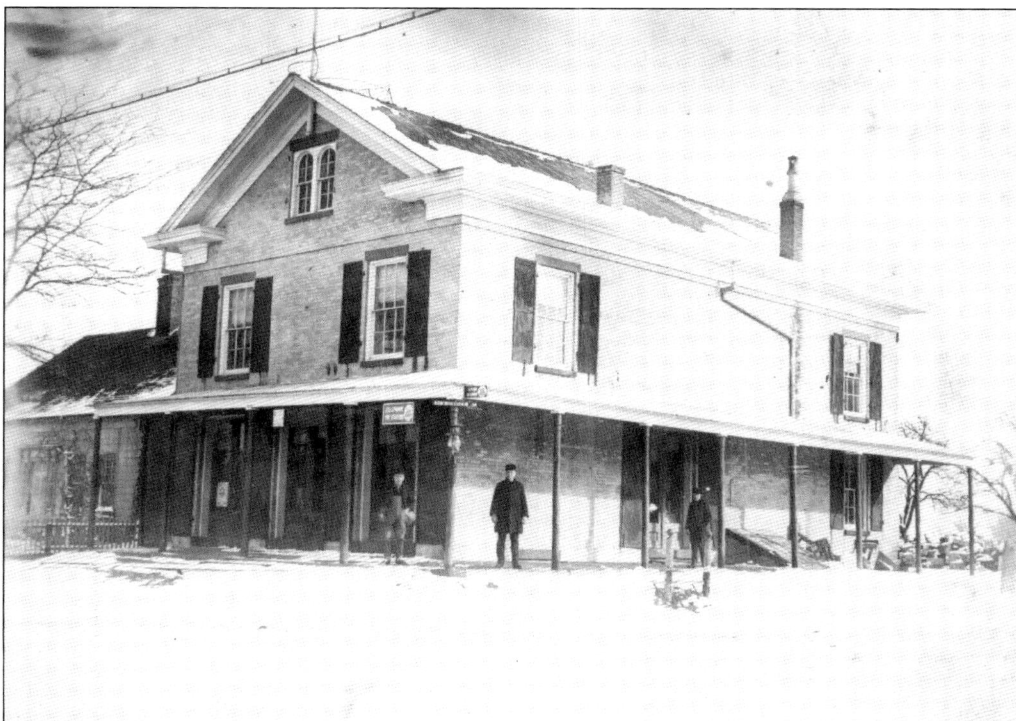

Goldsmith & Tuthill Store, c. 1900. The Cutchogue store was built by Ira Tuthill about 1828 at the corner of Main and New Suffolk Roads, a prominent corner at the center of the village. Constructed of brick, the large building boasted a wraparound porch supported with slender columns. After Ira's cousin Orrin T. Goldsmith joined the business around 1835, the enterprise changed its name to Goldsmith & Tuthill.

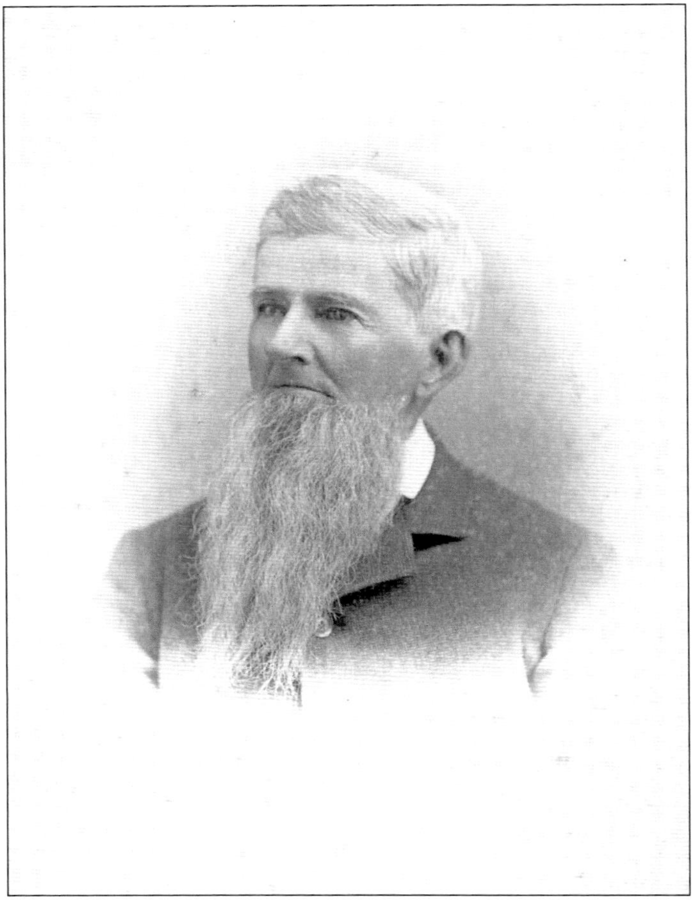

Orrin T. Goldsmith and Trade Card, c. 1875 and c. 1880. Orrin Tuthill Goldsmith (1818–1900) joined his uncle Ira Tuthill around the age of 17 in the operation of the Goldsmith & Tuthill store in Cutchogue. Goldsmith married Fanny Marie Tuthill in 1844 and had two children, Oliver and Emma. The general store that he operated in Cutchogue was the purveyor of all things useful and necessary, from fresh fruit and farm products to "store bought" and imported goods like hardware, tobacco, stoves, and bolts of fabric. Goldsmith & Tuthill, "dealers in L.I. Produce, Eggs, &c.," served not only as a center of village life and commerce, but also as the post office and trading center for goods that were brought in for barter.

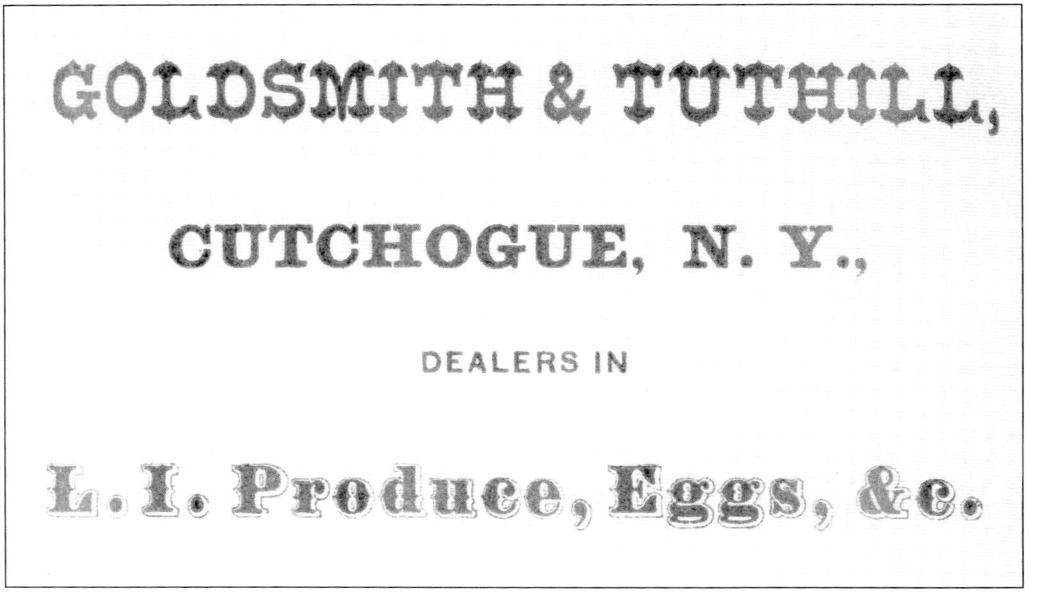

GOLDSMITH & TUTHILL,

CUTCHOGUE, N. Y.,

DEALERS IN

L. I. Produce, Eggs, &c.

New Boardinghouse Trade Card, 1840. Ira B. Tuthill, New Suffolk's greatest booster, built the hamlet's first hotel. He promoted the town as a destination for tourists and arranged steamboat service and a line of stages to facilitate travel to and from New York City. In his words, New Suffolk could not be surpassed for those "who may wish to pass the summer months out of the City."

NEW BOARDING HOUSE,

At New Suffolk, Long Island.

The subscriber would take this method to inform his friends and the public, that he has opened his house in New Suffolk, Southold, L. Island, which he has built and fitted up expressly for the accomodation of *Boarders*, where he will be happy to receive his friends and all others who may favor him with their patronage; and he pledges himself to use every exertion to please and gratify those who may find it convenient to call at his house. His charges will be moderate and such as he hopes will be satisfactory to all. The opportunities for communicating with the City, will be superior the coming season. A steamboat will leave New York daily for Port Jefferson, and from thence a line of stages will be formed to Riverhead and New Suffolk, thus enabling passengers to make the passage through in one day. There are also four packet sloops running between New York and New Suffolk, viz.: the Emperor, Capt. Goldsmith; the Suffolk, Capt. Tuthill; the Prudence, Capt. Booth, and the Swallow, Capt. Wells; from New Slip.

The village of New Suffolk is beautifully situated on a rising ground, commanding an extensive view of Peconic Bay and the adjacent villages. Its natural advantages for fishing, sporting and the healthiness of its location, are not surpassed by any village on the Island; and citizens who may wish to pass the summer months out of the City, will find it an advantageous and delightful summer retreat.

IRA B. TUTHILL.

New Suffolk, L. I., 27th February, 1840.

The subscribers cheerfully recommend the above house to those of their friends who are fond of a quiet and pleasant home and obliging hosts, pleasant and healthy location, good shooting, fishing, &c. and reasonable charges.

Jas. W. Pinckney, Henry Vandervoort, O. B. Goldsmith, B. W. Osborn.

Grant Houses, c. 1920. The three-story structures pictured here were built by village founder Ira B. Tuthill in 1840 as part of the New Suffolk Hotel. Operated in the 1870s by William McNish, the hotel was later cut into two sections and relocated across town. Known as the Grant houses, the "apartment houses" became residences for Portuguese laborers working on improving the Main Road in Cutchogue.

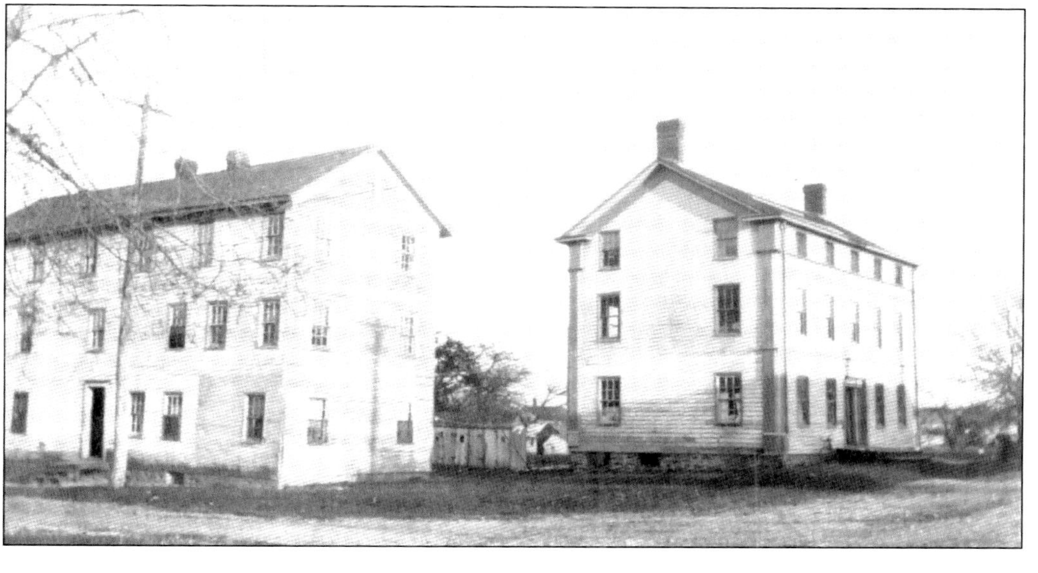

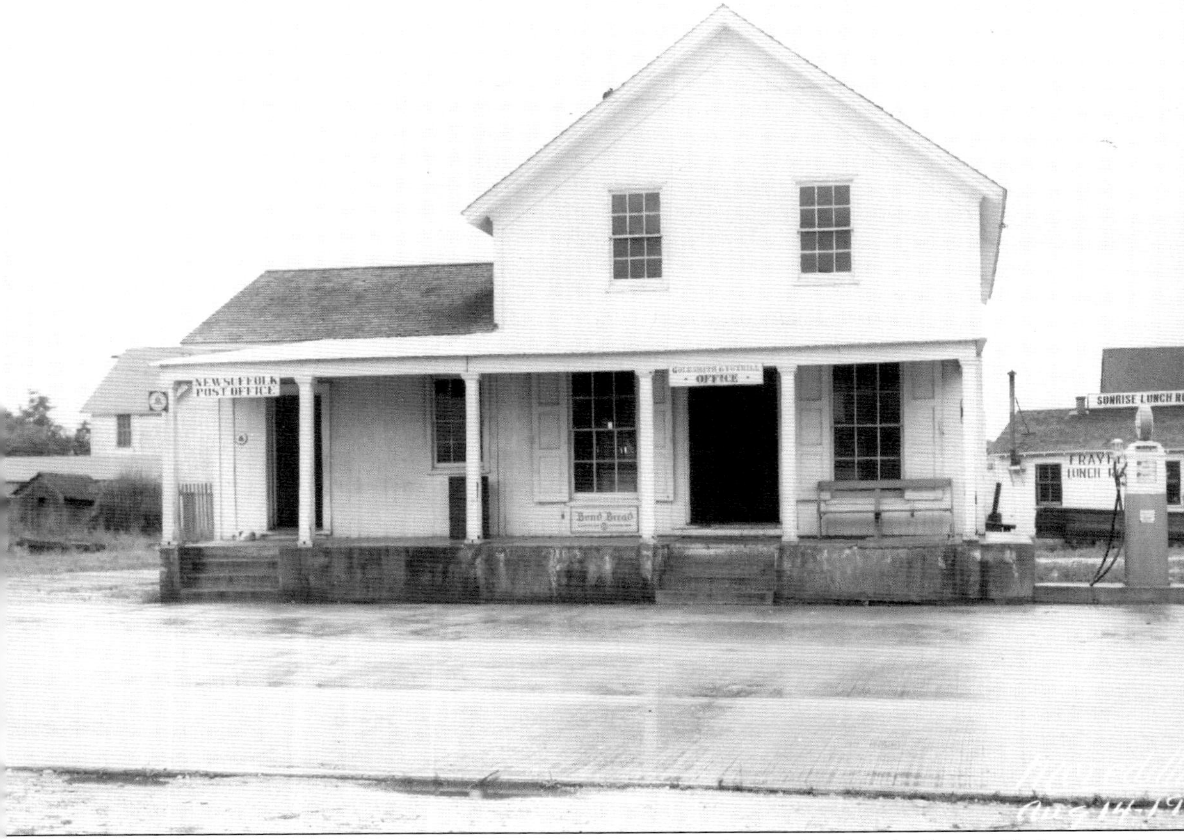

GOLDSMITH & TUTHILL'S, NEW SUFFOLK, 1942. Not to be confused with the establishment of the same name in Cutchogue, Goldsmith & Tuthill's second general store occupied a prominent location at the foot of Main Street in downtown New Suffolk. The store and ship chandlery was constructed in 1836 by New Suffolk's enterprising land developer and greatest booster, Ira B. Tuthill, who turned management over to his son Jeremiah in 1842. Ira was also influential in opening New Suffolk's first post office, a service that his store provided. After Ira served as the town's first postmaster for many years, his son Jeremiah assumed the job until 1898. Although a catastrophic fire destroyed the original building in 1872, the store was rebuilt within the year and continued to operate under family management until its sale in 1966. In this 1942 Charles H. Meredith photograph, Lou Frayher's Sunrise Lunch Room can be seen at right, behind the gas pumps.

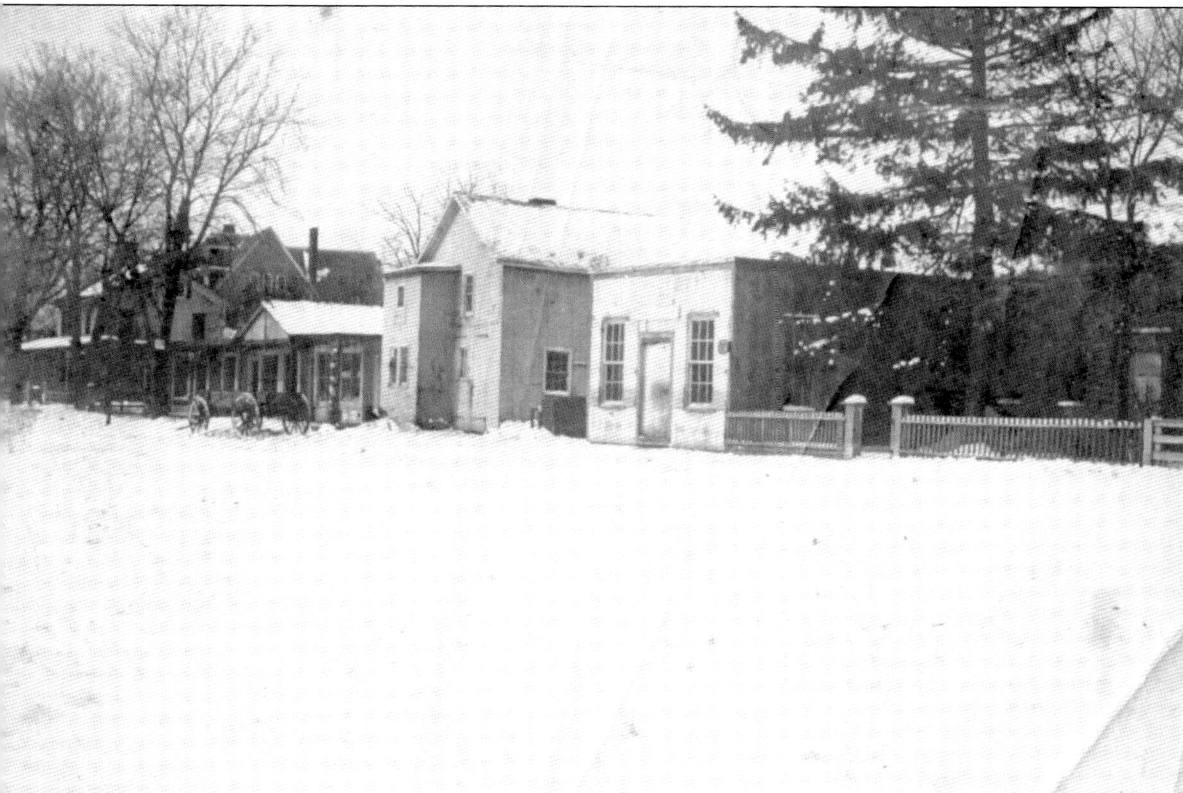

Blacksmith Shop, c. 1900. Central to local commerce before the automobile age was the village blacksmith, often located near other essential commercial enterprises, as in this view of downtown Cutchogue around 1900. The blacksmith worked primarily with wrought iron, manufacturing and repairing wheels, springs, and fasteners for carriages and other conveyances, horseshoes, hoops for barrels, a wide variety of agricultural tools and household implements, hardware, and decorative objects. By the early 20th century, however, the blacksmith's trade was fading with the advent of manufactured goods that could be shipped quickly and cheaply across the country. Seen in the left distance is Sacred Heart Church and Rectory, the only Main Street buildings in this photograph that are standing today. (Courtesy of a private collection.)

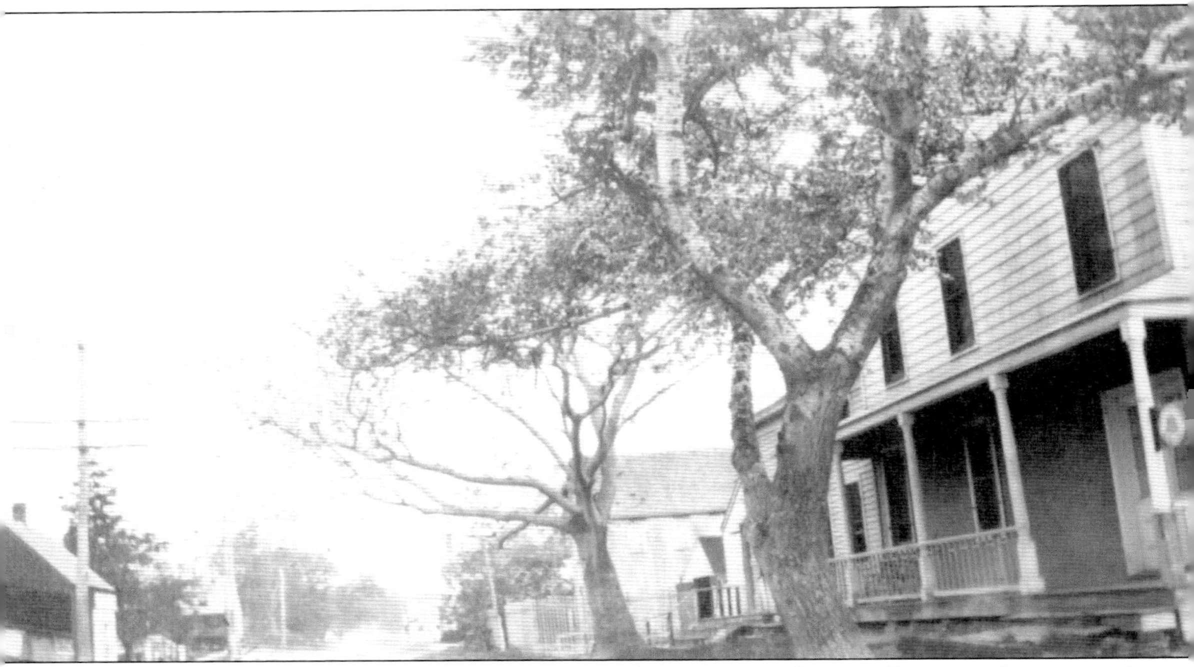

New Suffolk, c. 1925. Just as Main Street in Cutchogue remained a mix of houses and commercial enterprises in the early 1900s, downtown New Suffolk retained its residential feel despite the bustling waterfront for which it was better known. In this photograph facing north along First Street, Emlen Johnson's store is at the far left. A fixture of downtown New Suffolk for many years, Johnson's store began business on School House Creek in the early decades of the 20th century, furnishing supplies primarily to fishermen. Johnson's store grew with the New Suffolk population, expanding its product line to keep pace with an ever-changing clientele. Farther north on the left are the King and Raynor residences. The King family was among the first to settle New Suffolk, and it is perhaps no coincidence that a street is named for them. At far right is Frank Jacob's Hotel. The "hotel" was a popular saloon conveniently located near New Suffolk's wharf. The wraparound porch and familiar telephone sign are indications of its public purpose, although the building had likely started out as a private residence.

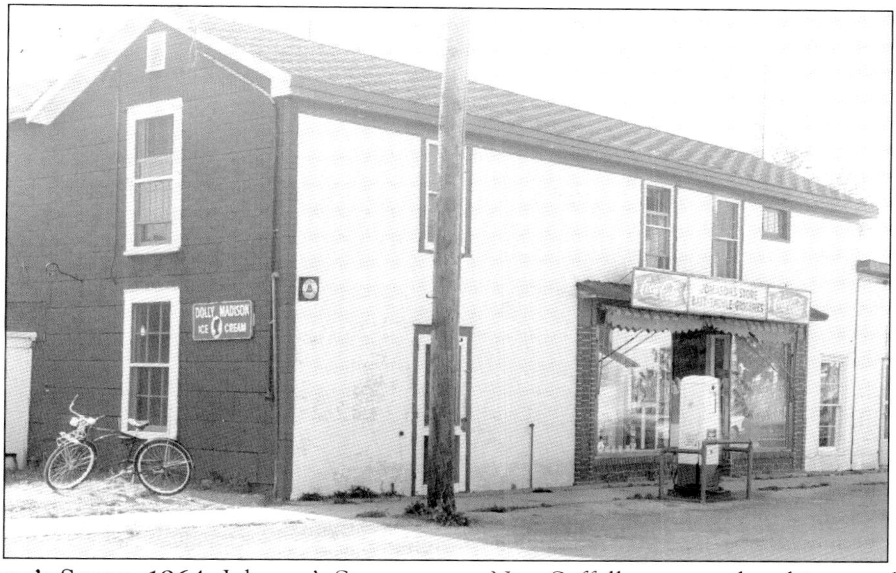

JOHNSON'S STORE, 1964. Johnson's Store grew as New Suffolk prospered and its population expanded to include commercial fishermen, "summer people," and year-round residents. The new Johnson's Store of the mid-20th century (above) offered a wide range of goods and services, including Coca-Cola, Dolly Madison ice cream, groceries, and bait and tackle, as well as gasoline and a public telephone. The interior (below) was typical of its era: a modest variety of canned and bottled goods line the narrow shelves, while refrigerated floor units offer cold cuts, perishables, and the ice cream advertised out front. The store's wood flooring and hand-built shelving became relics of an earlier time, however, and Johnson's Store would soon close as modern "supermarkets" in nearby Cutchogue claimed its business. (Courtesy of the Southold Historical Society.)

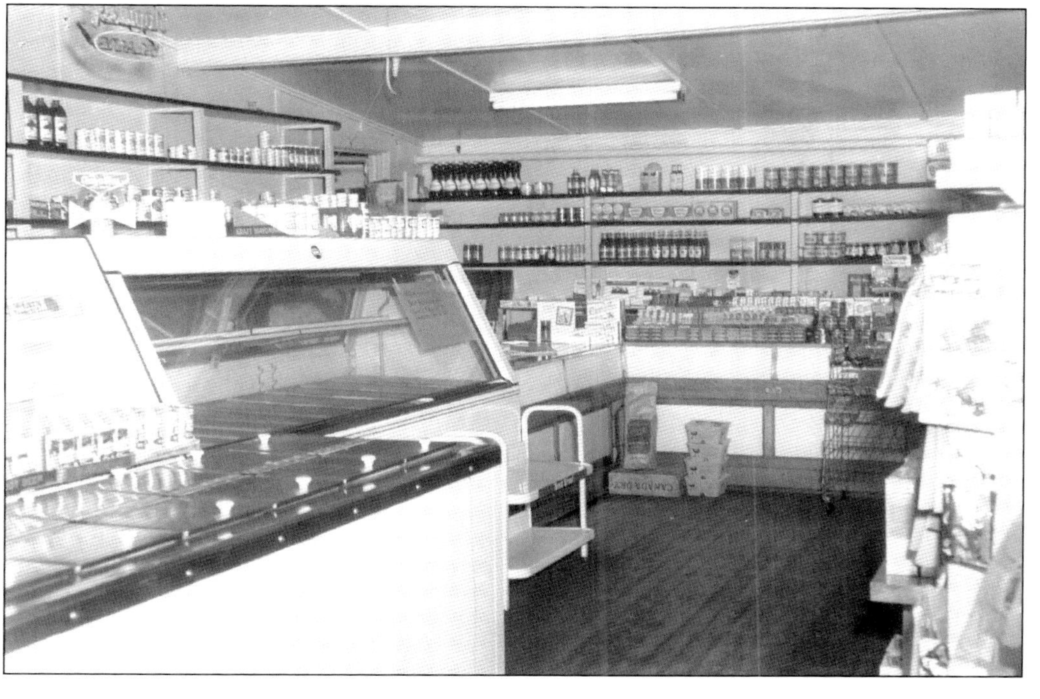

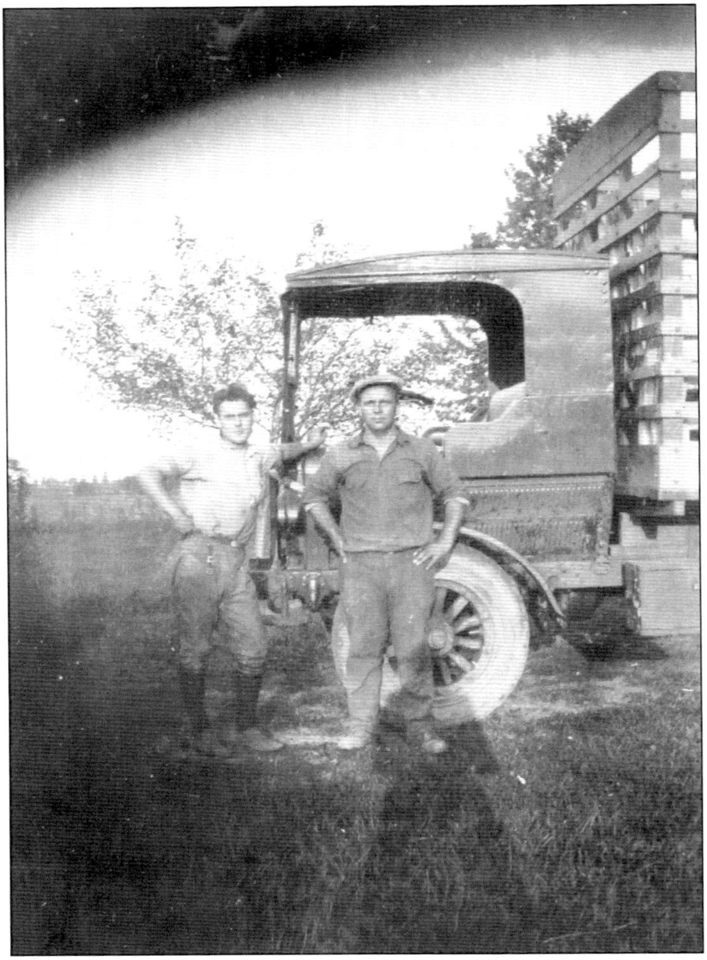

Shipping Produce by Truck, c. 1925. The G&D Motor Express Company was founded in Cutchogue in 1920 by John E. Gee (right) and his brother-in-law, Al Denzler. Financed by Gee's mother, Agnes, the firm became a major commercial trucking business and employed over 30 trucks and 60 men by the 1930s. Gee had gained experience during World War I repairing aircraft engines. After the war, he returned to Cutchogue and went into business with Denzler, converting a surplus Army vehicle into a freight truck. Their initial competition was the Long Island Rail Road, but as roads improved between eastern Long Island and metropolitan New York, so too did the trucking business. After its fleet of trucks was confiscated to settle an accident claim, the company was driven into bankruptcy by the Great Depression.

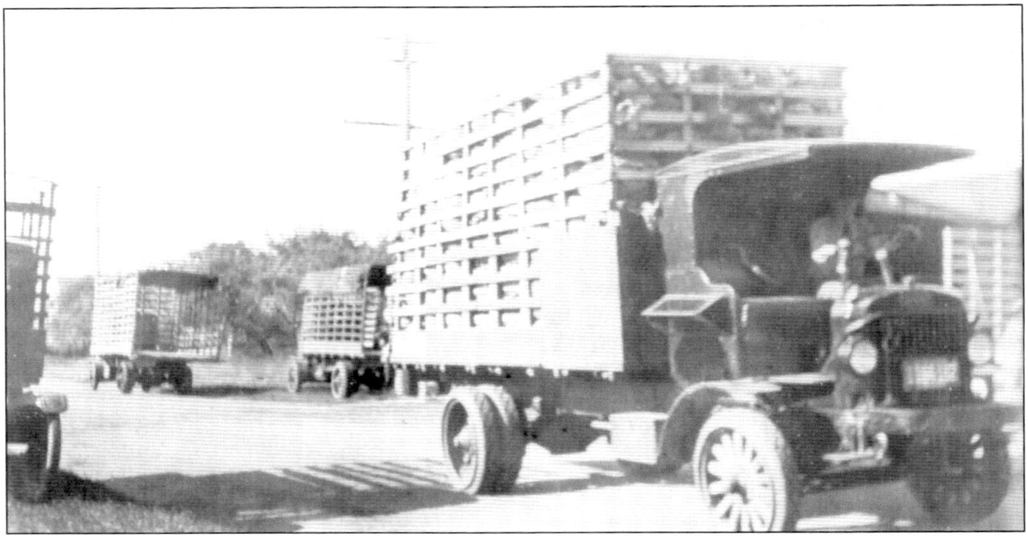

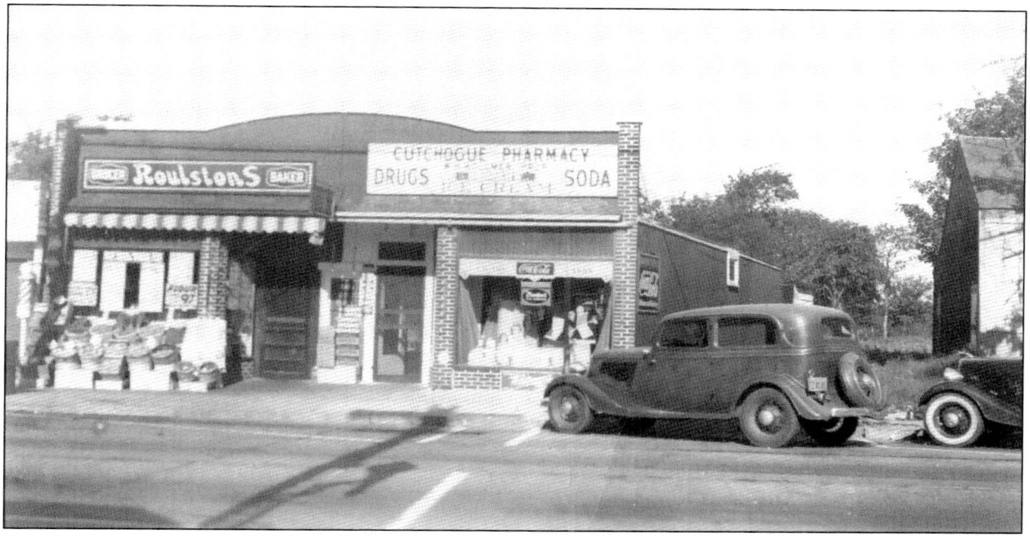

Downtown Cutchogue, c. 1930. Roulston's Store and the adjoining Cutchogue Pharmacy share a common storefront, and an old frame dwelling remains standing next door, in the above photograph of downtown Cutchogue from around 1930. Roulston's combined groceries with baked goods and was managed by Arthur Johnson. The pharmacy next door was run by W.H. Kollmer. A barbershop, out of view on the left but marked by a classic striped pole, was owned by B.L. Tomaszewski, who employed three barbers in the shop's heyday. In the c. 1930 postcard below, facing west down the center of the Main Road, the rooftops of older residential structures protrude above the storefronts. (Above, courtesy of a private collection.)

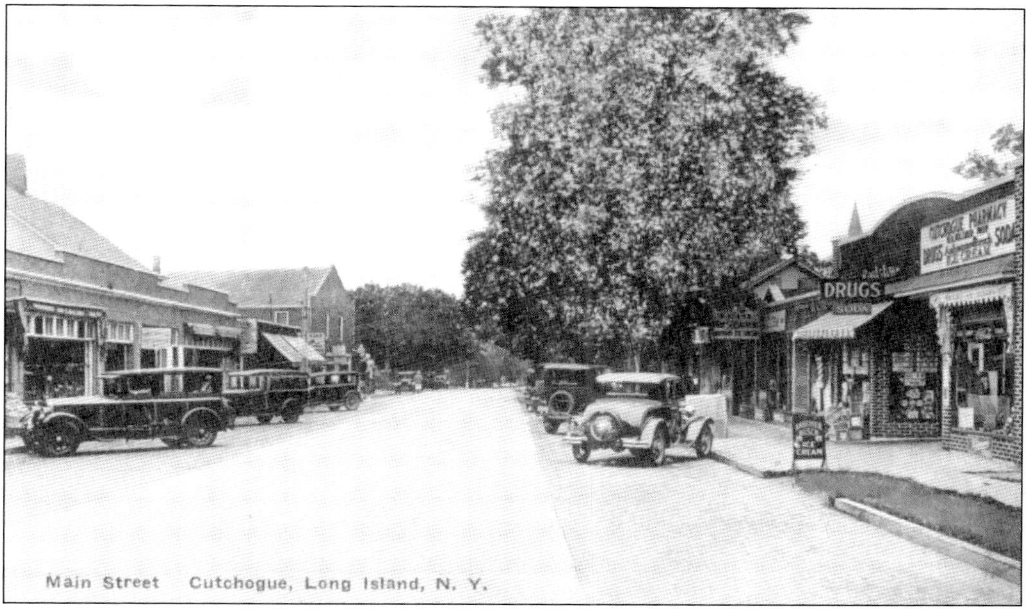

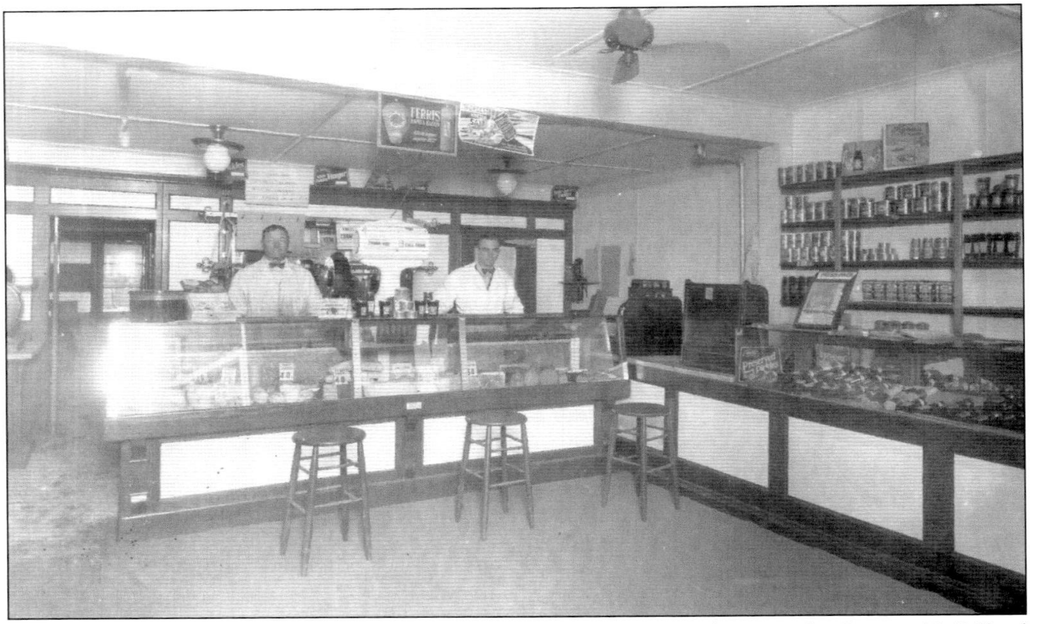

Billard's Market and Main Street, c. 1935. In the above photograph, George T. Billard (1870–1954) (left) and his youngest son, Ellis Francis Billard (1904–1982), mind the family meat market on Cutchogue's Main Road around 1935. George was the second of two children born to Theodore B. Billard and Cynthia Conklin. His dad was born in Brookhaven, but after marrying a local Southold girl, George settled in Cutchogue and opened the family business. The Ben Franklin Store featured in the postcard of Cutchogue's Main Street (below) was part of a chain of five-and-dime stores once common in small towns across America. The chain was organized on the franchise model in 1927, with each store owned and operated by an independent proprietor. W.E. Walty was the proprietor of the Cutchogue store.

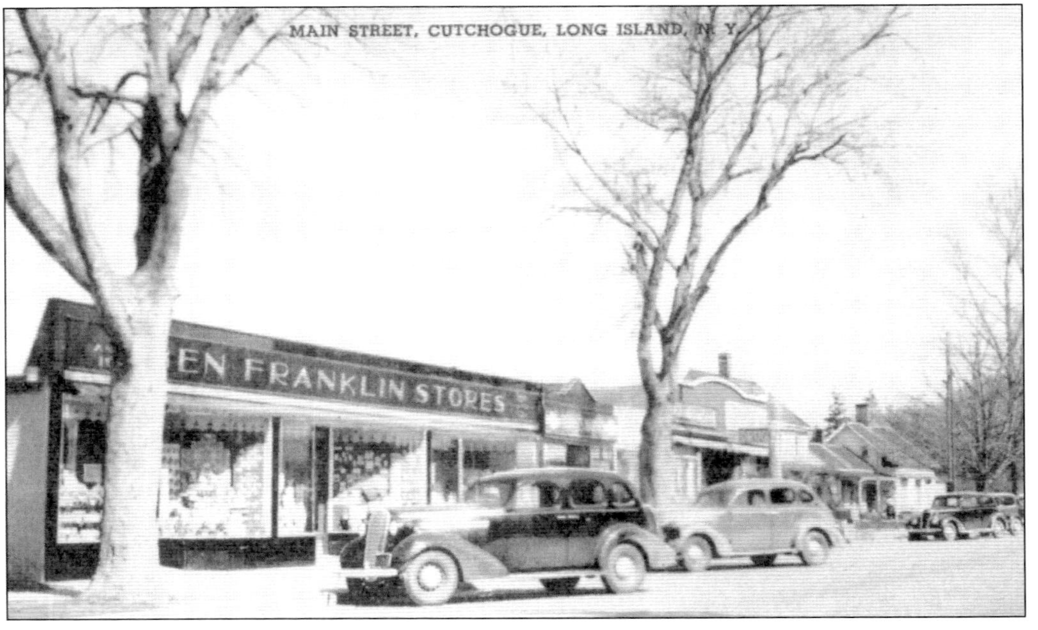

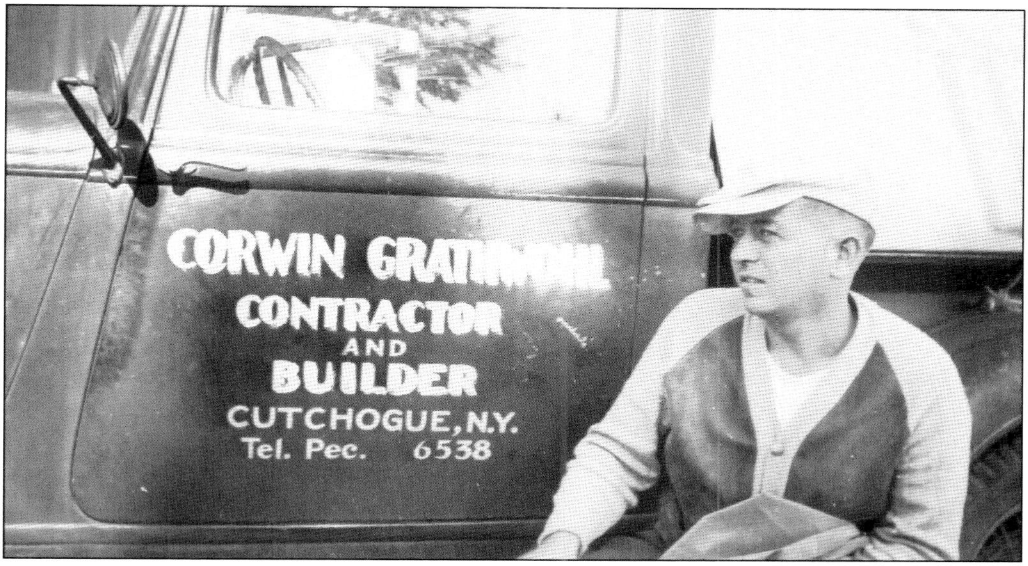

CORWIN GRATHWOHL, c. 1935. Corwin C. Grathwohl (1907–1985), a well-known Cutchogue builder and carpenter, kept his shop in his house at the corner of Main Road and Alvah's Lane. He was civic-minded, serving as president of the chamber of commerce, a member of the parks commission, and founding president of the Cutchogue–New Suffolk Historical Council in 1960. (Courtesy of James F. Grathwohl.)

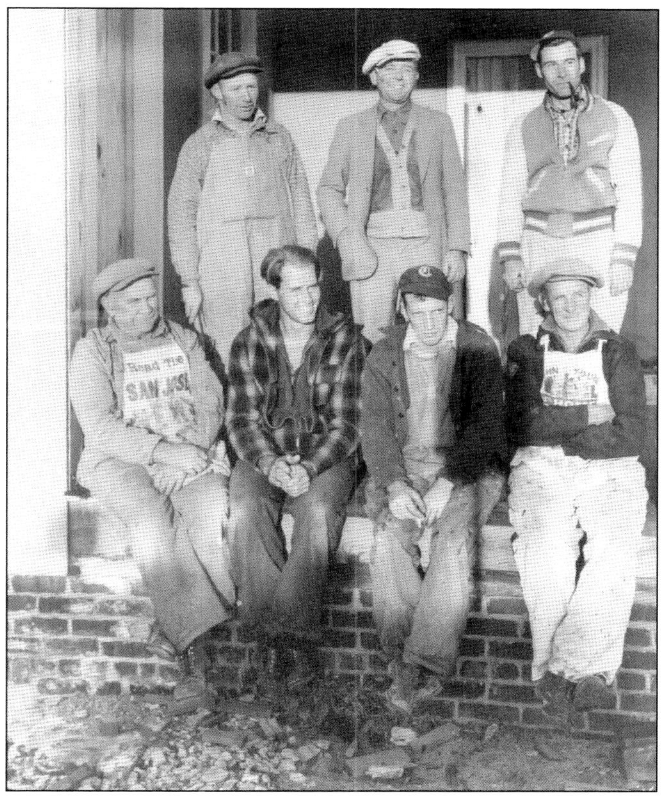

GRATHWOHL'S CONSTRUCTION CREW, c. 1941. Corwin C. Grathwohl and his construction crew assemble for a group portrait around 1941. Shown here are, from left to right, (first row) Harry Marrois, Harold Weggland, Edward (Red) Grathwohl, and Tyson Bond; (second row) Francis (Mac) McCaffery, Corwin Grathwohl, and Dick Horton. The photograph was taken while the crew was working on the Breaker estate in Mattituck. (Courtesy of Virginia McCaffery.)

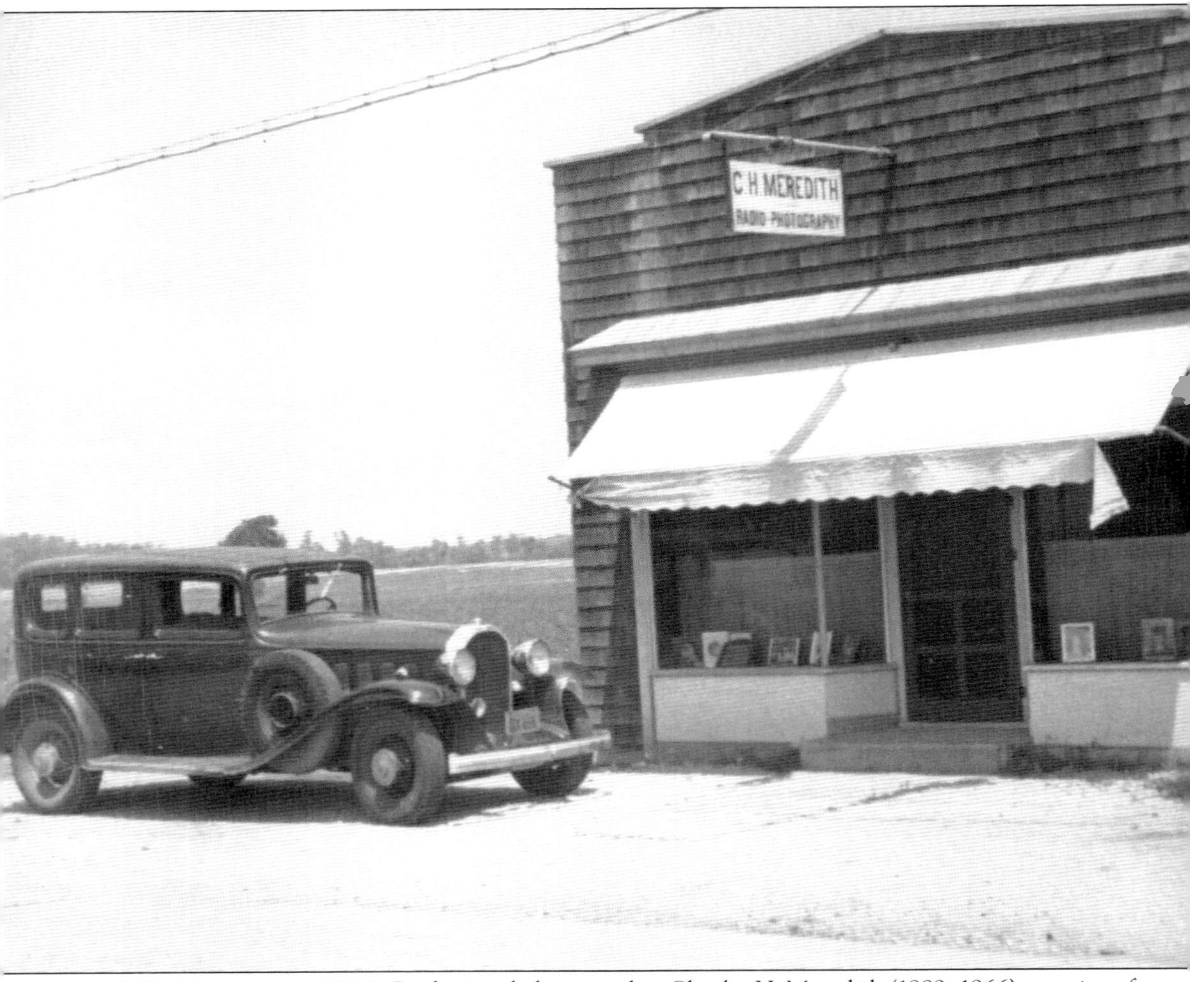

C.H. MEREDITH, c. 1940. Professional photographer Charles H. Meredith (1889–1966), a native of Vancouver, Canada, came to the village of Peconic on eastern Long Island as an employee of the Long Island Rail Road. Working first as an agent and telegraph operator of the station, Meredith maintained the railway's signaling and communications system. He became a "lightning slinger," as telegraphers of the day were known, providing an essential link in the railroad's communications system. He later developed a photography business, for which he is primarily known today. Meredith's workshop and studio were located on Depot Lane, Cutchogue, where he repaired radios and managed a photography business that generated thousands of images of everyday life, special events, and transition in this rural community. Many of Meredith's photographs appear in this book. (Courtesy of the Southold Historical Society.)

A&P Store, Cutchogue, 1941. Charles H. Meredith appreciated the visual power of brand merchandizing, as shown in this store display of "Dexo," the hydrogenated vegetable shortening that was "guaranteed 100% pure." Dexo shortening was A&P's own brand, its labels promoting special recipes for cakes, "grandma's pumpkin pie," and even the "tastiest fried chicken under the sun!" (Courtesy of the Southold Historical Society.)

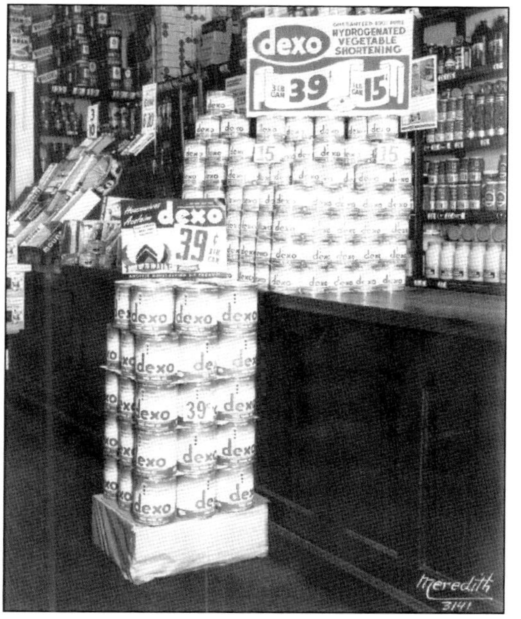

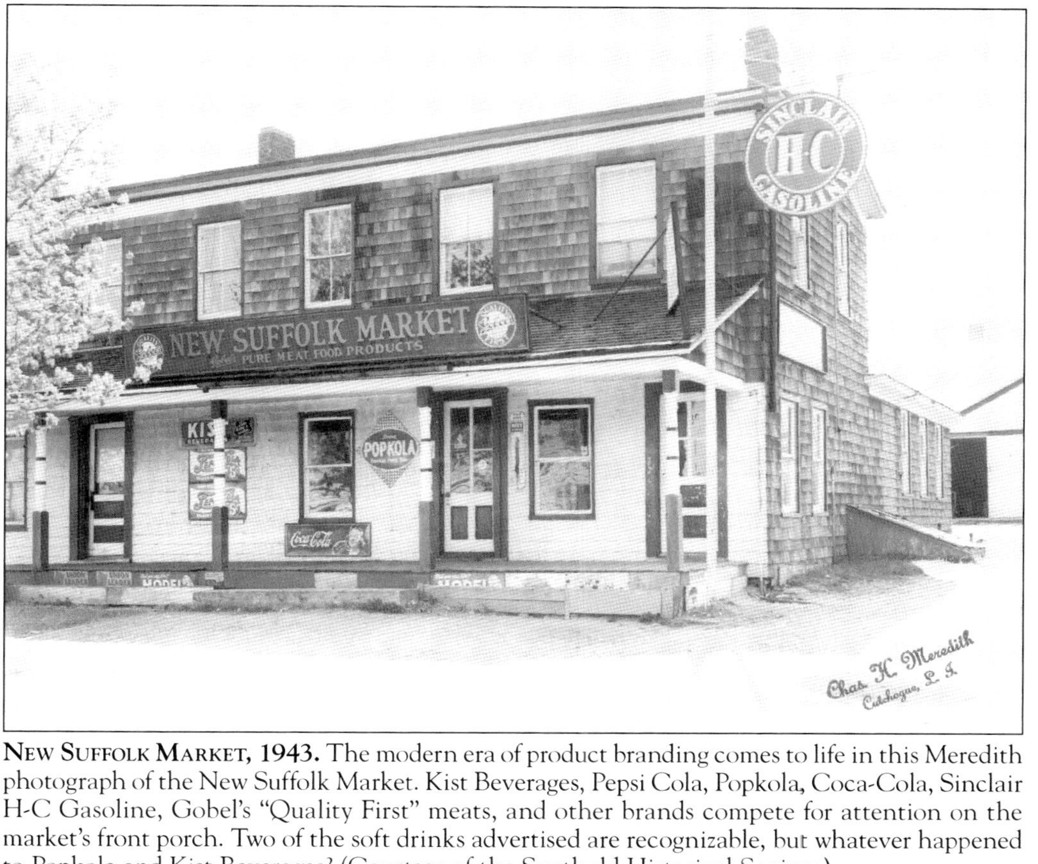

New Suffolk Market, 1943. The modern era of product branding comes to life in this Meredith photograph of the New Suffolk Market. Kist Beverages, Pepsi Cola, Popkola, Coca-Cola, Sinclair H-C Gasoline, Gobel's "Quality First" meats, and other brands compete for attention on the market's front porch. Two of the soft drinks advertised are recognizable, but whatever happened to Popkola and Kist Beverages? (Courtesy of the Southold Historical Society.)

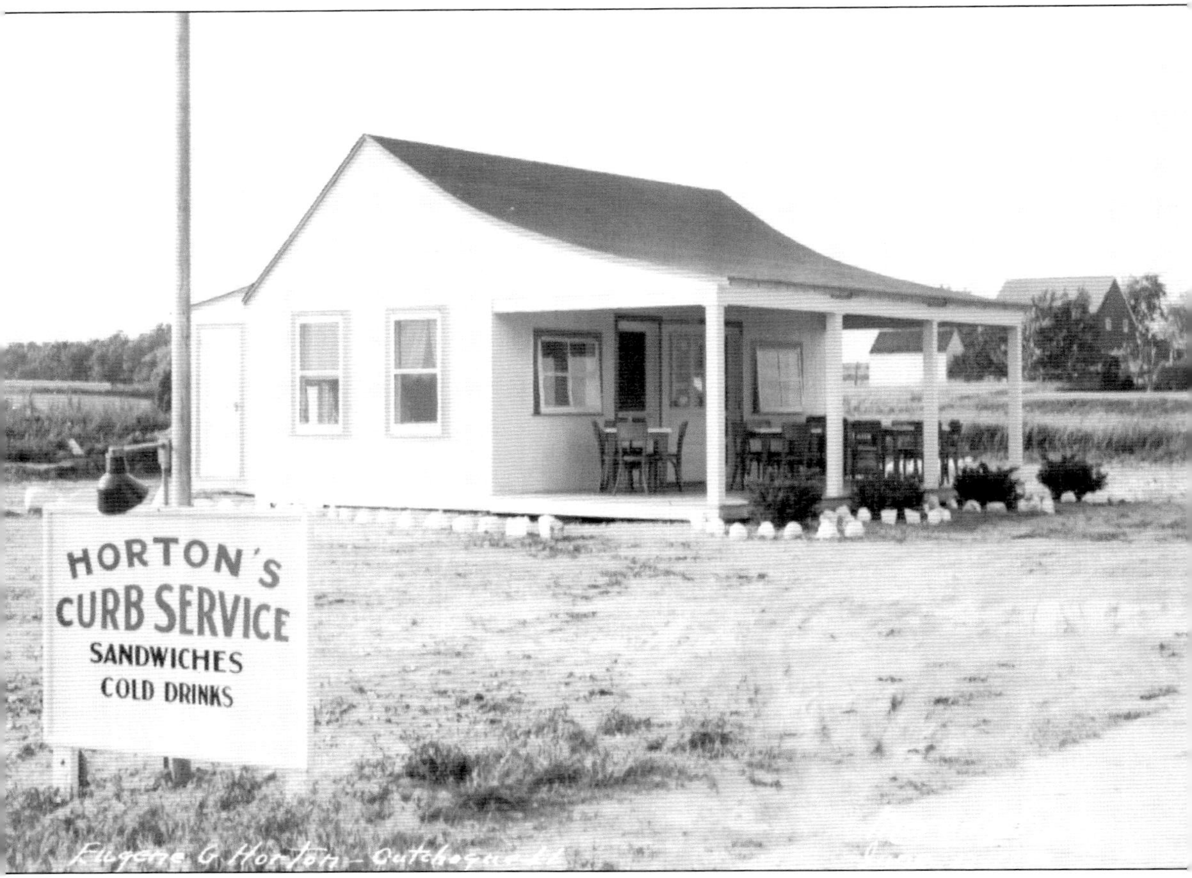

Horton's Curb Service, 1940. Eugene G. Horton (1911–1983) was a descendant of one of Cutchogue's earliest settlement families. He proved himself to be an up-to-date entrepreneur, however, by opening this roadside snack bar in an era that witnessed the phenomenon of increased tourism and an influx of "city people." Out-of-town folks sought wholesome food at a reasonable price in a natural setting, and what could be more convenient than a roadside restaurant? The farmhouse and barns in the background provided a casual and authentic setting for this impromptu dining opportunity. Surrounded by farm fields, Horton's tidy little food stand offered alfresco dining by the side of the road at no extra charge! (Courtesy of the Southold Historical Society.)

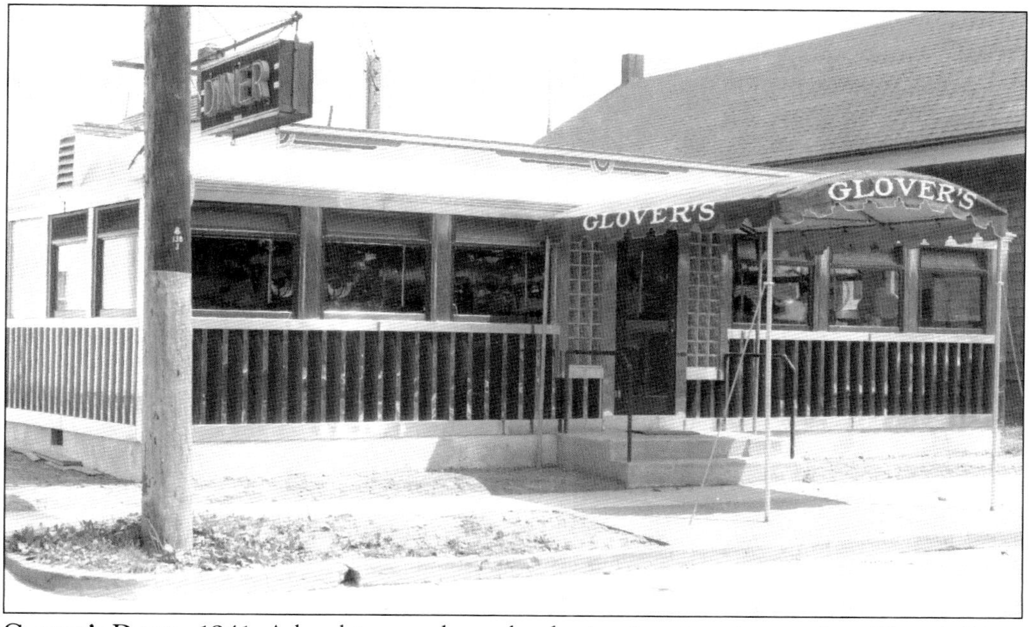

GLOVER'S DINER, 1941. A local icon and popular destination since its opening, Glover's Diner was located on the Main Road in downtown Cutchogue. Akin to Horton's Curb Service snack bar nearby, Glover's offered "family dining" and "counter service" to visitors and vacationers. The landmark eatery remains in business today, a favorite stop for many travelers en route to the Orient Point Ferry. (Courtesy of the Southold Historical Society.)

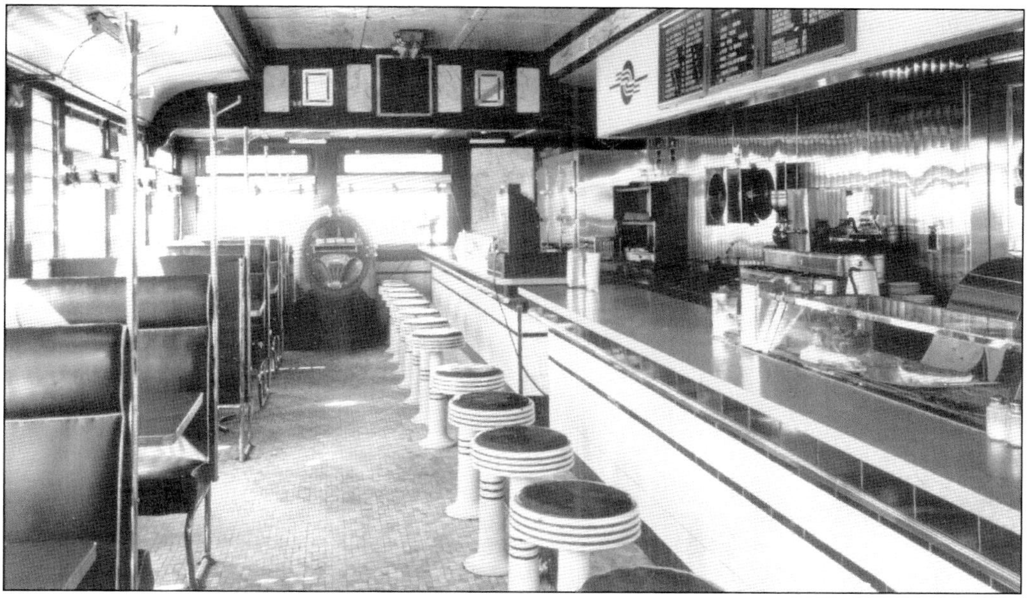

AL'S CUTCHOGUE DINER, 1948. Albert C. Harker acquired Glover's Diner in 1948, but the interior remained unchanged, as it does to this day. The tiled floor and counters, vinyl-covered benches, sleek aluminum backsplashes, and jukebox are all classic features of the American diner. Harker's ancestors were among the original settlers of Southold Town in 1640. (Courtesy of the Southold Historical Society.)

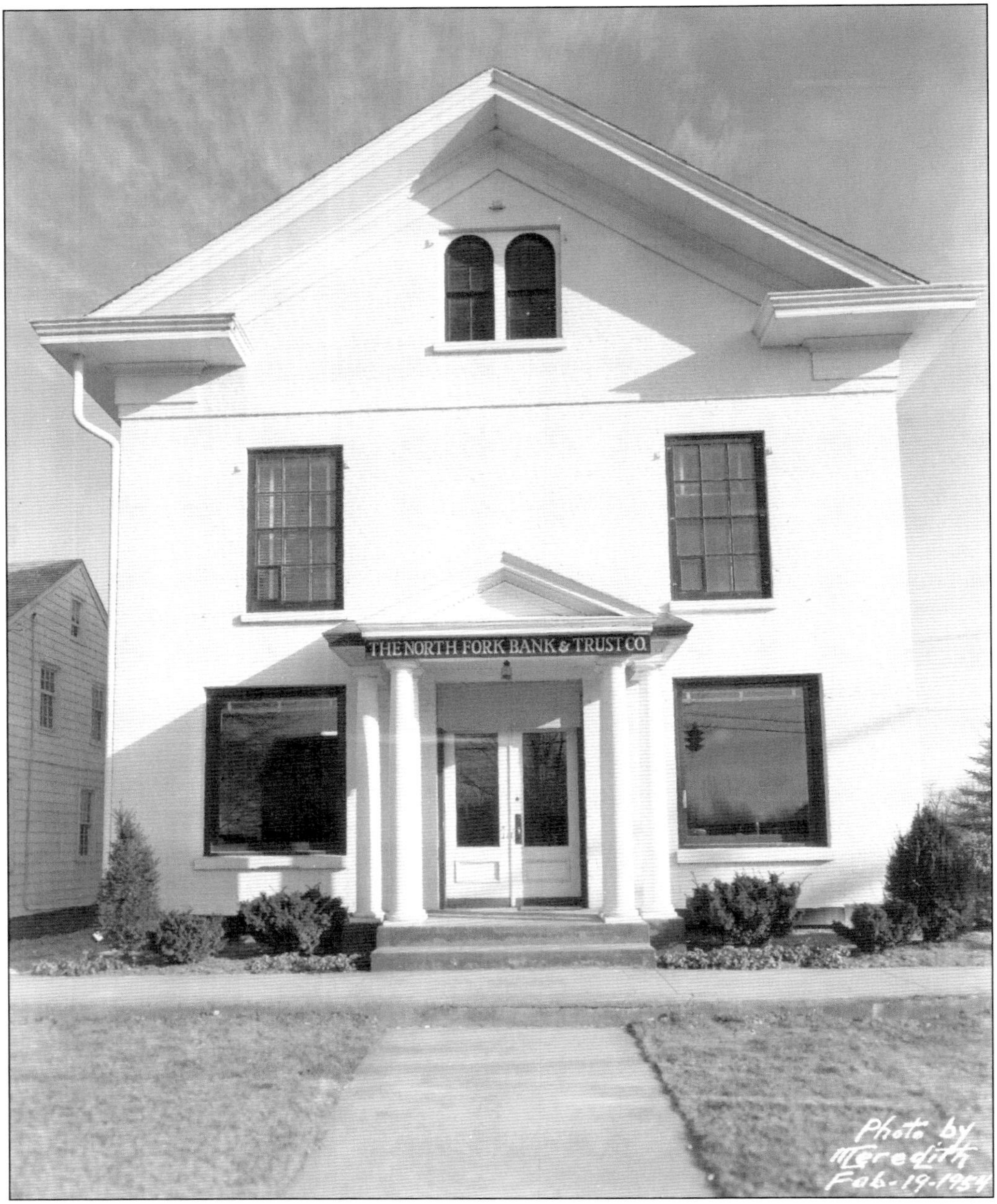

NORTH FORK BANK & TRUST CO., 1954. Looking stark in a fresh coat of white paint and with the old window sashes devoid of shutters, the former Goldsmith & Tuthill general store at the corner of Main and New Suffolk Roads took on a new appearance after adaptive reuse for the North Fork Bank & Trust Company in 1950. The removal of the old wraparound porch and construction of a smaller and more formal portico at the front door completed the transformation. The bank assumed its name after the consolidation of the old Mattituck Bank (founded 1905) and the First National Bank of Cutchogue (founded 1924). The North Fork Bank & Trust Co. was in turn absorbed by Capital One Bank in 2008, thus ending a long tradition of locally owned savings and commercial banks on Long Island's North Fork. (Courtesy of the Southold Historical Society.)

Five

Getting Around

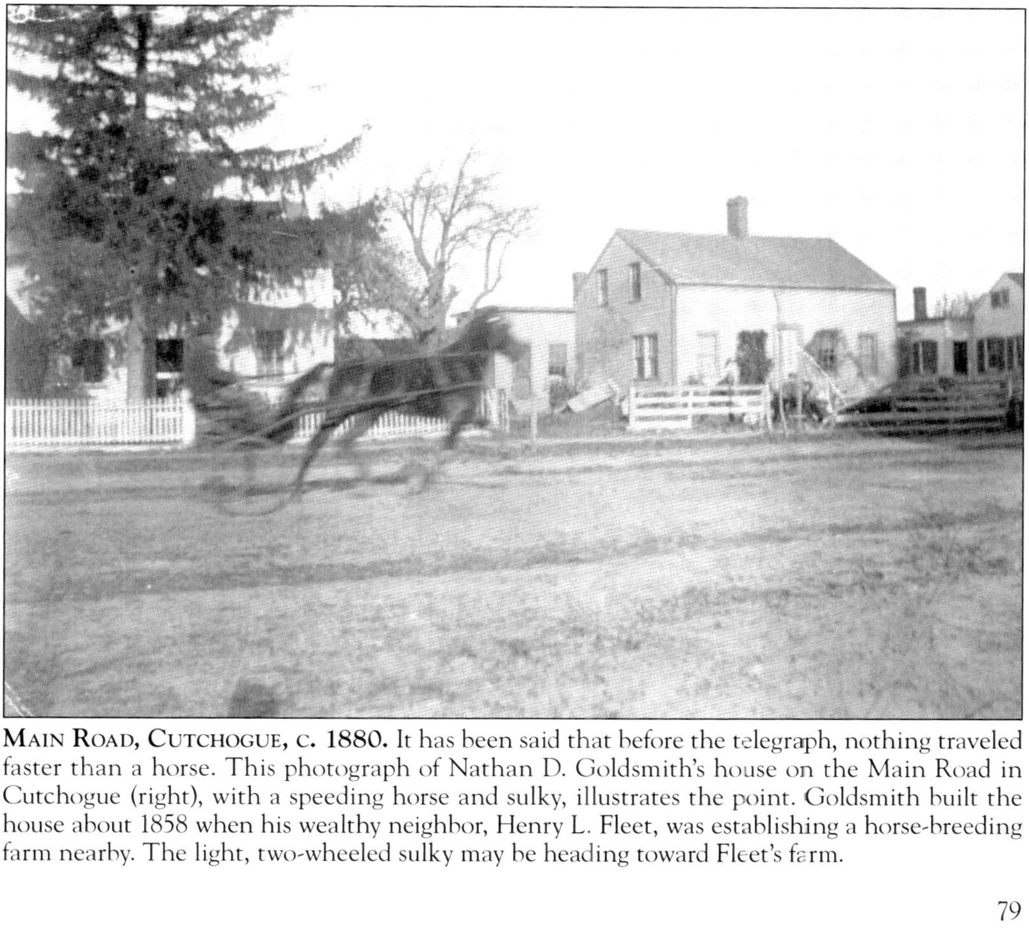

Main Road, Cutchogue, c. 1880. It has been said that before the telegraph, nothing traveled faster than a horse. This photograph of Nathan D. Goldsmith's house on the Main Road in Cutchogue (right), with a speeding horse and sulky, illustrates the point. Goldsmith built the house about 1858 when his wealthy neighbor, Henry L. Fleet, was establishing a horse-breeding farm nearby. The light, two-wheeled sulky may be heading toward Fleet's farm.

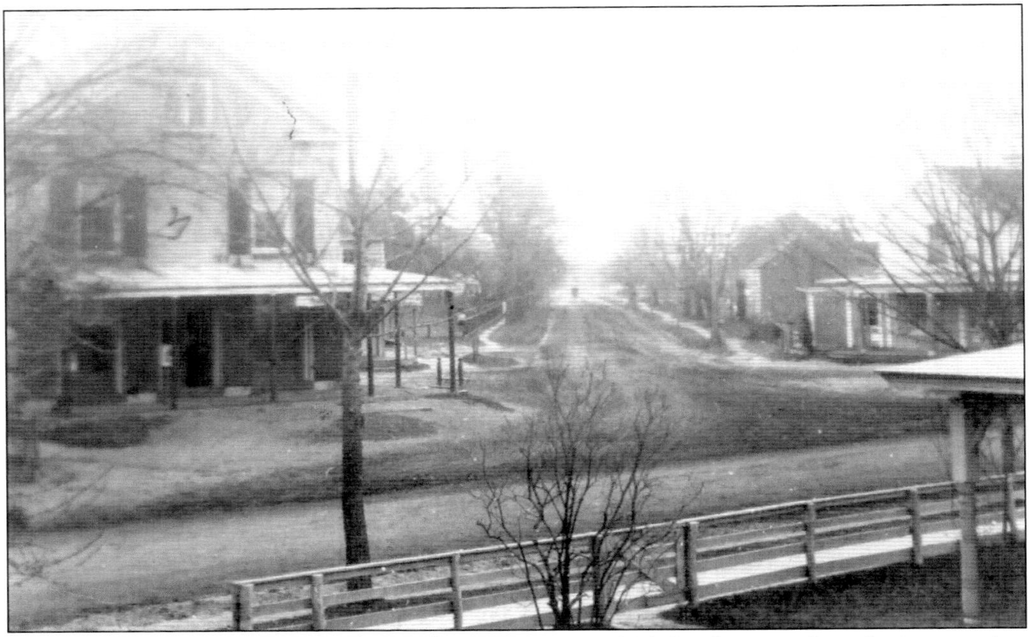

MAIN ROAD AND NEW SUFFOLK ROAD, CUTCHOGUE, C. 1900. Looking south at the intersection of Main and New Suffolk Roads, this photograph of Cutchogue's future business district captures its rural simplicity before the arrival of automobiles. The dirt roads are bordered by grassy, tree-lined verges. Goldsmith & Tuthill's store (left) and Bett's Hotel (right) flank the turnoff from the Main Road to New Suffolk.

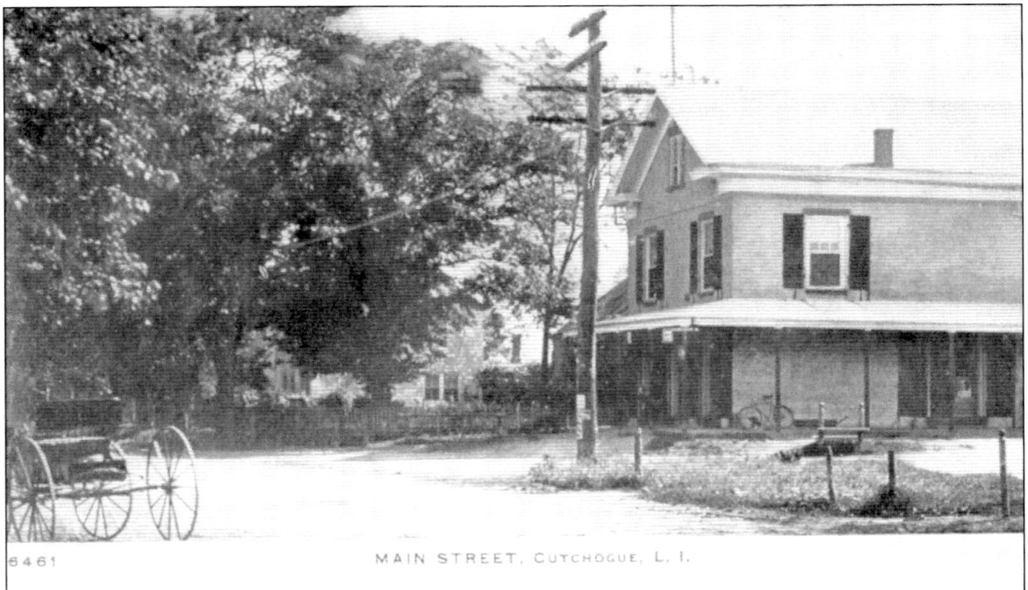

MAIN ROAD, CUTCHOGUE, C. 1900. The surrey on the left in this c. 1900 photograph of Main Road and New Suffolk Avenue illustrates how long the transition lasted from horse-drawn vehicles to the automobiles and trucks of the modern age. Silhouetted against Goldsmith & Tuthill's store is a mounting block that was indispensable for climbing aboard horse-drawn vehicles.

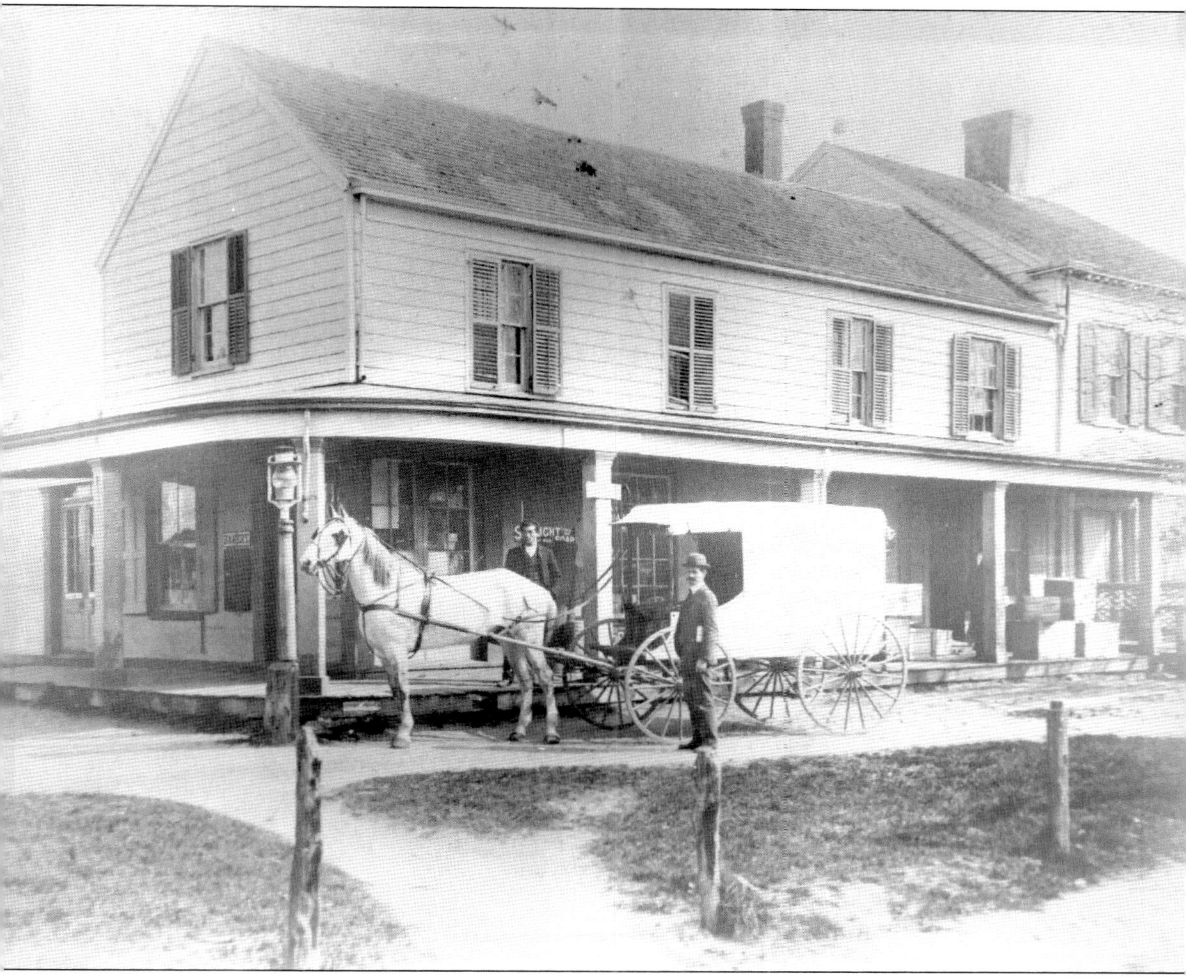

WILLIAM HARRISON CASE RESIDENCE, C. 1890. The large and imposing residence of William Harrison Case, built in the mid-1800s, serves as the backdrop in this photograph for Morrell Brother's grocery wagon. The Case residence stood at the southwest corner of the Main Road and New Suffolk Road, in the heart of downtown Cutchogue. The long easterly extension of the house and its wraparound porch were important features of a late-19th-century hotel, store, and delivery station. The original house, seen at the right, was evidently enlarged with a later addition to the left. Later in the 19th century, the expanded structure became known as Bett's Hotel, and by the turn of the century, a portion of it was removed from the main building and restored as a residence on New Suffolk Road.

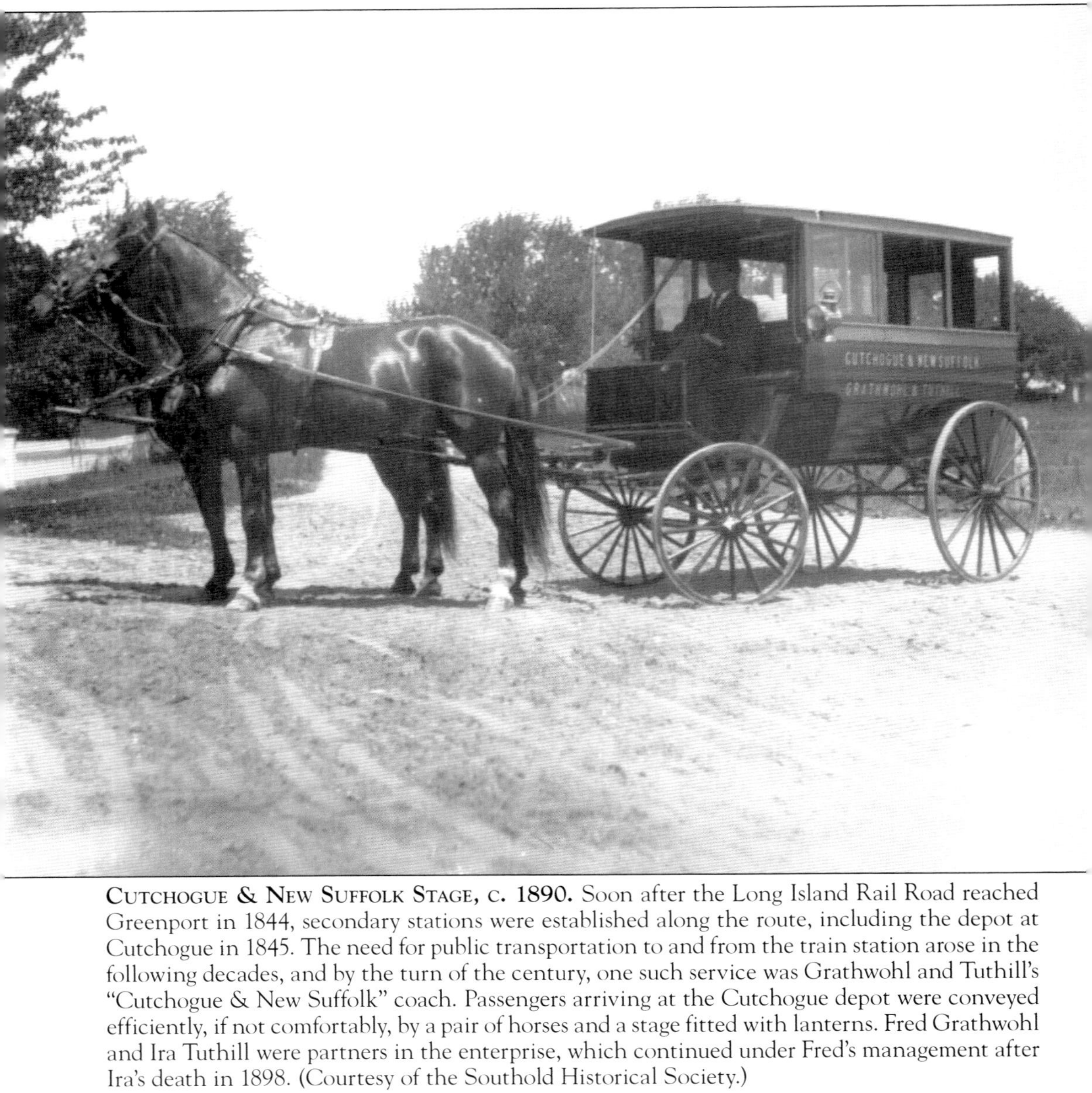

CUTCHOGUE & NEW SUFFOLK STAGE, C. 1890. Soon after the Long Island Rail Road reached Greenport in 1844, secondary stations were established along the route, including the depot at Cutchogue in 1845. The need for public transportation to and from the train station arose in the following decades, and by the turn of the century, one such service was Grathwohl and Tuthill's "Cutchogue & New Suffolk" coach. Passengers arriving at the Cutchogue depot were conveyed efficiently, if not comfortably, by a pair of horses and a stage fitted with lanterns. Fred Grathwohl and Ira Tuthill were partners in the enterprise, which continued under Fred's management after Ira's death in 1898. (Courtesy of the Southold Historical Society.)

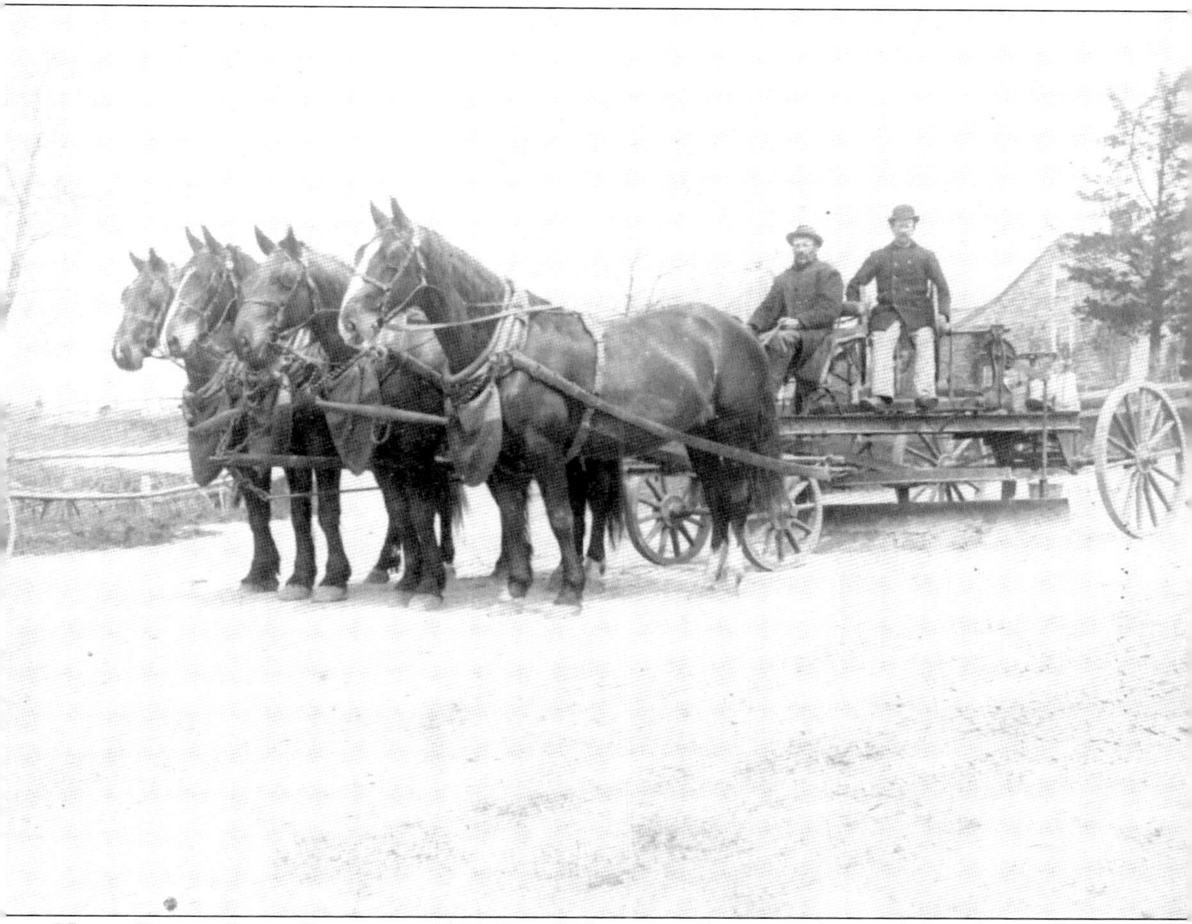

HORSE-DRAWN ROAD GRADER, C. 1900. It took four strong horses, and a steady hand to guide them, to traverse Cutchogue's country roads at the turn of the century. Pictured here (right) is George H. Fleet (1858–1932), one of Henry L. Fleet's four sons and an avid horseman like his father. George served as Southold Town's superintendent of highways. At the time of this photograph, the vast majority of local roads were still dirt, and their maintenance was an ongoing challenge. One way that George supervised the maintenance of the highways was by riding along with the road-grading crew and their apparatus, which employed a weighted cart fitted with a wide blade that leveled the roadway. As automobiles became more commonplace and better driving surfaces were required, main roads across the country were macadamized or improved with poured concrete, and horse-drawn graders such as this one were relegated to secondary and private dirt roads. (Courtesy of a private collection.)

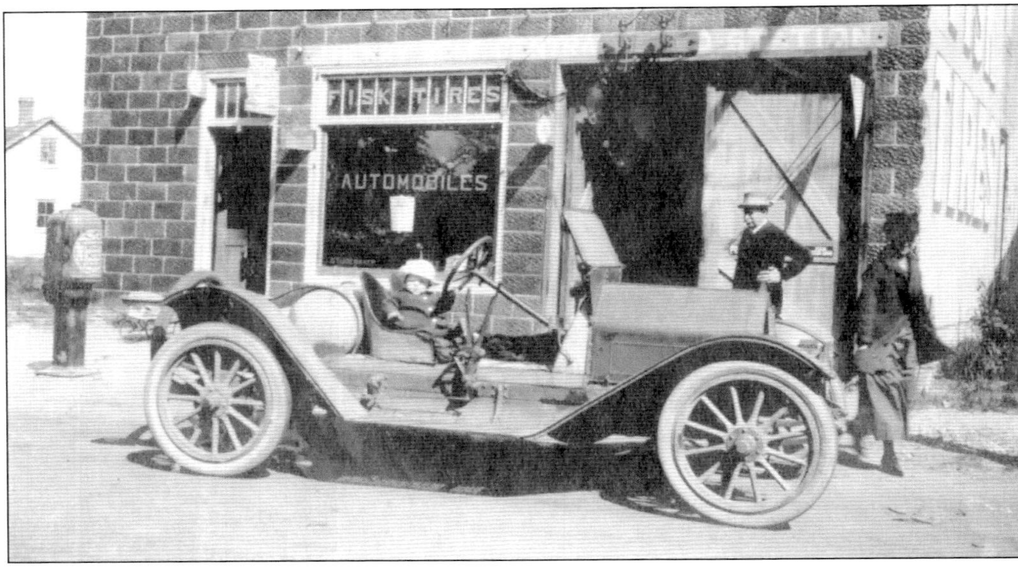

Wolf's Garage, c. 1915 and c. 1920. J. Henry Wolf was the proprietor of the Central Auto Station in Cutchogue in the early 1900s (above). In 1916, he advertised "supplies, storage, repairs" and his dealership in Hudson and Studebaker cars in *Scarborough's Tour Book*, a reliable guide for tourists seeking adventure on the open road. Wolf's garage also advertised Fisk tires, manufactured between 1899 and 1940. Upstairs was a space devoted to musical entertainment, known for many years as Wolf Hall. In the photograph below, Wolf's name is displayed on the side of a truck of the Fulton Motor Truck Company, for which he also served as agent. The company was located in Farmingdale, Long Island. Like hundreds of small, regional companies that failed to establish a national market, it was short-lived (1916–1925). (Courtesy of a private collection.)

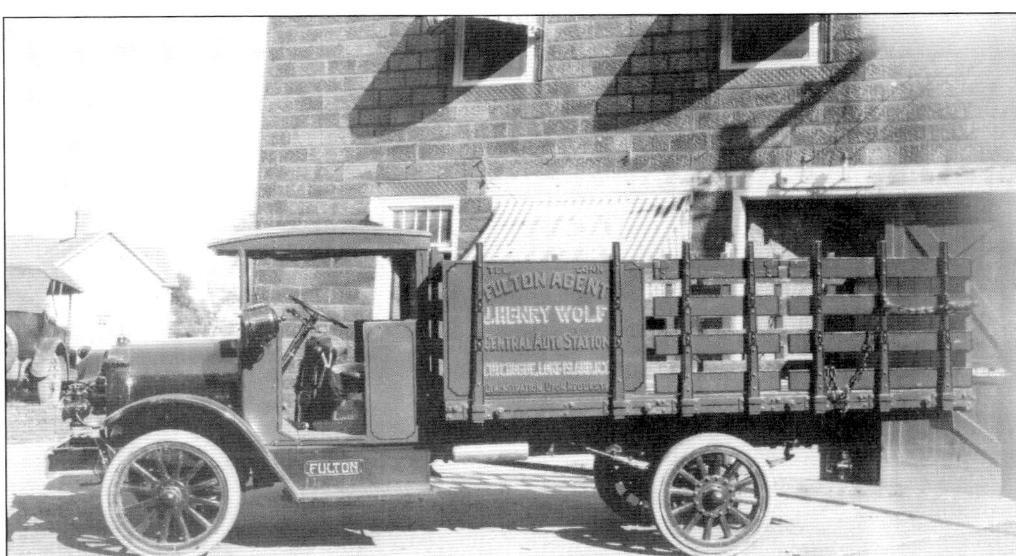

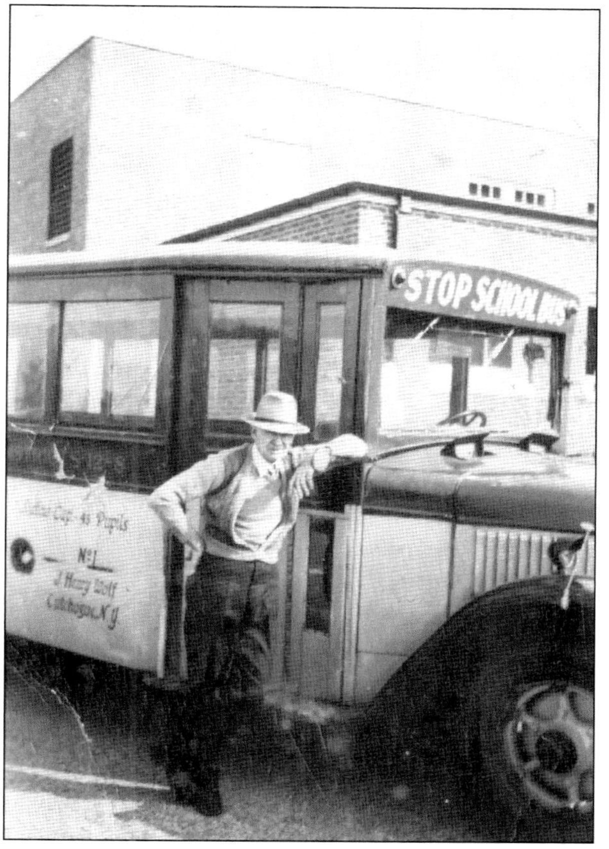

School Bus No. 1, c. 1930. The Cutchogue School District, which would later merge with the adjoining community of Mattituck to form the Mattituck-Cutchogue School District, began busing its own students to school in the late 1920s. As the student population grew, the district consolidated to a "central" school. J. Henry Wolf, already a local agent for the Fulton Truck Company, was a natural choice for operating the school bus franchise. In the 1930s, the school bus evolved from an adaptation of existing vehicles, such as wagons, carriages, and trucks, into a vehicle type of its own. (Photograph courtesy of a private collection.)

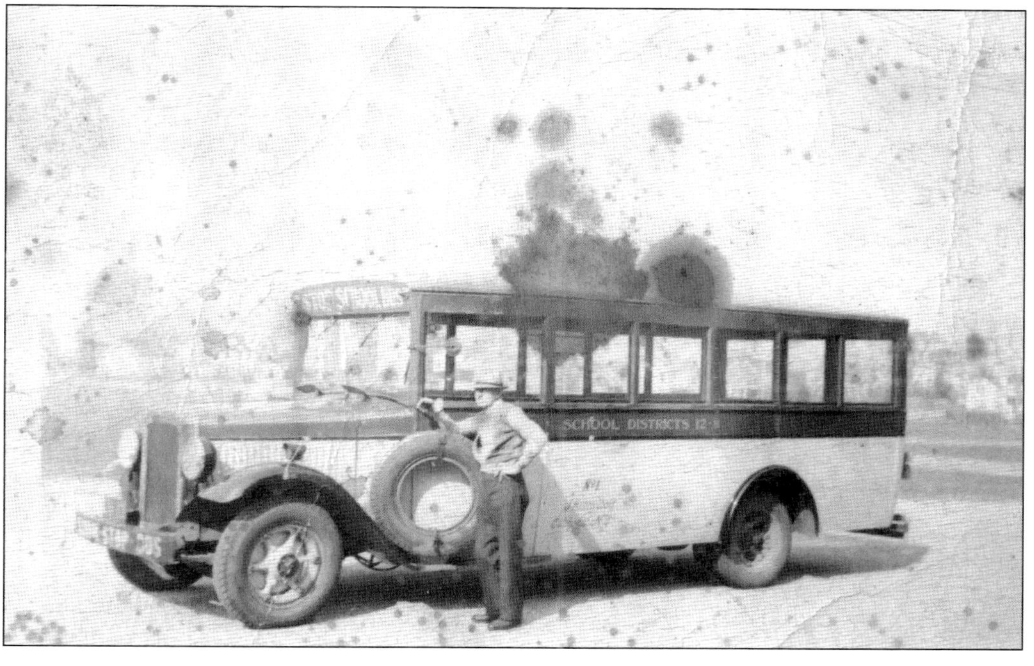

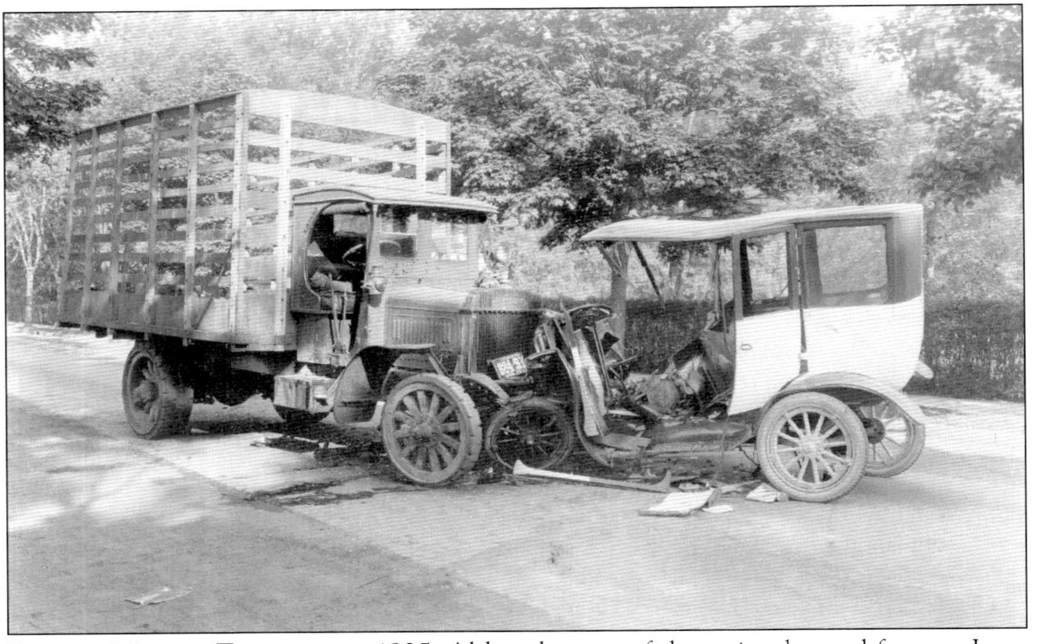

FARM-TO-MARKET TRUCKING, C. 1925. Although many of the major thoroughfares on Long Island were paved with concrete or macadam by the 1920s, mishaps, such as the one shown above, abounded due to inexperienced drivers, unmarked pavements, and the lack of directional signage. Oftentimes, truckers were blamed for accidents simply because of the size of their vehicles. The G&D Motor Express Company, whose trucks are shown on this page, took matters into their own hands by employing local photographers to document incidents in anticipation of litigation. Their trucks were also sidelined due to mechanical breakdowns (below) in an era when service stations were few and far between.

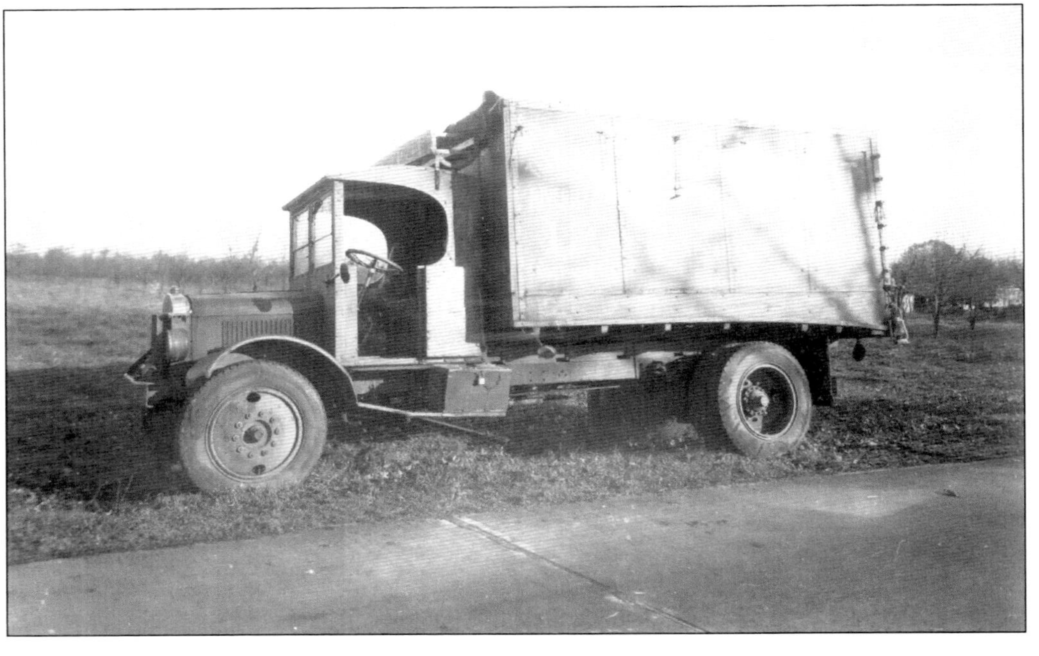

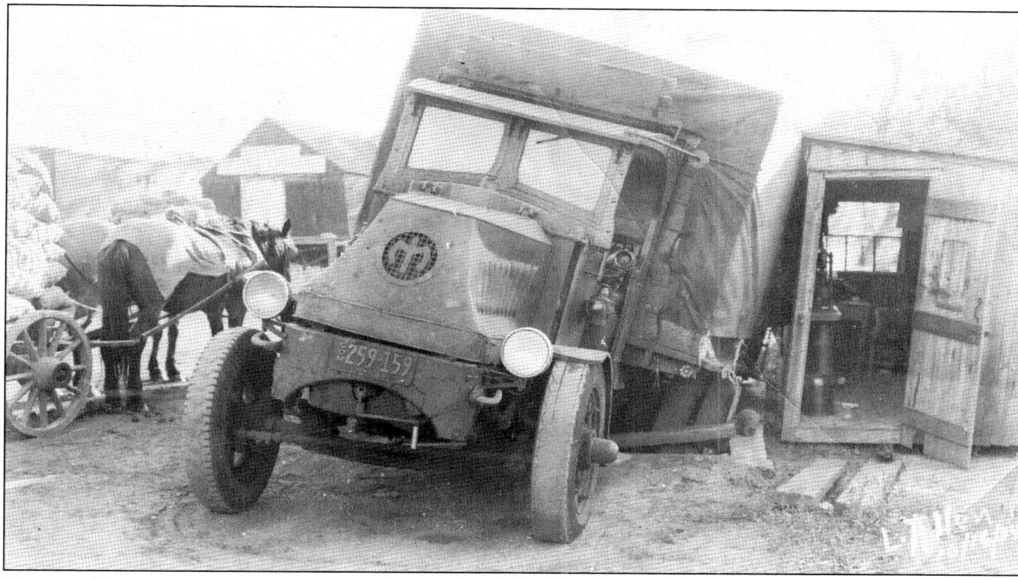

POTATO TRUCK MISHAP, 1934. The transition from horse-drawn wagons to motorized trucks that grew in size and weight every year was not always easy, as illustrated by this 1934 accident at a potato-weighing station. In the above photograph, the horse-drawn rig at the left stands in mute testament to the days when wooden platforms adjacent to the weigh stations (below) were built to handle their payloads. Another casualty of the emerging trucking industry was the Long Island Rail Road, which had traditionally carried potatoes and other farm products to urban markets. As trucks grew larger and dirt roads across Long Island were macadamized, the railroad lost its monopoly. The unmistakable logo of Mack Truck appears on the front of the vehicle. The bulldog was adopted as a corporate symbol in 1922, but it was not until 1932 that the now-familiar hood ornament was patented and put into service.

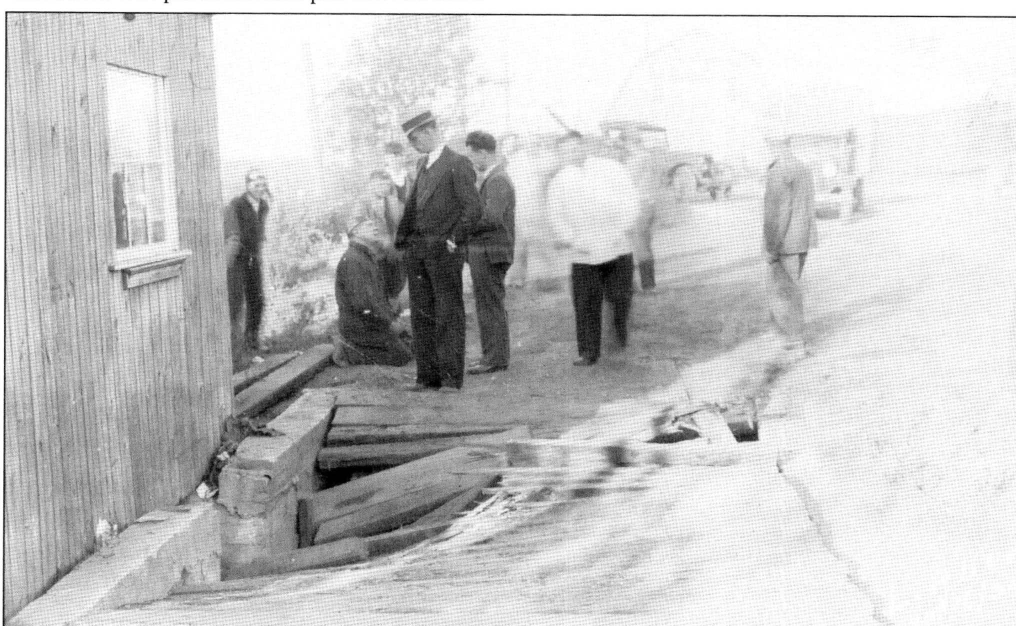

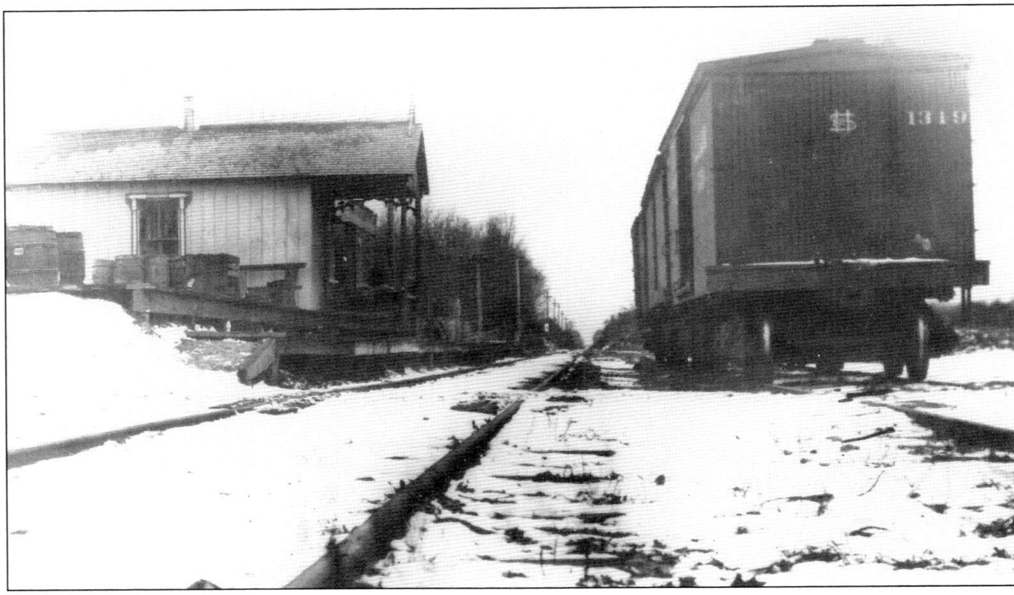

LONG ISLAND RAIL ROAD, C. 1879 AND 1905. The Long Island Rail Road was conceived in the 1840s as the quickest passenger route from Brooklyn to Boston, via ships that completed the commute across Long Island Sound at Greenport. The Cutchogue station was built on the original route, which had pushed through to its eastern terminus at Greenport in 1844. The above photograph shows the first of three Cutchogue stations, all built at the intersection of Depot Lane. The small board-and-batten structure faced the tracks and carried decorative roof cresting typical of the era. By the turn of the century, the Cutchogue station had been rebuilt (below), and its two functions—freight and passenger service—were segregated into separate buildings. The freight depot appears in the background. The passenger depot's long, open platform features support posts that branch at the top like trees to support a ribbed and ornamented roof. (Courtesy of Ron Ziel.)

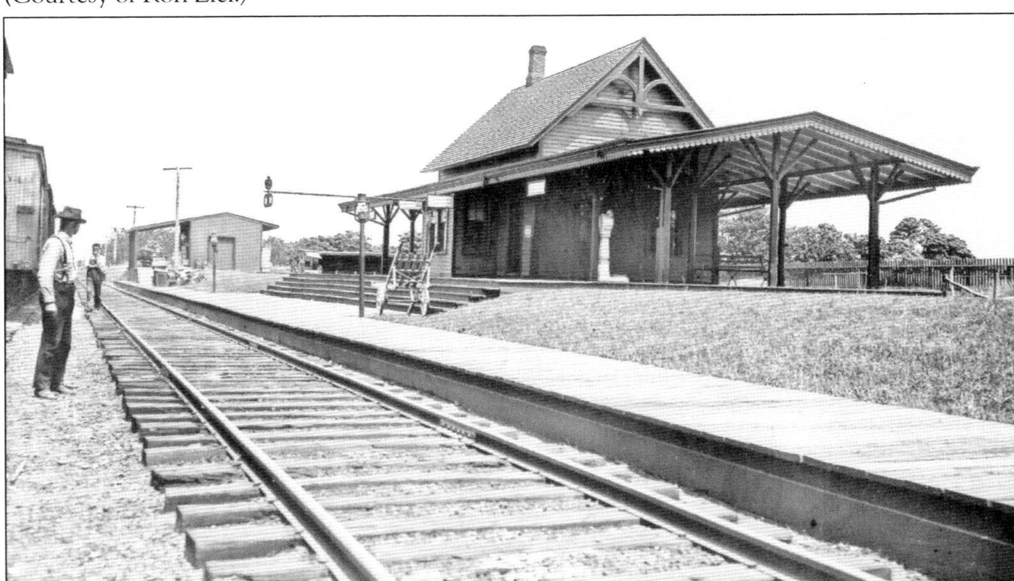

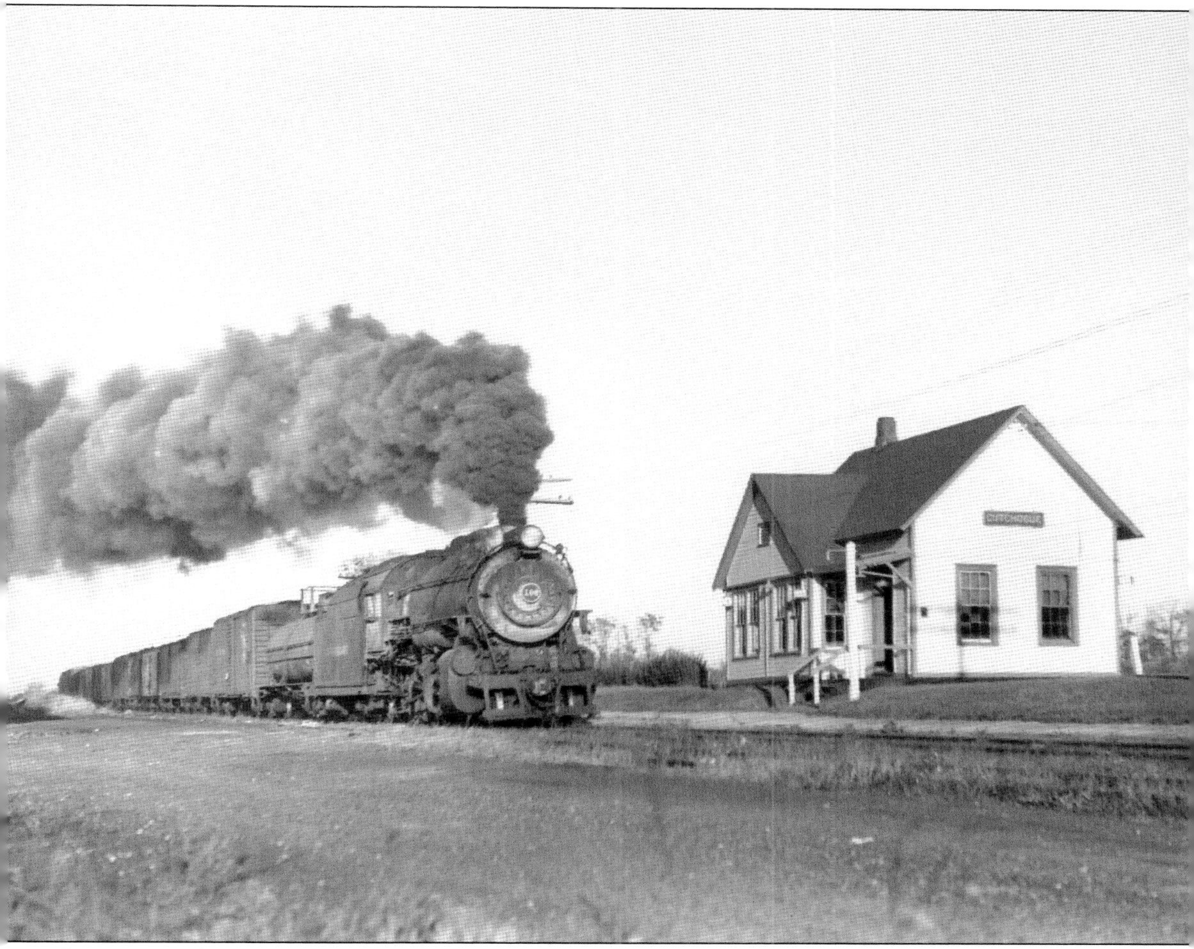

CUTCHOGUE STATION, LONG ISLAND RAIL ROAD, C. 1953. Until it closed in 1962, the Cutchogue train depot provided a convenient and profitable link to urban markets for farmers whose produce, including locally grown broccoli, cauliflower, and potatoes, found their way to metropolitan New York homes and restaurants. But as the number of passengers dwindled, so too did the need for freight service, and the station stop was decommissioned in 1962. The station house had been rebuilt a second time, its small and unassuming design reflecting the great changes that had taken place in the railroad industry since its heyday at the turn of the century. Despite these changes, there was one constant: the stationmaster, Jim Hand, had been on the job for nearly 50 years. (Photograph courtesy of Ron Ziel.)

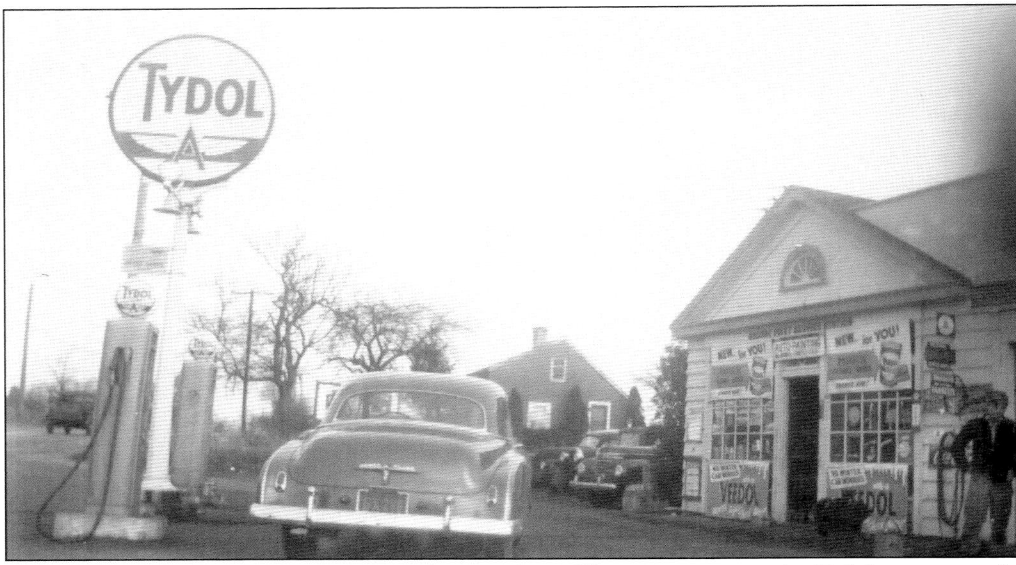

TYDOL SERVICE STATION, C. 1940. Cutchogue's first "filling" station was the Tydol station, at the corner of Main and Eugene's Roads. Tidewater Oil, founded in New York State in 1887, was initially known for its world-famous motor oil brand Veedol. Tidewater entered the gasoline market about 1915, and by 1920, it was marketing all along the Eastern Seaboard under the Tydol brand.

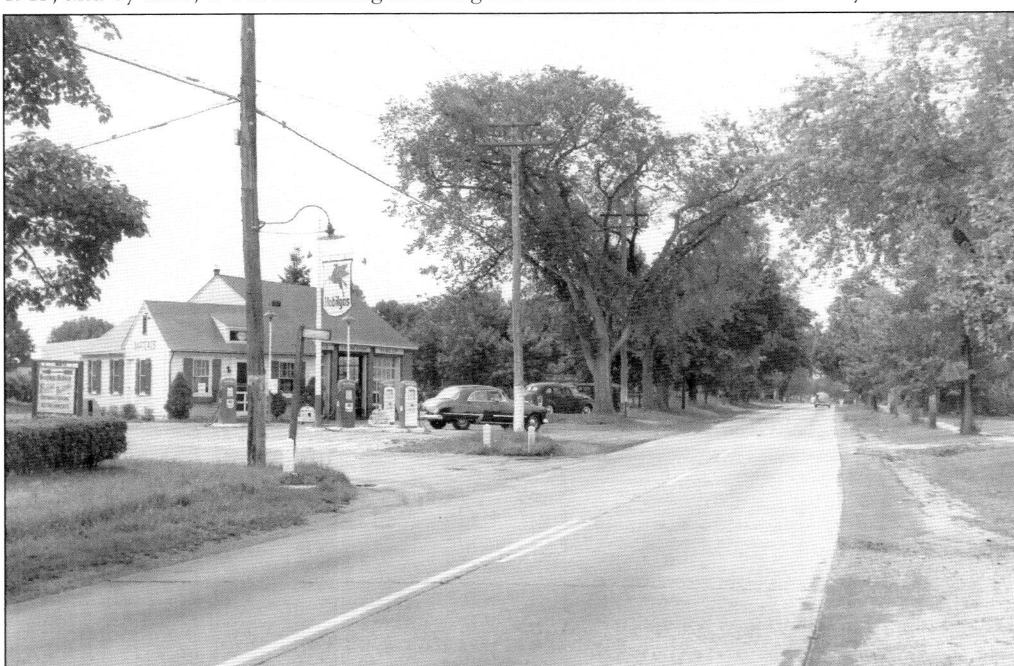

MOBILGAS SERVICE STATION, C. 1949. With the breakup of Standard Oil in 1911, the Standard Oil Company of New York ("Socony") was formed, along with scores of other companies. In 1920, the company registered the name "Mobiloil" as its trademark. Through the years, Mobil became one of the largest sellers of gasoline and motor oils in the United States, holding the top spot during the 1940s and much of the 1950s.

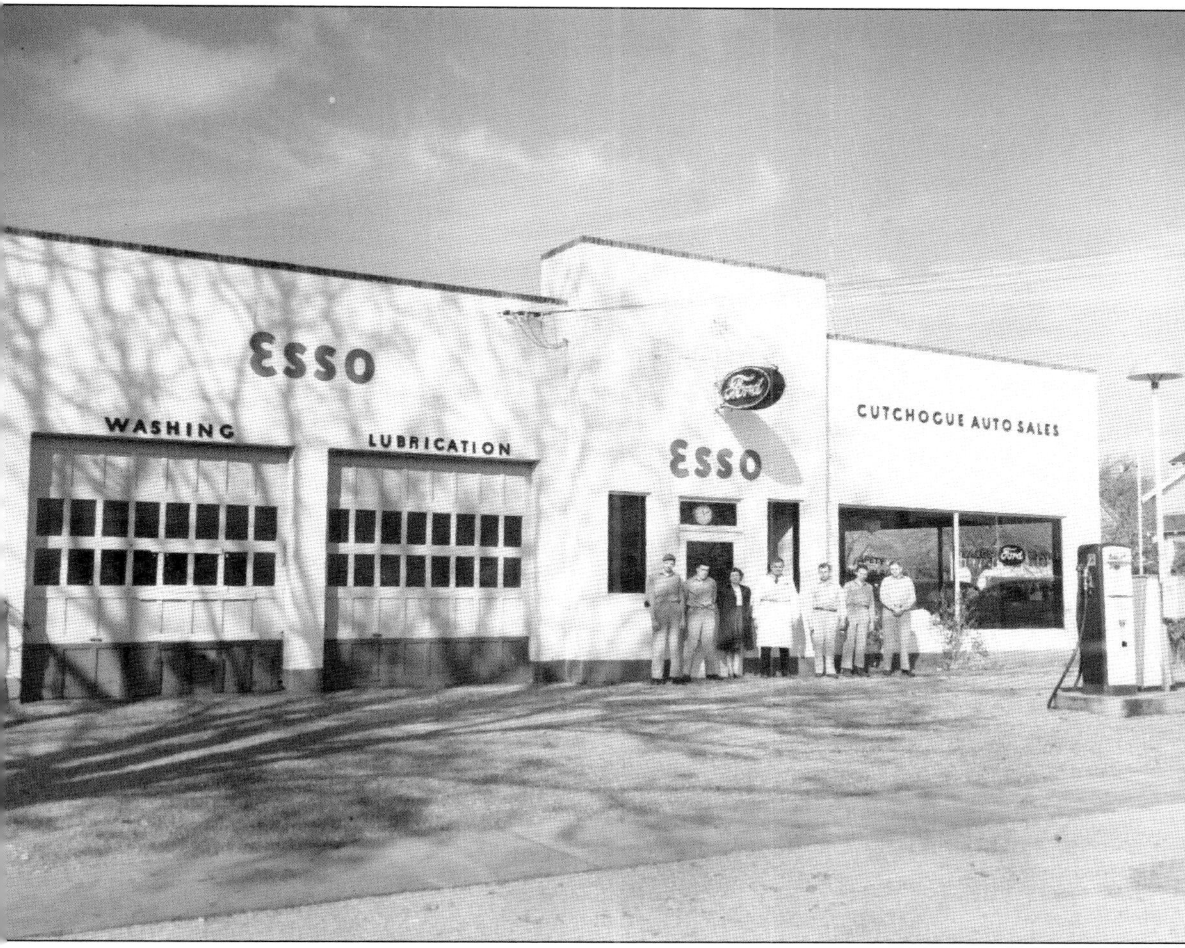

ESSO SERVICE STATION, C. 1947. Ultramodern, clean, and uncluttered, the Esso service station on the Main Road was also a Ford automobile dealership. Pictured out front is the original workforce, including proprietors Felix Doroski and his brother Martin. The white, stuccoed structure stood in stark contrast to its nearby competitors, Tydol and Mobilgas, whose service stations were built in the Colonial "cottage" style. Esso (like Socony) was a product of the breakup of Standard Oil in 1911. One of the largest companies to emerge had been Standard Oil of New Jersey, whose Esso brand name was a phonetic spelling of the "S" and the "O" of Standard Oil. The old Esso station, still standing today, is now a Citgo station. It has expanded for use as a convenience store. (Courtesy of the Southold Historical Society.)

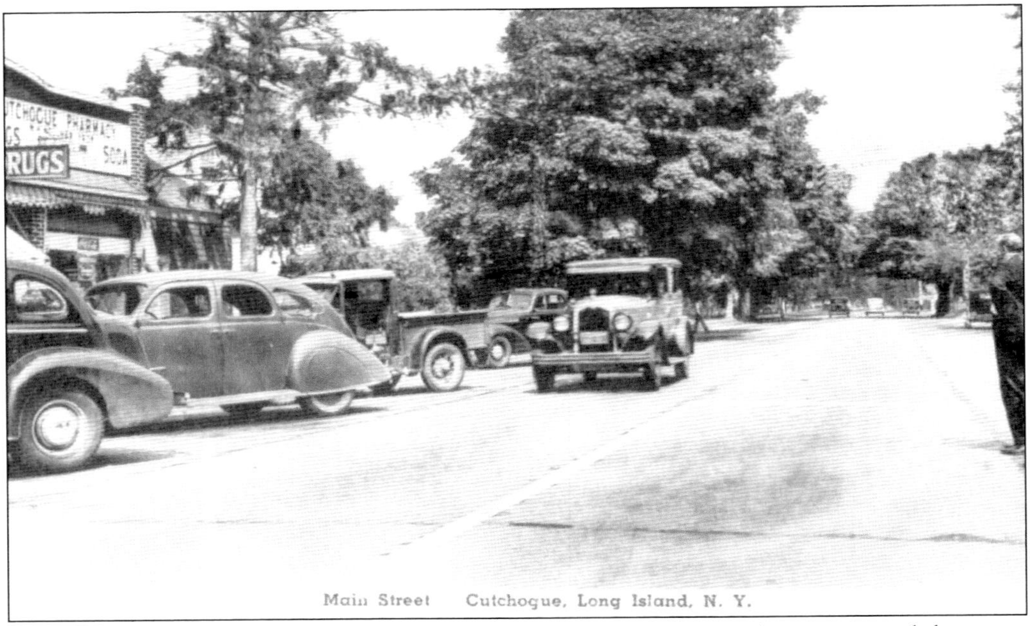

MAIN STREET, CUTCHOGUE, C. 1930. The Main Road is concrete, the commercial district is emerging, and competition for parking has become the norm by 1930. A painted centerline and the word "STOP" at New Suffolk Road pass for traffic control in an era that has yet to see traffic lights. But the volume of traffic was clearly on the rise, leading to a proliferation of service stations in the village and a concern over congestion that lingers today.

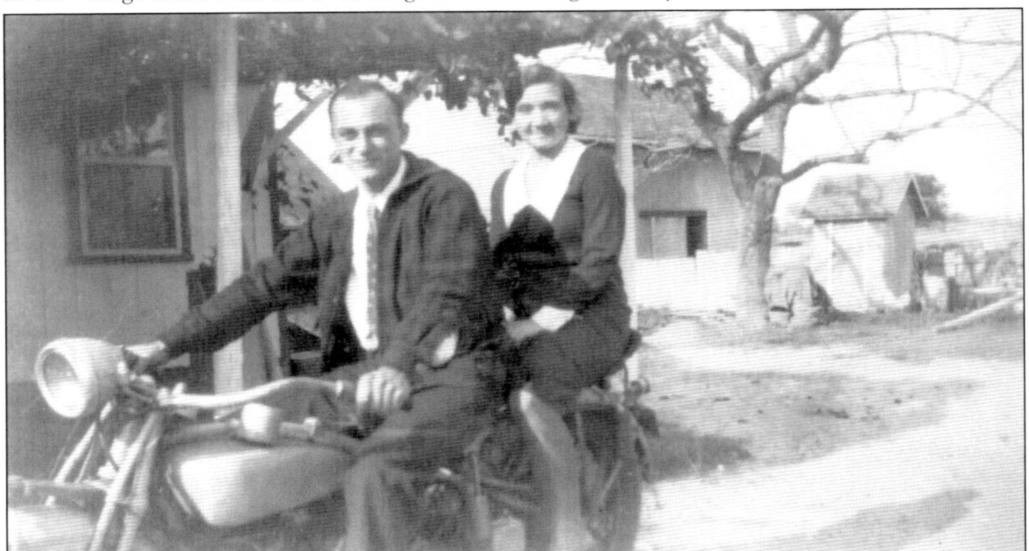

NELLIE DRUM AND FRIEND, C. 1930. With all the attention given to trucks and automobiles, it is easy to overlook the impact of motorcycles on the American driving culture. Motorcycles were a novelty in farming communities when Nellie Drum went for a ride on her father's cauliflower farm on Oregon Road with an unidentified companion. Nellie was the daughter of James H. and Nellie Drum, Irish immigrants who came to Long Island as farmers in the mid-1800s. Nellie married Frances McCaffery in 1936. (Photograph courtesy Virginia McCaffery.)

Six

LEISURE TIME

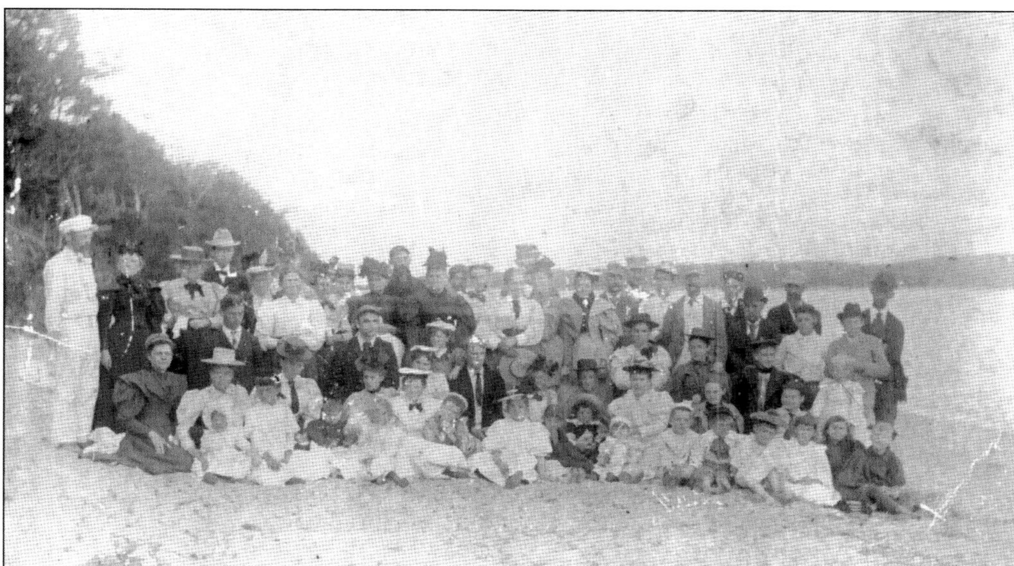

PICNIC ON FLEETS NECK, C. 1898. C.P. Tuthill organized this picnic on Fleets Neck around 1898. The Tuthill name is synonymous with the history of both Cutchogue and New Suffolk. By the size of this family group, it seems the entire clan showed up for this reunion! Fleets Neck is a peninsula to the east and south of Cutchogue that fronts on Little Peconic Bay. It is bounded by New Suffolk to the west and Nassau Point to the east.

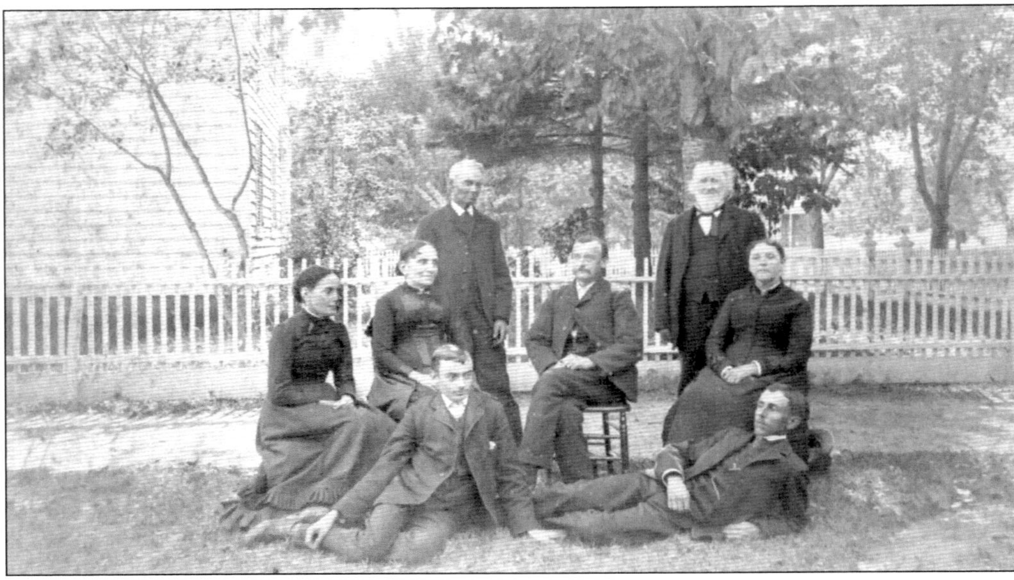

GATHERING ON THE LAWN, C. 1900. Three couples—Mr. and Mrs. Harvey Howell, Mr. and Mrs. Eugene Goldsmith, and Mr. and Mrs. John Smith Howell—and two unidentified young men gather on the front lawn of a Cutchogue home around 1900 (above). The tidy picket fences defined not only the well-ordered yards, but also the well-ordered lives of these Victorian ladies and gentlemen. Eugene H. Goldsmith owned an extensive farm that stretched for acres south of the Main Road in Cutchogue, surrounding the Old Burying Ground. The Howells were neighbors who lived on the north side of the Main Road. Below, a group of elderly couples are assembled in the front yard of the Goldsmith residence in Cutchogue at about the same time as the gathering shown above. Note the small area rug that has been brought out from the house to cover the path.

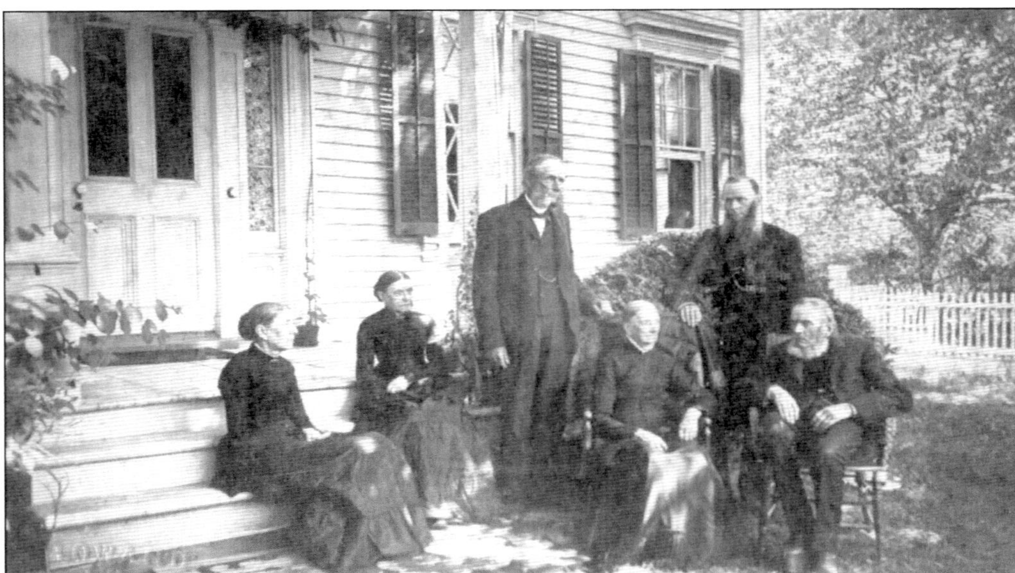

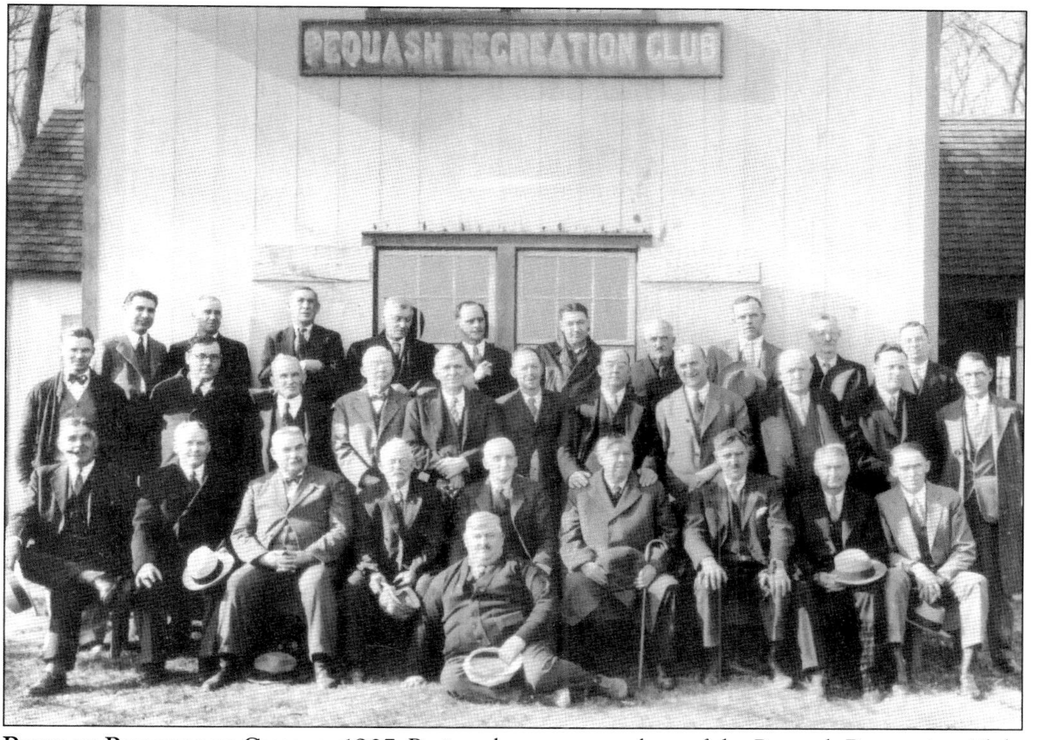

PEQUASH RECREATION CLUB, C. 1907. Posing above are members of the Pequash Recreation Club, a group of men who enjoyed cooking together and celebrating their status as born-and-bred "locals." Shown below is the group's bay-front clubhouse. Outsiders were not recommended for membership in this unusual "country" club. Founded around 1889, the group of 30 or so members hailed from professions as diverse as banker and farmer, teacher and contractor, but all shared a love for hearty, single-dish meals such as clam chowder and scallop stew. The group met on alternating Saturdays throughout the year, and a "rations committee" performed the ritual of preparing the noontime meal, with hefty fines doled out to those who failed to please the other members with their culinary abilities. Wives were invited, but only once a year, in June, when they brought fruit pies and helped the men scrub up the clubhouse for another year.

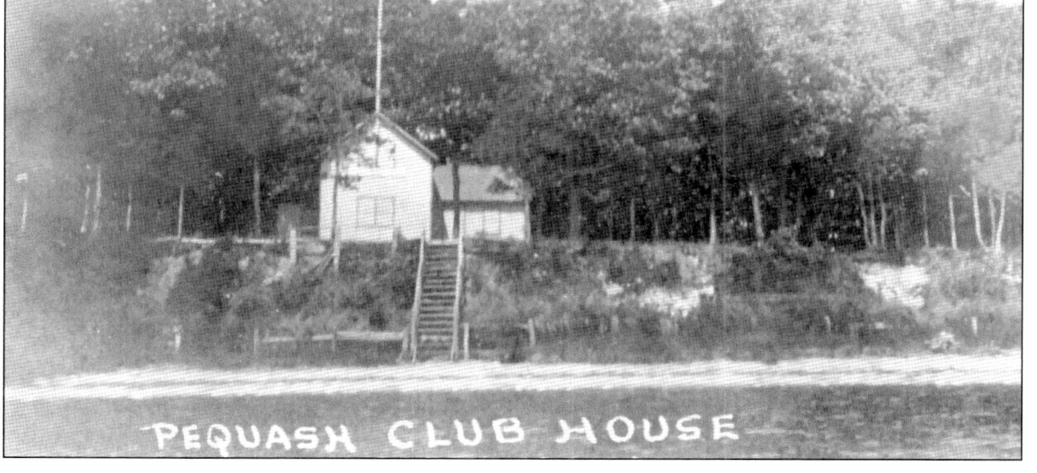

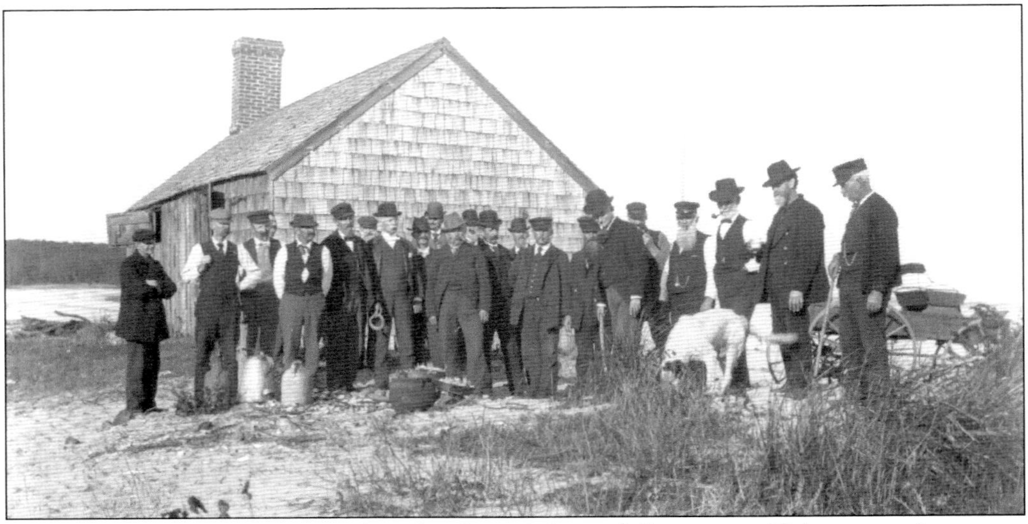

OLD CROWS CLUB, C. 1910. Rivaling Cutchogue's Pequash Recreation Club was another group, the Old Crows Club. The men were farmers who fished for "bunkers," or menhaden, which was used to fertilize crops. Club members caught the bunkers by using large seines or nets that required the collaboration of several men to toss, gather, and retrieve. The catch was loaded onto wagons and pulled by horse to the fields, where it was shared by club members. (Courtesy of the Southold Historical Society.)

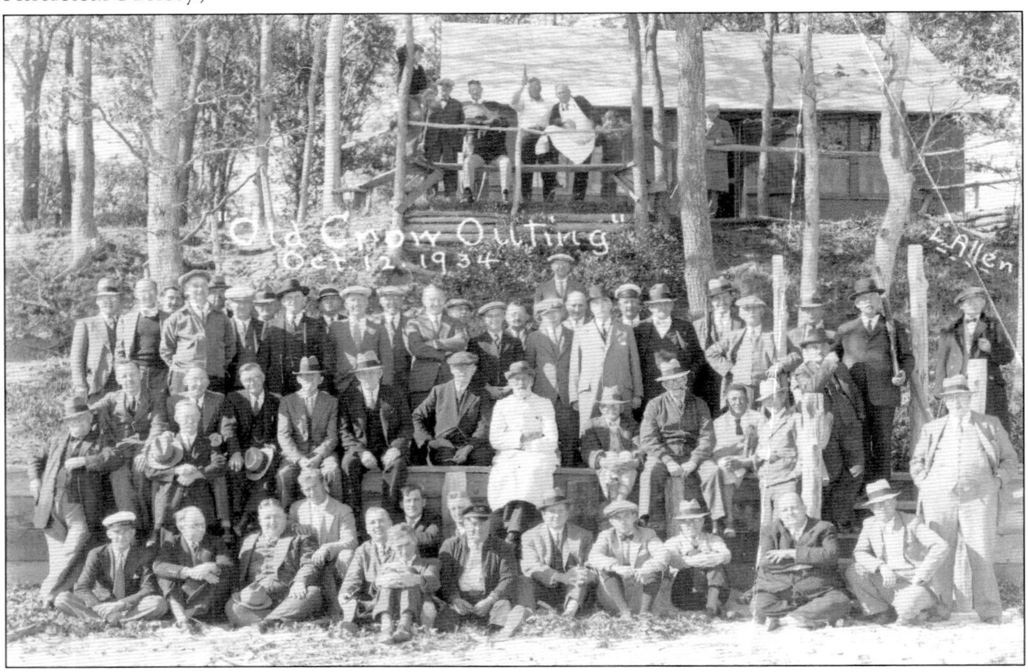

OLD CROWS OUTING, OCTOBER 12, 1934. The ranks of the Old Crows Club had increased considerably by the time local photographer Linnaeus Allen recorded members on an outing in 1934. The club's purpose, unchanged since the turn of the century, was that of catching "bunkers" to spread as fertilizer. It is thought that Native Americans had used these small, oily fish for the same purpose and passed their knowledge to white settlers in the 17th century.

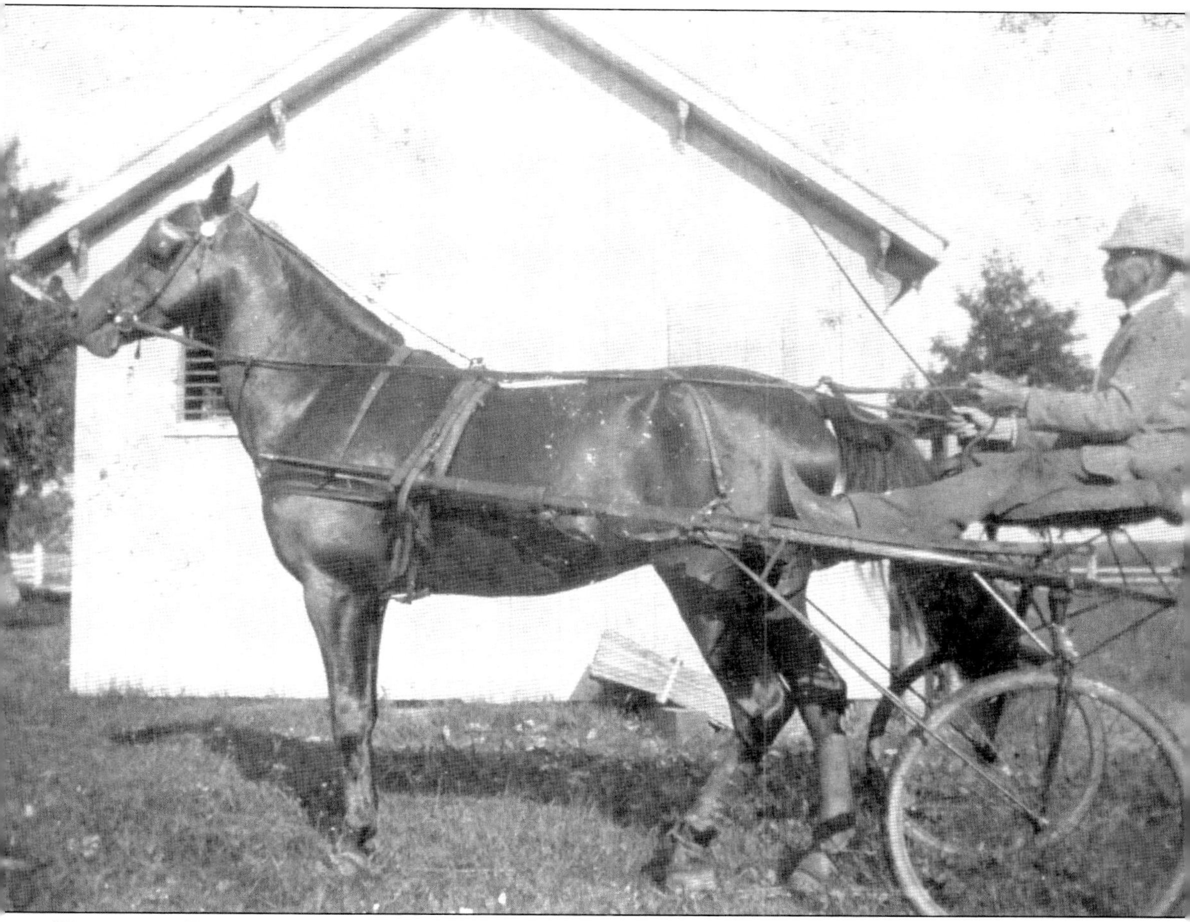

Horse and Driver, c. 1890. The sulky, or two-wheeled racing cart, seen in this photograph on the Fleet Farm, is identified as an older version. Its wheels are larger than those of a later era. The driver sits high above the lightweight wooden frame. The wheels take advantage of recent developments in bicycle technology that introduced wire spokes and pneumatic tires, a great advance on the wooden spokes and solid rims of earlier times. (Courtesy of a private collection.)

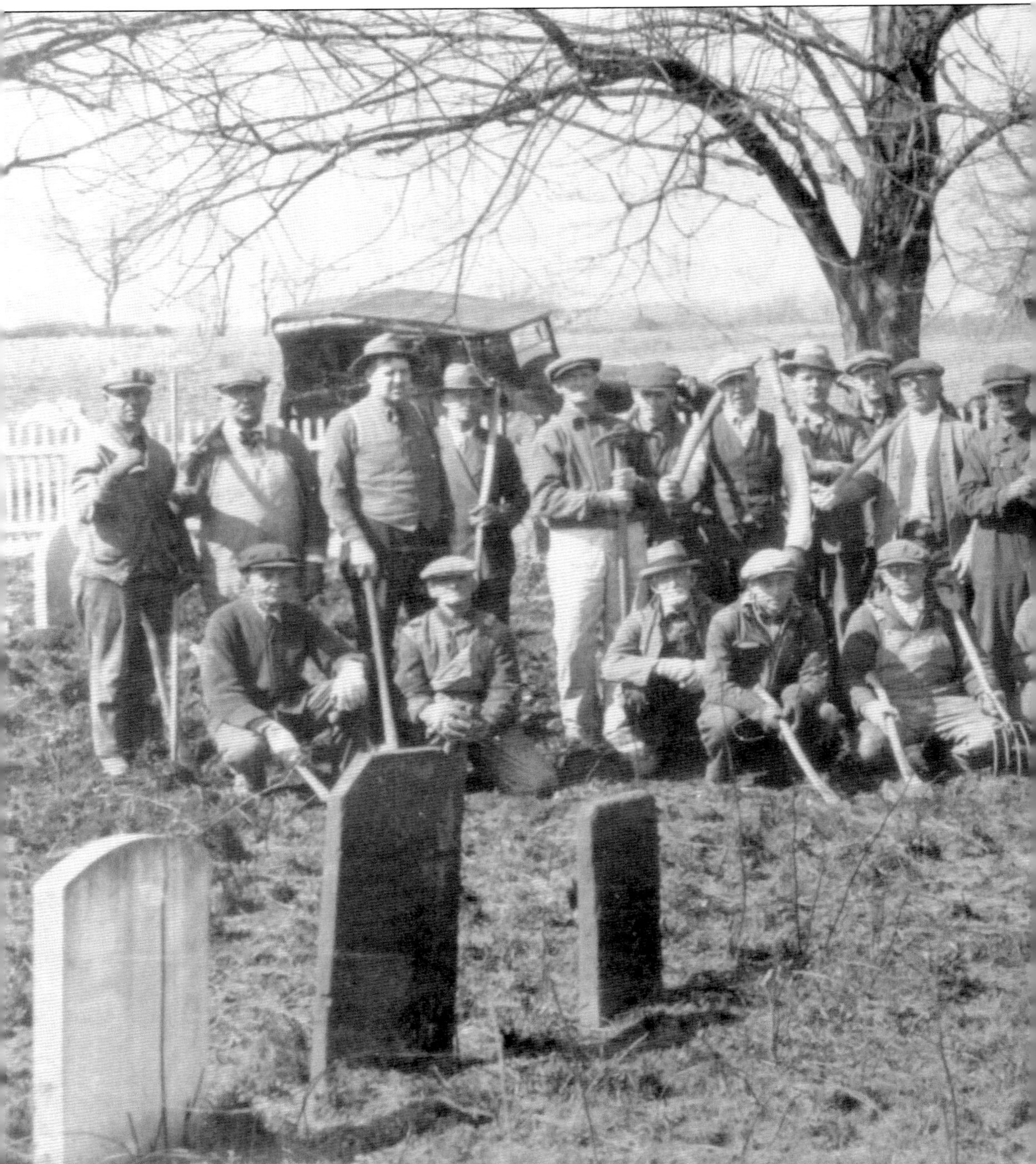

Old Burying Ground Cleanup, c. 1925. Members of Cutchogue families pause for a group portrait during their annual cleanup of the Old Burying Ground. The cemetery was the final resting place for many of the original settlers and their descendants beginning in the early 1700s. The oldest surviving headstone is that of Phebe Wells, the daughter of William and Easter Wells,

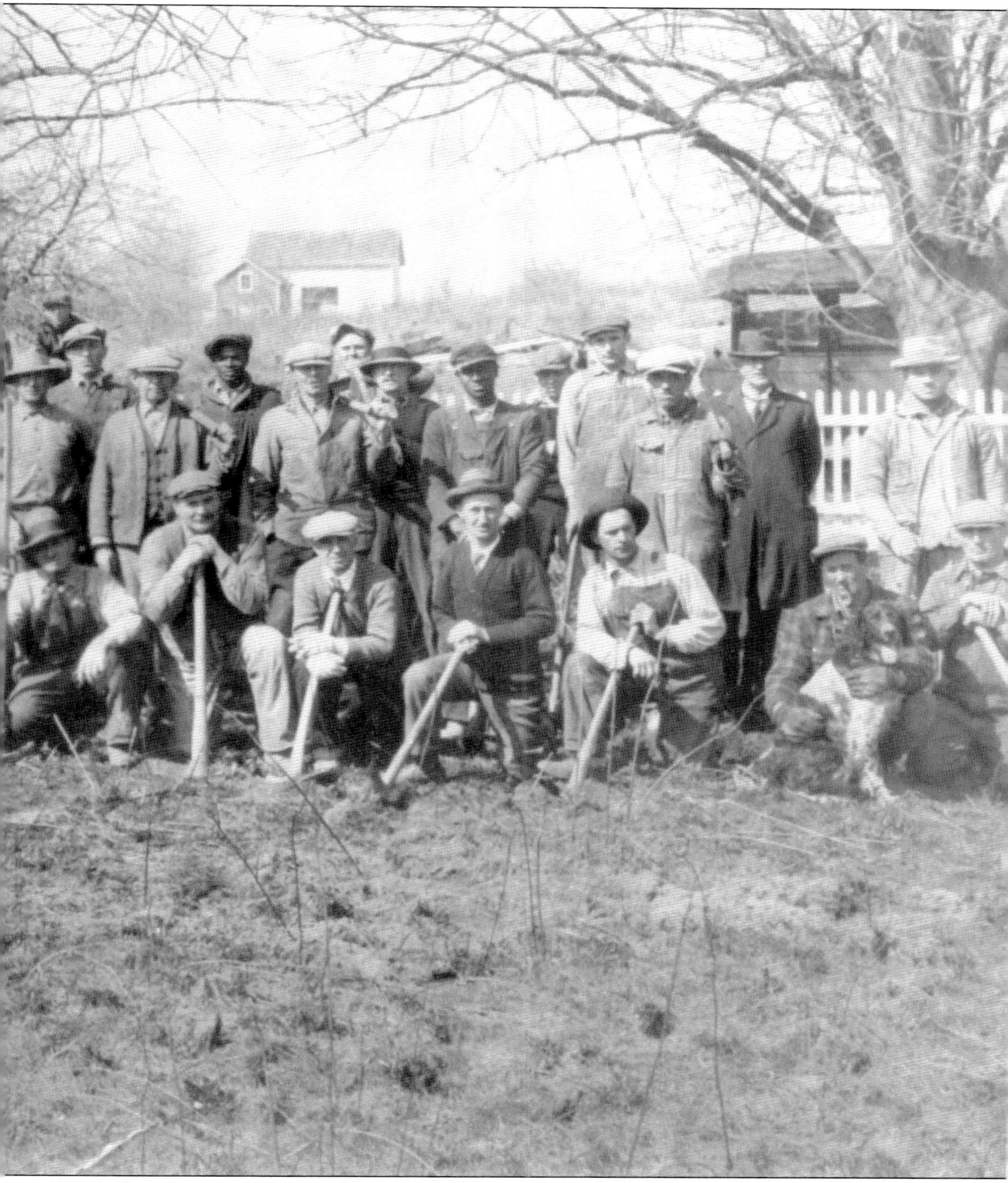

who died at the age of one in 1717. Originally a municipal burying ground, the site became the property of the Cutchogue Presbyterian Church, which later transferred ownership to the Cutchogue–New Suffolk Historical Council. The council maintains and interprets the site for the general public.

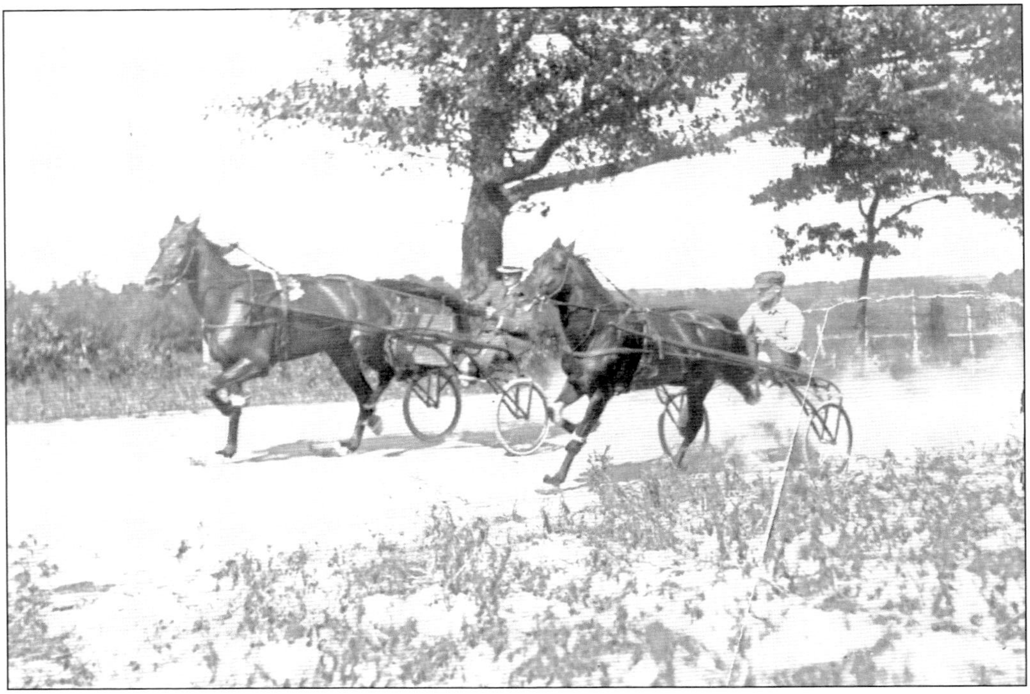

Training Harness Horses, c. 1920. Henry L. Fleet's horse-breeding and training farm remained active long after his death in 1894. His son, George H. Fleet (1858–1932), is shown at left above, racing a trotter believed to be Island Girl, while Bingle, son of Bingen and great-grandson of the famed Hambletonian, is driven by his friend George Billard. Island Girl was one of the Fleet farm's prized brood mares. Below, George Billard is again shown racing Bingle, while George Fleet (left) and another gentleman pace their speed in an automobile. Such trial heats developed the speed and agility of both horse and driver. (Courtesy of a private collection.)

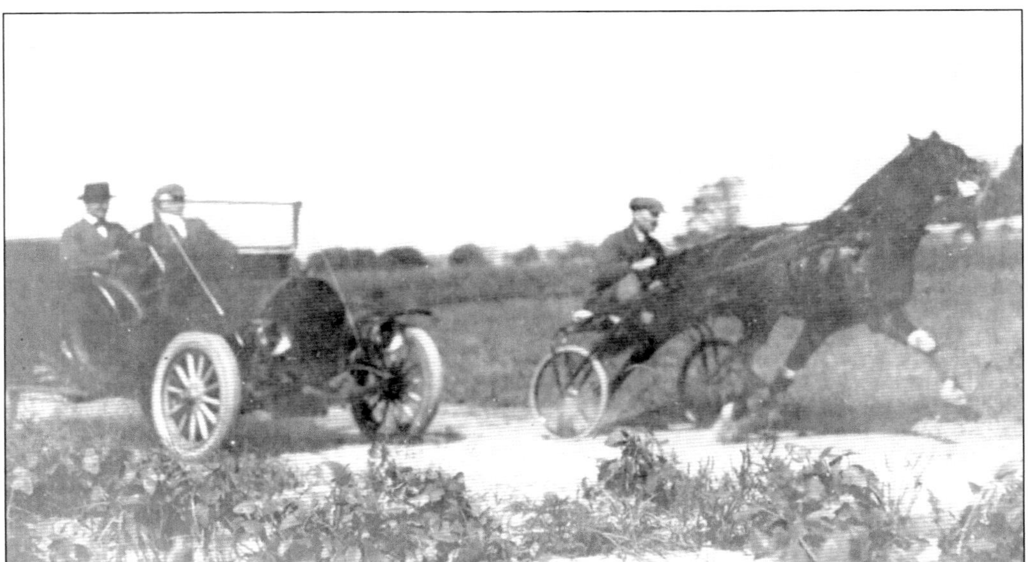

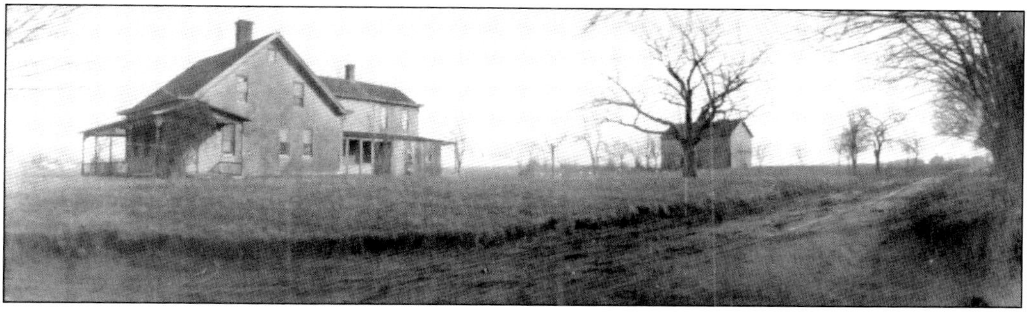

North Fork Country Club, c. 1910 and c. 1925. Opened on July 4, 1912, by local summer residents Charles B. Hudson and Stuart Hull Moore, the North Fork Ccuntry Club occupied a large tract of former farmland on the south side of the Main Road in Cutchogue. It was the area's first professional golf club. The club boasted an 18-hole course designed by renowned architect Donald J. Ross. The original clubhouse, adapted from the old Calvin Moore farmhouse (above), was redesigned and enlarged (below) for club use by architect John Petit. He also built the freestanding "Locker House"—a pro shop, residence, and bar—as well as a garage that accommodated 12 automobiles, a caddy room, and a tool shop. The original clubhouse stood for little more than a decade, however, and burned beyond repair on Labor Day of 1925.

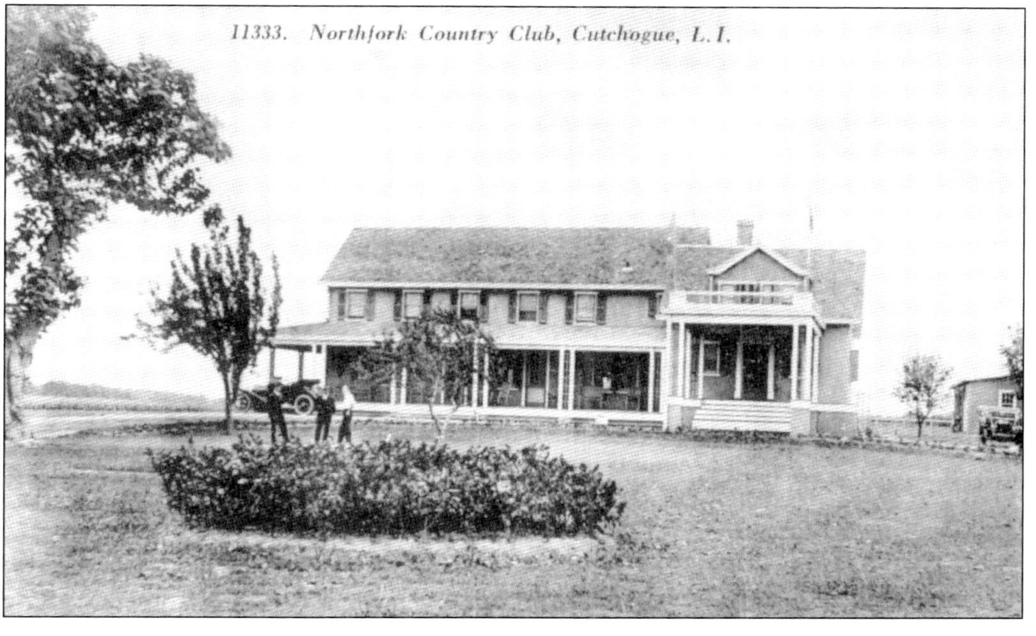

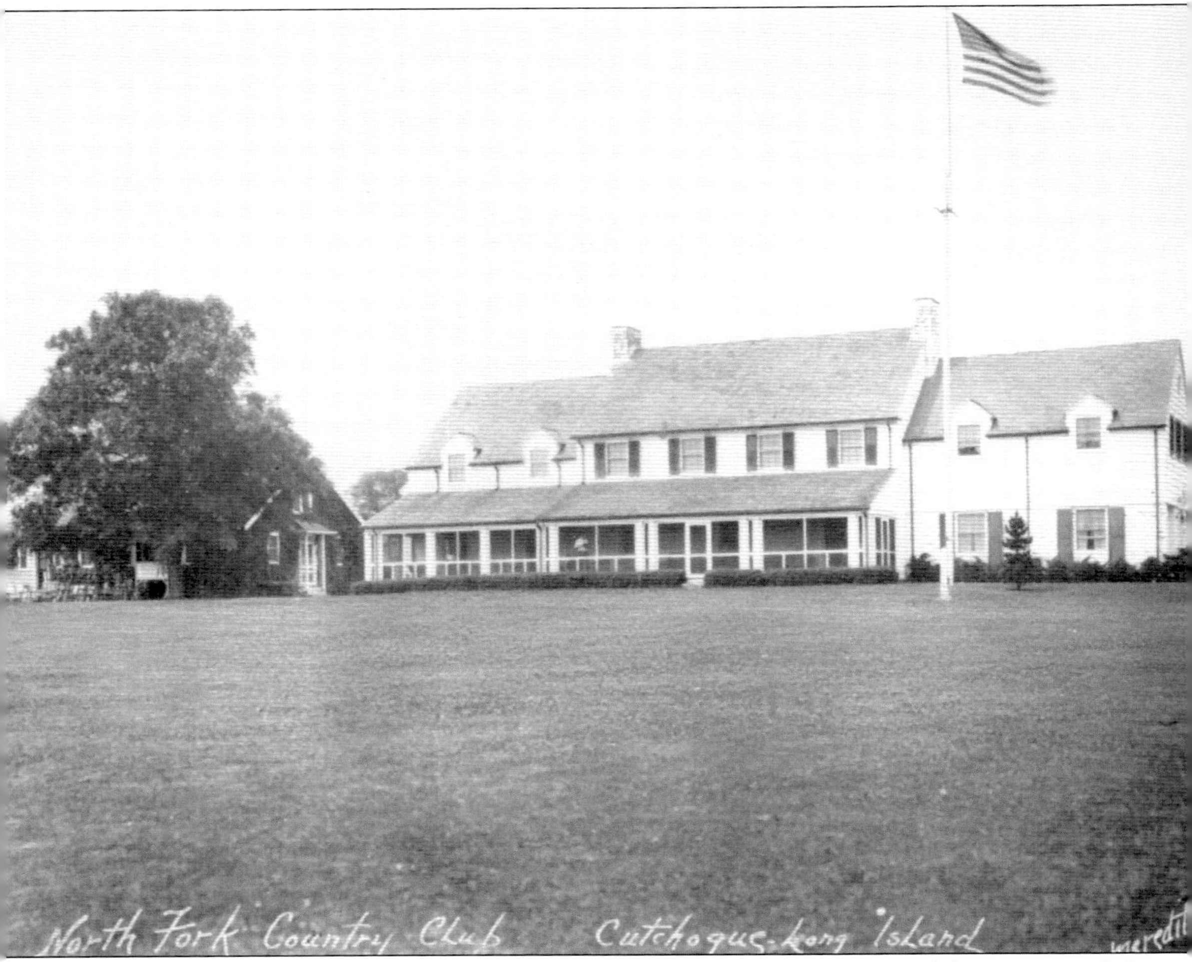

North Fork Country Club, 1941. Activities at the North Fork Country Club were suspended in 1926 due to the fire that destroyed the clubhouse. In the meantime, a new clubhouse was built, and it opened on July 2, 1927. Fortunately, the adjacent Locker House (to the left of the tree in this Meredith photograph of 1941) was spared in the 1925 blaze. Serving as men's and women's locker rooms, pro shop, bar, and quarters for the help, as well as a business office, it, too, would burn to the ground in 1985. The main clubhouse was rebuilt by C. Morrison Wines of Mattituck, whose design followed the classic lines of an old Long Island farmhouse. Sadly, this second clubhouse would also succumb to the June 1985 blaze, which left the North Fork Country Club with the task of rebuilding yet again. (Courtesy of the Southold Historical Society.)

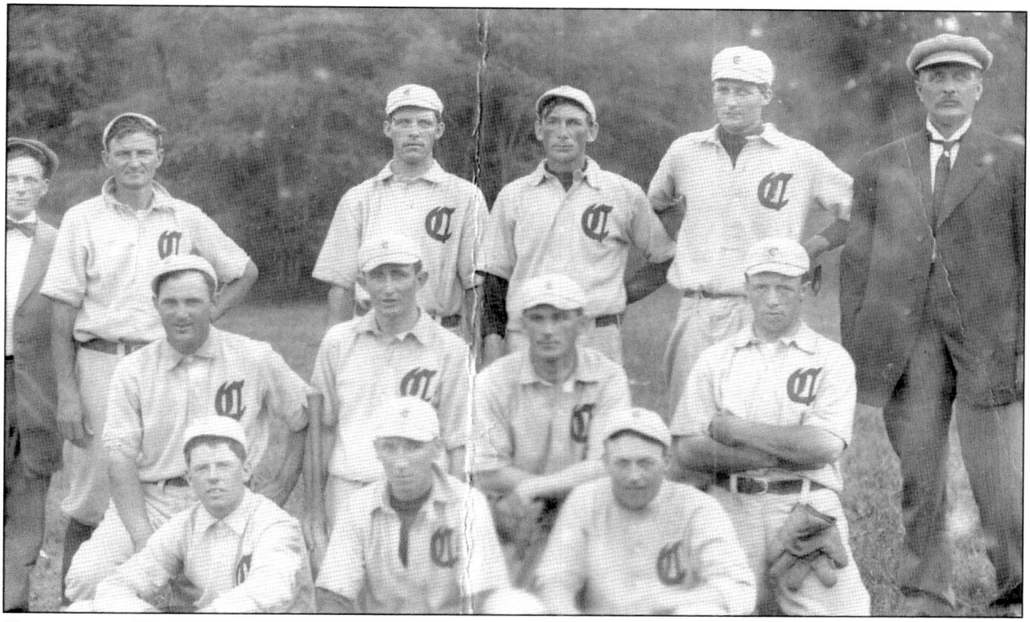

CUTCHOGUE BASEBALL, c. 1930 AND c. 1940. Many North Fork communities sponsored competitive baseball teams in the early to mid-1900s, including nearby Mattituck, Southold, Peconic, and even Oregon. The Cutchogue team shown above around 1930 included, from left to right, (first row) Gil Horton, Les Case, and Jim Dixon; (second row) Al Davids, Ben Drumm, Jim Hand, and Tom McCaffery; (third row) Raymond Tuthill, Charles Hannabury, Sherwood Beebe, Pete Hand, Jed Fleet, and William M. Beebe. Below, a team poses around 1940. Shown are, from left to right, (first row) Ed Skwara, Jack Tuthill, Chester Zaneski, Walter Kaelin, Henry Kane, Adolf Rysko, and Bennett Orlowski; (second row) Wesley Stepnoski, Al Doroski, Harry Waite, Bernard McCaffery, and Richard Horton. Active until World War II, the local teams were discontinued by the 1950s. (Below, courtesy of the Southold Historical Society.)

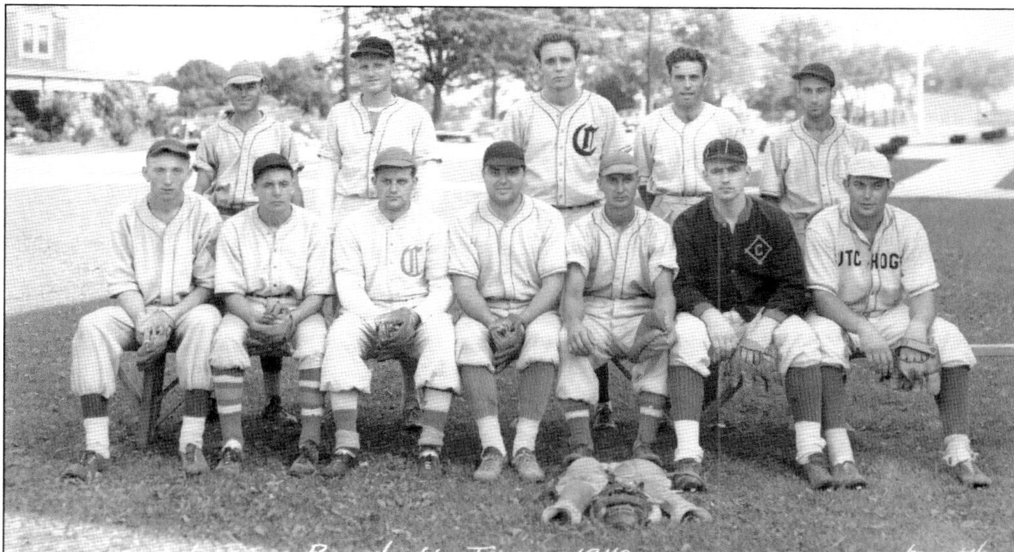

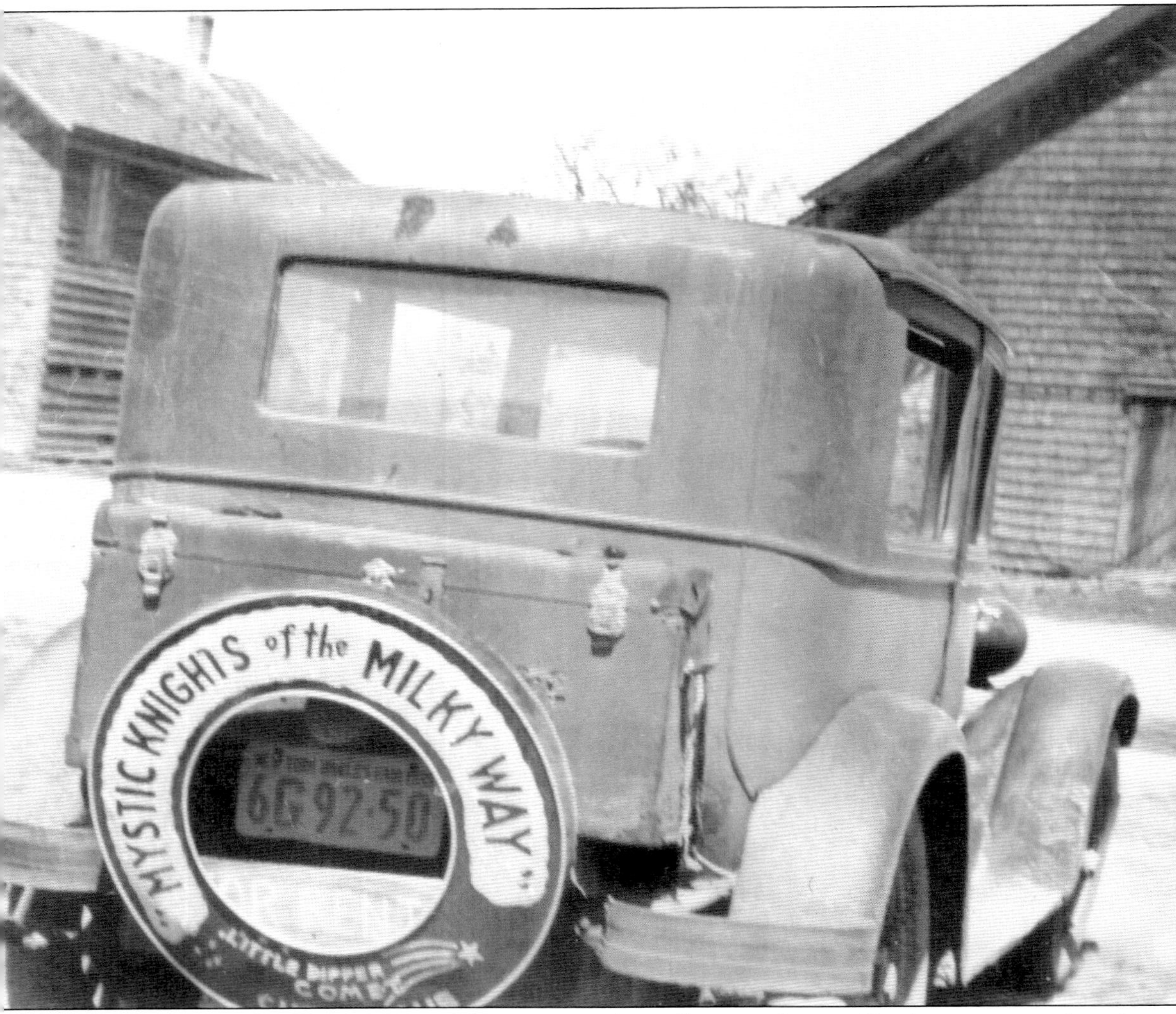

Mystic Knights of the Milky Way, c. 1939. A small group of young Cutchogue men gathered on a March night in 1939 to form a new club, which they dubbed the Mystic Knights of the Milky Way. The officers of the club were: Head Mystic Moonbeam, Stanley Ambroski; Exalted Big Dipper, Walter Kaelin; Exalted Little Dipper, Edward Grathwohl; Taurus, Chester Zaneski; and Venus, James Horton. The club was possibly a spoof on one of the active fraternal organizations that were popular among older men at the time, such as the Freemasons and Knights of Columbus. The nearest Masonic lodges were those at Greenport, chartered in 1855, and Riverhead, chartered in 1867. Perhaps the rituals associated with this ancient fraternal organization inspired these young men to start a club of their own. Its purpose remains as mysterious as the name, however, and it ceased meeting soon after forming, so its mission may never be known. (Courtesy of Cutchogue Fire Department.)

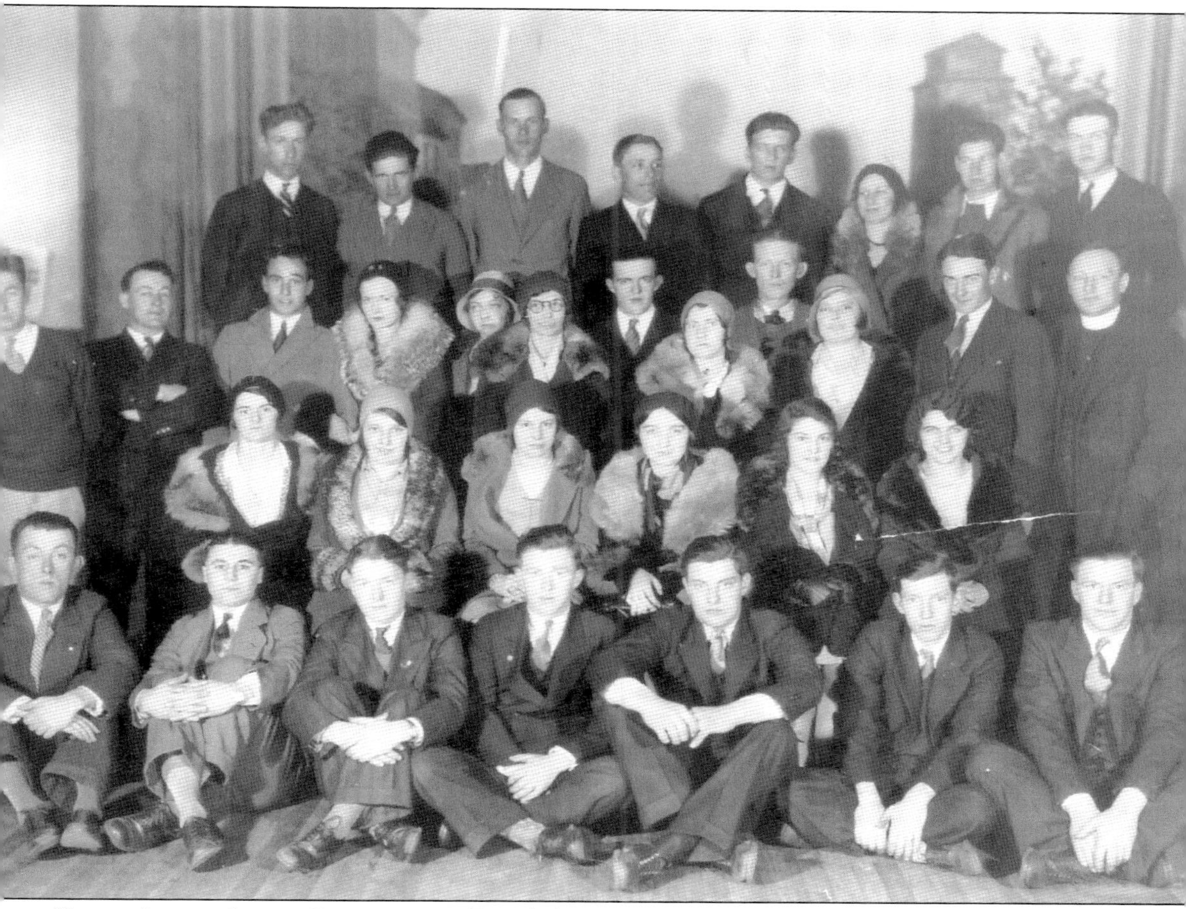

YOUNG ADULTS SOCIAL CLUB, C. 1929. Founded in 1901, Sacred Heart was a parish of the Diocese of Brooklyn, New York. Rev. John C. Brennan (third row, far right) was pastor of the parish and the inspiration for its youth group, the Young Adults Social Club, pictured here around 1929. Sacred Heart was initially a mission of St. Patrick's Roman Catholic Church, Southold. In 1873, Rev. John McKenna bought property that became the site of the church and rectory. The church was built in 1878, and on October 3, 1901, Sacred Heart was set up as a distinct parish, with Rev. James H. Lynch as its first pastor. (Courtesy of Peggy Kaelin.)

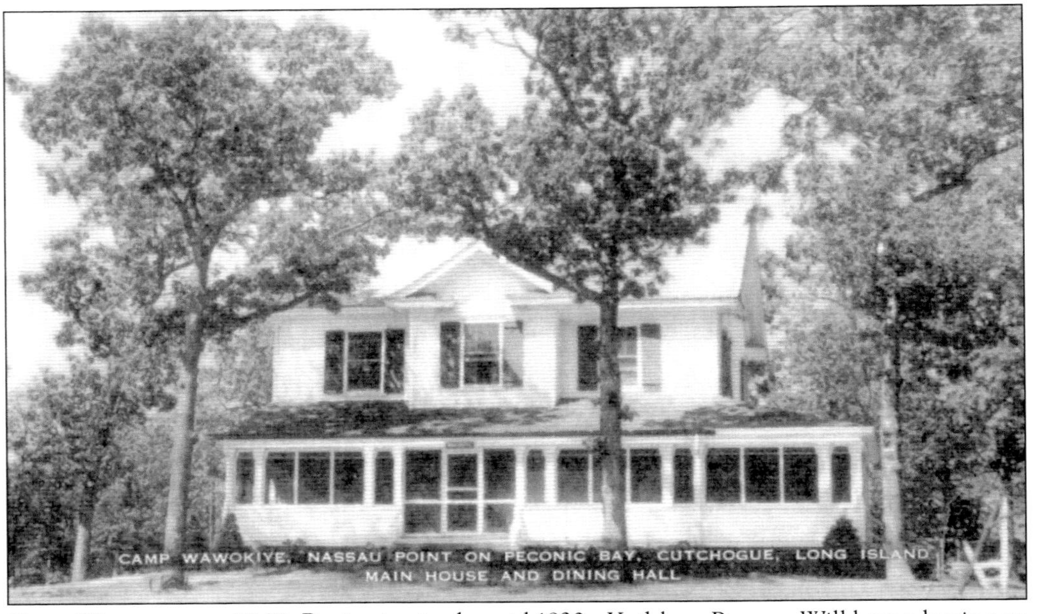

CAMP WAWOKIYE, C. 1940. Beginning in the mid-1930s, Kathleen Pearson Will began buying up land on Nassau Point. She established Camp Wawokiye on about eight acres of land overlooking the bay. The old Carpenter house, built around 1865 as a private residence for Dr. Benjamin Carpenter, served as both the hub of camp life and as the dining hall, while six redwood cabins, all with "Indian" names like Netab and Opelachi, were built nearby. The cabins had running water and toilets for the 70 campers, who ranged in age from five to about sixteen. The camp boasted a strong staff-to-camper ratio and a full-time nurse, and the daily routine emphasized old-time family values and self-reliance. Getting back to nature was a central theme, and sitting around a campfire under the stars each night reinforced the message. Camp Wawokiye remained active until 1979.

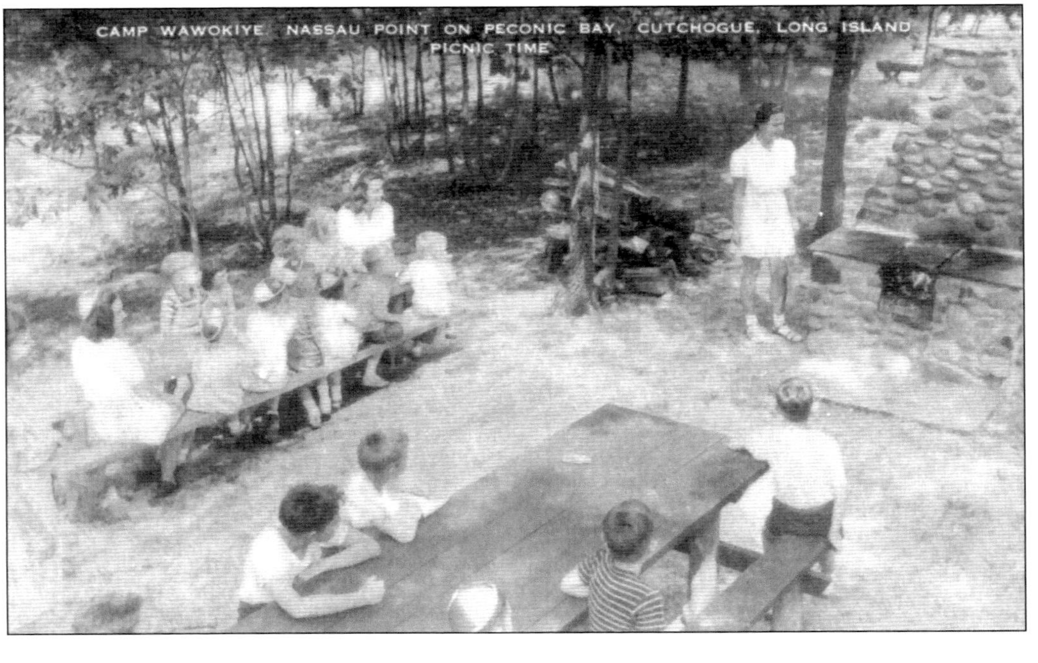

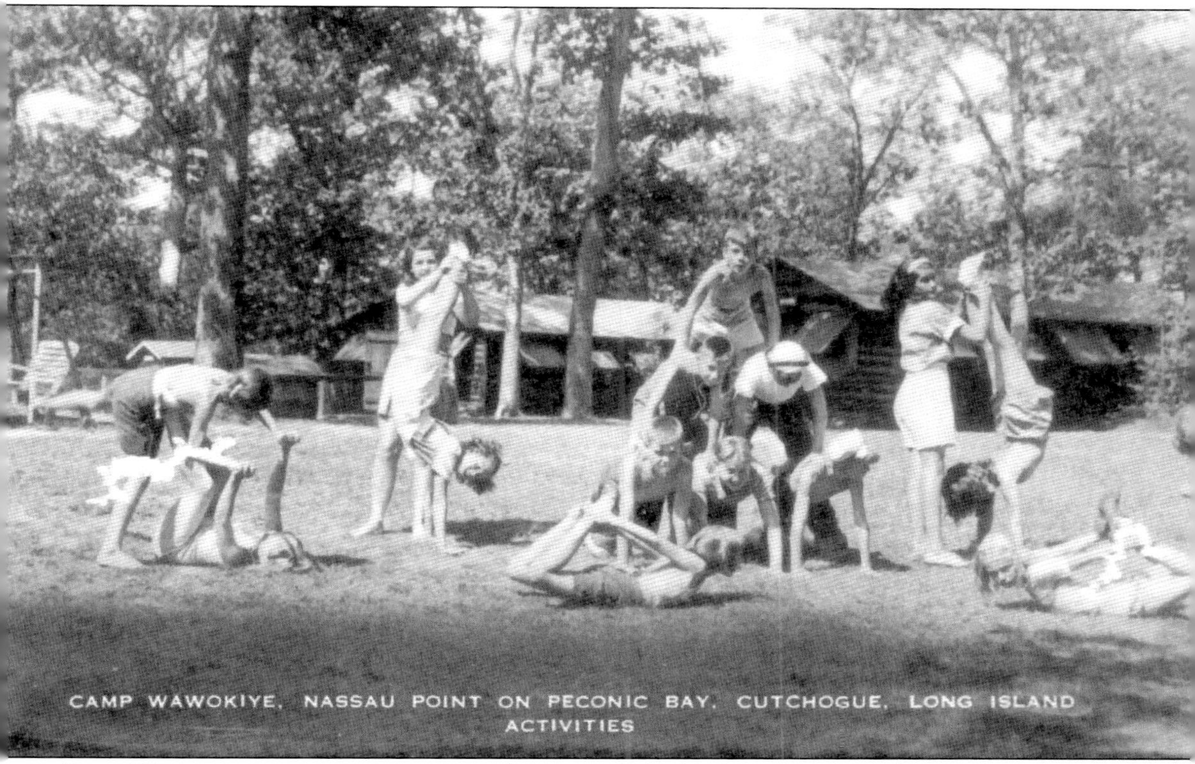

CAMP WAWOKIYE, C. 1940. Camp Wawokiye provided a healthy dose of outdoor exercise and activities for summer campers, and it served on occasion as a meeting place for one of Cutchogue's social groups, the Mums Club. Camp Wawokiye grew to include not only the main clubhouse, but also adjacent properties that provided the camp with cabins, a recreation hall, an arts and crafts center, and a ball field. The decade in which Camp Wawokiye was created saw major changes in sports and physical education on a national scale. In the post-Depression economy, few could afford to attend spectator sports. A major shift resulted in favor of participatory sports, especially at the local level. Youth sports, including the opportunities afforded by summer camps, increased exponentially. It was in this larger national context that Charlie and Kathleen Will created Camp Wawokiye. After running the camp for two decades, it was sold to Kevin and Maureen Kist in 1964.

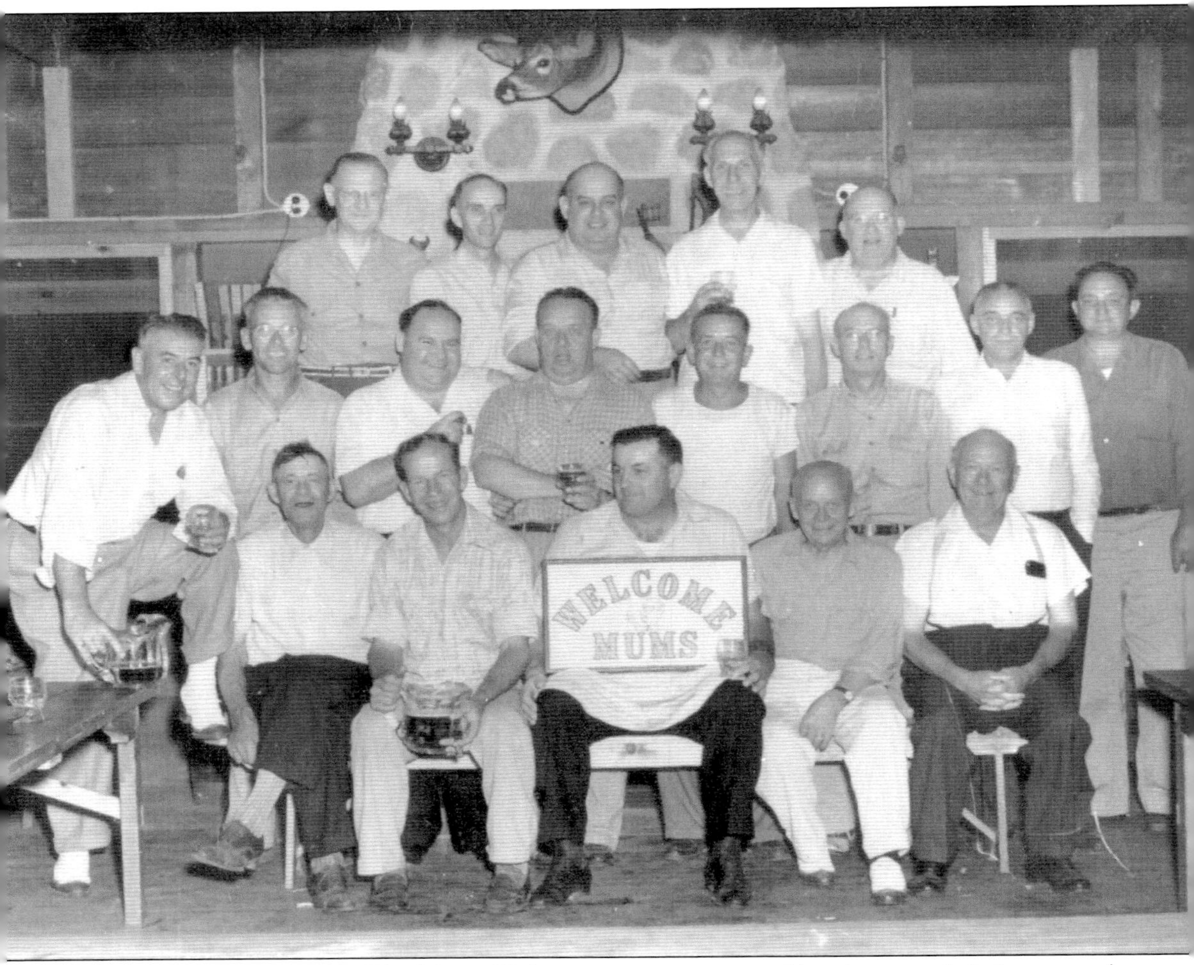

Mums Club, c. 1950. The Mums Club was an organization of local men and their guests who met annually in the spring and fall to enjoy clam chowder and beer. For this group portrait, the club met at Camp Wawokiye on Nassau Point in Cutchogue. They were hosted by club member Charlie Will, the owner of the camp. Shown gathered in front of the stone fireplace of the clubhouse's meeting room are, from left to right: (first row) unidentified guest, Roy Hallock, Irv Wells, Charlie Miska, Charlie Will (club owner), and Ed Gallagher; (second row) Cliff Polhemus, Howard Berry, George (Ike) Tuthill, Corwin C. Grathwohl, Gordon MacNish, Harold Grathwohl, and unidentified guest; (third row) unidentified guest, Arthur Fanning, Spencer (Spen) Butterworth, Harold (Bummy) Hudson, and Walter MacNish. Two of the most active members were local builder Corwin C. Grathwohl (1907–1985) and his older brother Harold (1895–1958). The club disbanded in the 1950s.

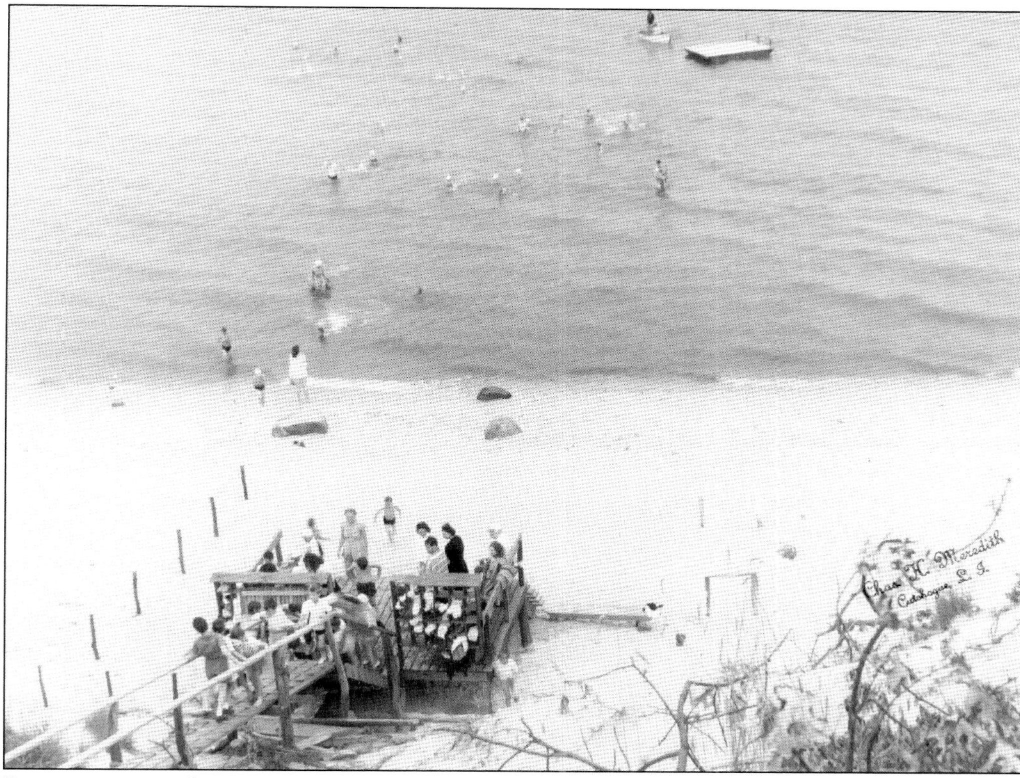

BATHING IN THE SOUND AND BAY, c. 1943. For swimming or sunning on the beach, nothing could beat bathing in Long Island Sound along Cutchogue's northern shore (above). Due to the steep cliffs that characterize much of the coastline, long ladder-like stairs were used to reach the beach, as seen in this Charles Meredith view. As an alternative to Long Island Sound, the Peconic Bay to the south offered opportunities for sun bathing, too (right). Summer resident Anna Wurzbacher Kohn enjoyed a sunny afternoon framed by one of New Suffolk's iconic landmarks, the oyster house. Anna and her cousin Josie Spitzmiller were Brooklyn residents who visited summers at their Aunt Elsie's boardinghouse, later known as White Cap. Elsie and her husband, Johnny, were also from Brooklyn, but had relocated in the 1930s to operate the New Suffolk boardinghouse. (Above, courtesy of the Southold Historical Society.)

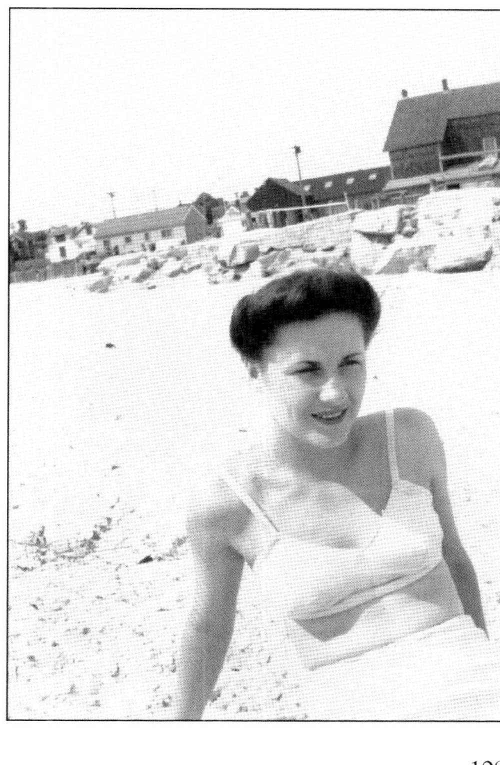

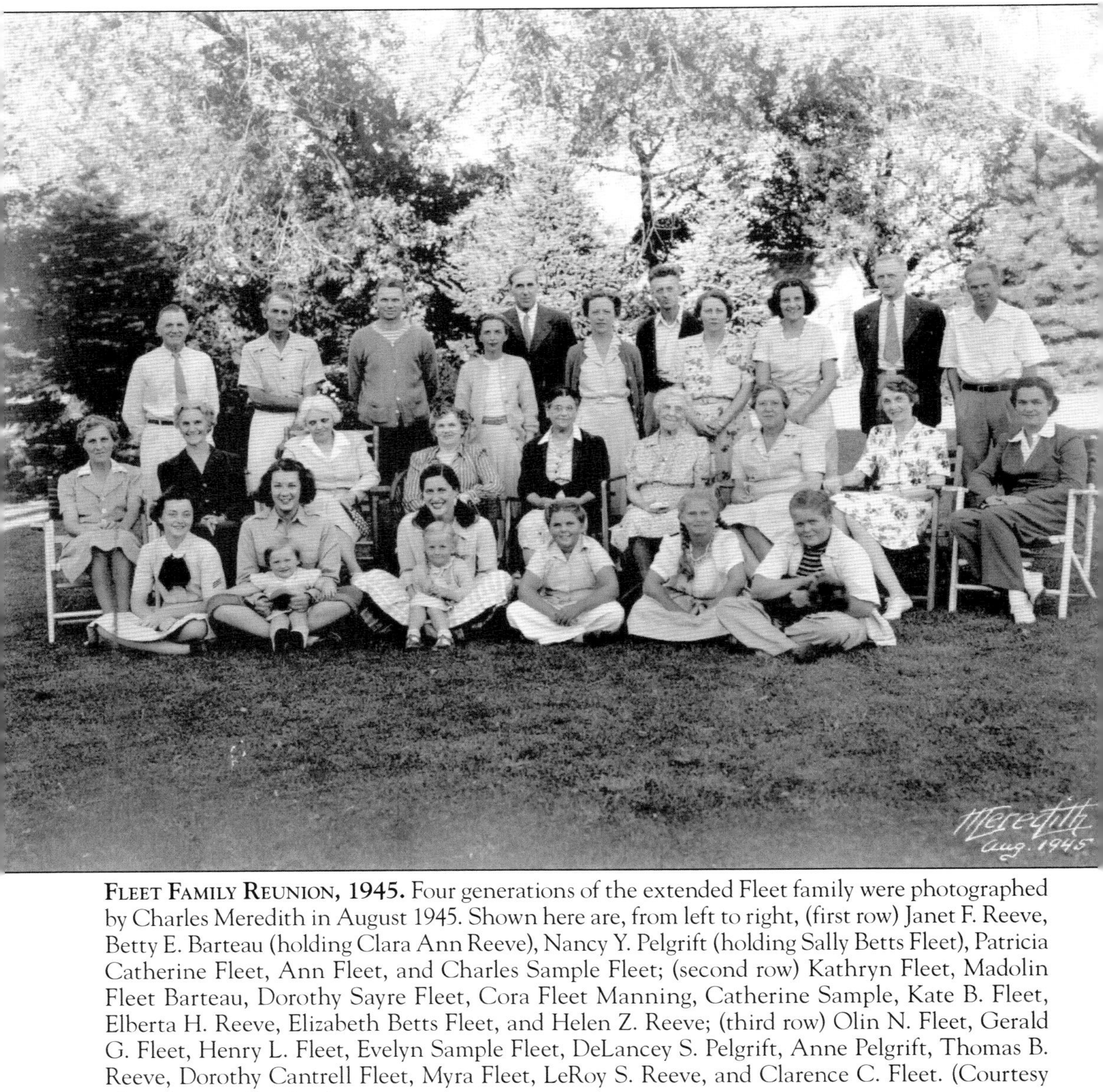

Fleet Family Reunion, 1945. Four generations of the extended Fleet family were photographed by Charles Meredith in August 1945. Shown here are, from left to right, (first row) Janet F. Reeve, Betty E. Barteau (holding Clara Ann Reeve), Nancy Y. Pelgrift (holding Sally Betts Fleet), Patricia Catherine Fleet, Ann Fleet, and Charles Sample Fleet; (second row) Kathryn Fleet, Madolin Fleet Barteau, Dorothy Sayre Fleet, Cora Fleet Manning, Catherine Sample, Kate B. Fleet, Elberta H. Reeve, Elizabeth Betts Fleet, and Helen Z. Reeve; (third row) Olin N. Fleet, Gerald G. Fleet, Henry L. Fleet, Evelyn Sample Fleet, DeLancey S. Pelgrift, Anne Pelgrift, Thomas B. Reeve, Dorothy Cantrell Fleet, Myra Fleet, LeRoy S. Reeve, and Clarence C. Fleet. (Courtesy of a private collection.)

CORCHAUG INDIAN REENACTMENTS, C. 1940. The so-called Contact Period, when white colonists from New England displaced the local Indian population in the 1640s, was re-created in Southold Town's tercentenary celebrations of 1940. In the Linnaeus Allen photograph at right, taken during the celebrations, John White (left), Jesse Lyons (center), and Andrew Lewis (right) dressed the part of Native Americans. The parade float (below) included a tepee, Native Americans, and their naturalistic setting—all on wheels! The early Corchaugs were a dwindling presence in the region when Cutchogue, Southold's first satellite community, was established in the 1660s. Excavations undertaken between 1936 and 1996 by Ralph S. Solecki, Lorraine E. Williams, and other archeologists confirmed the existence of Fort Corchaug on the Downs farm in Cutchogue, the tribe's last stronghold. Fort Corchaug was declared a National Historic Landmark in 1999. (Below, courtesy of Cutchogue Fire Department.)

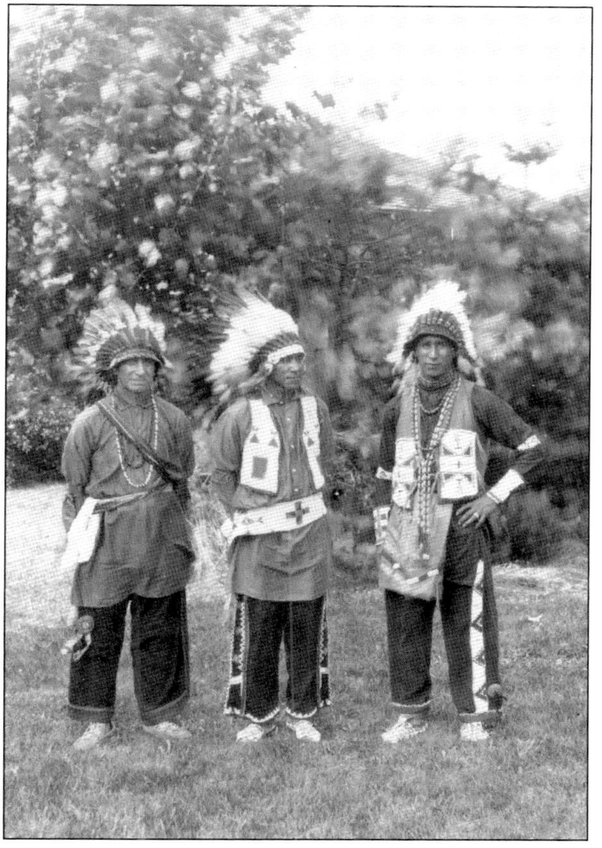

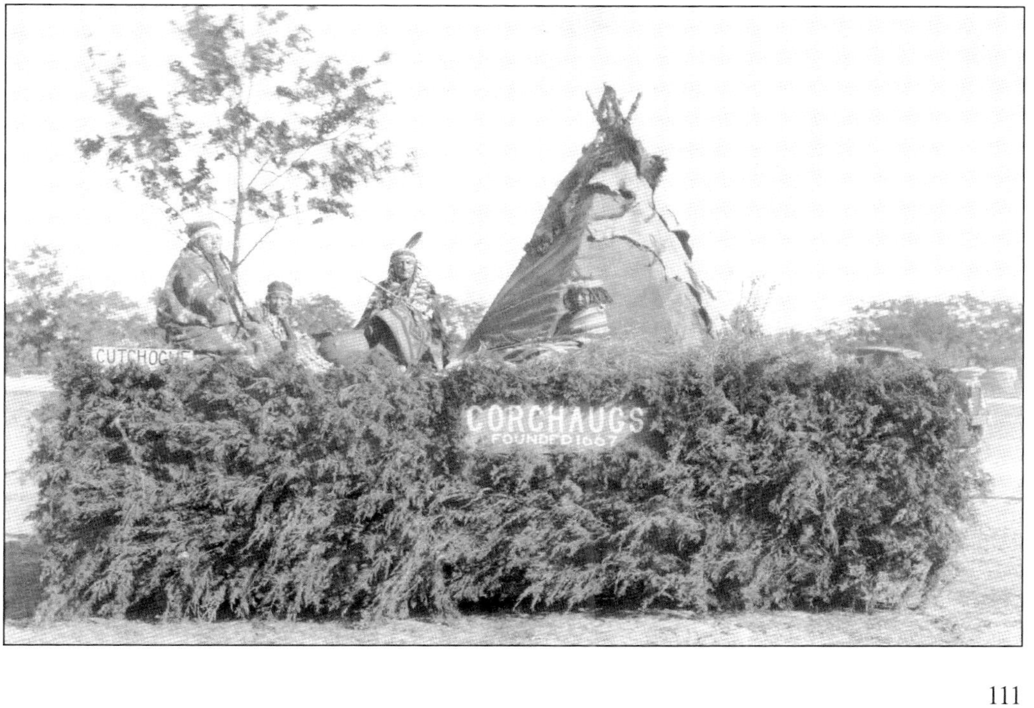

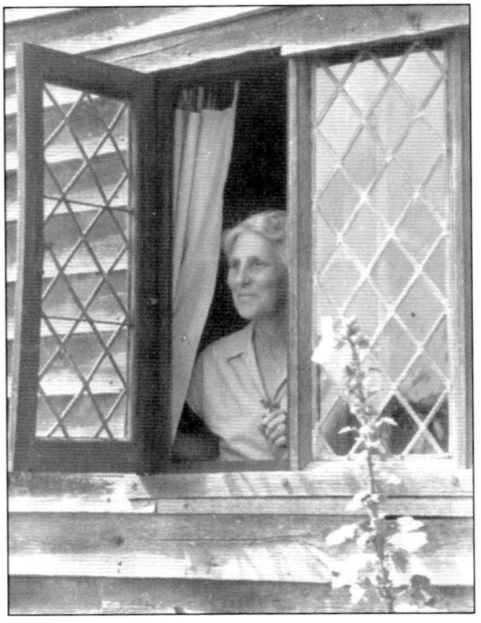

Kathryn Fleet at the Old House, 1954. Kathryn Fleet (1897–1994) was the youngest child of George H. Fleet. Her grandfather, Henry L. Fleet, had made his Cutchogue farm renowned for breeding and training race horses, a tradition that lasted well into the 20th century. Kathryn's older sister Madolin was a docent at the Old House after its restoration in 1940, and both sisters were frequent visitors to Cutchogue's most famous landmark. (Courtesy of a private collection.)

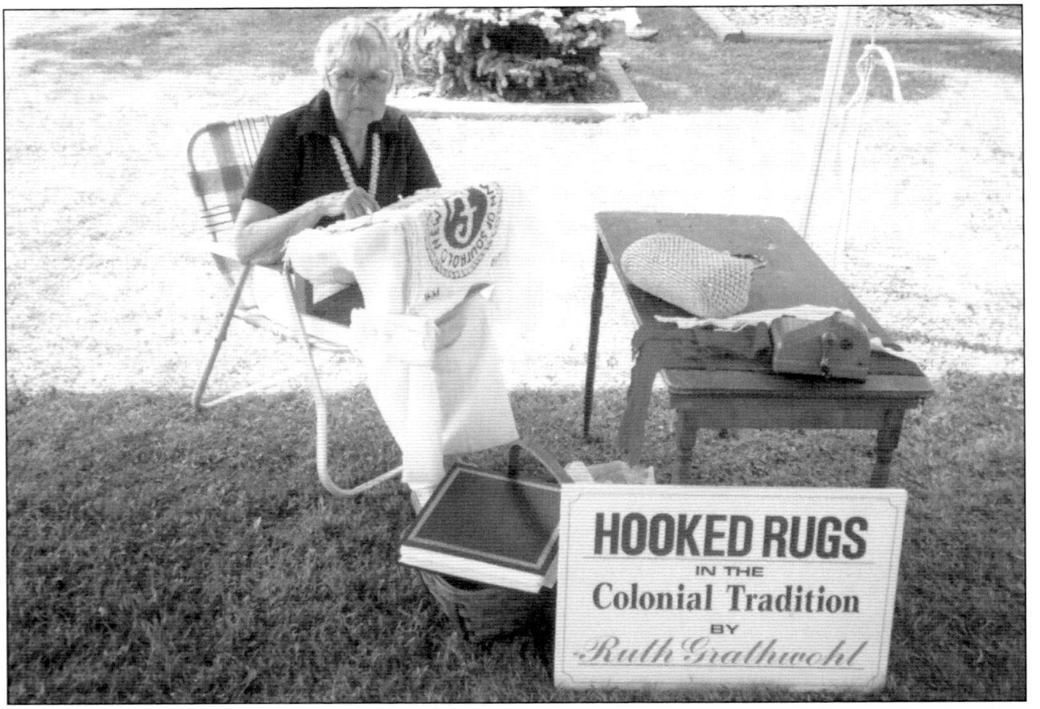

Hooked Rugs in the Colonial Tradition, c. 1975. One of the founders of the Cutchogue–New Suffolk Historical Council in 1960, Ruth G. Grathwohl (1906–2005) displays the "colonial tradition" of hooking rugs. Grathwohl was active in the Old Town Arts and Crafts Guild, founded in 1949 and dedicated to showcasing the works of local artists and artisans. She was married to Corwin Grathwohl, a local builder and contractor, and was descended from the Gildersleve family, early Southold settlers. (Courtesy of Emily Victoria.)

Seven

INVENTION AND INNOVATION

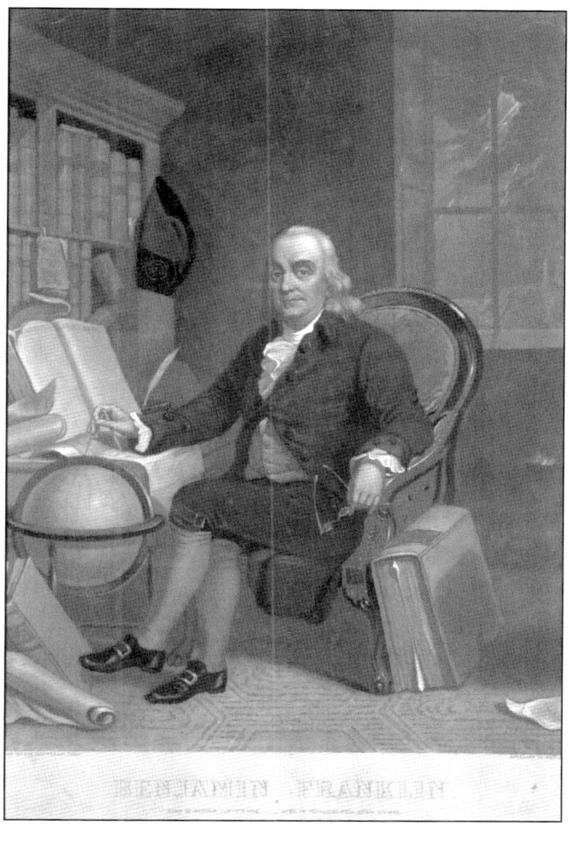

BENJAMIN FRANKLIN. Statesman, inventor, author, scientist, and diplomat, Benjamin Franklin (1706–1790) is one of the most renowned and beloved of the Founding Fathers. Few realize that Franklin also served as postmaster to the colonies before the Revolution. During his tenure, he improved postal routes by installing mile markers that measured distances between major cities. One such route was the Main Road through Cutchogue, where four of his mile markers survive today. (Courtesy of the American Philosophical Society, Philadelphia.)

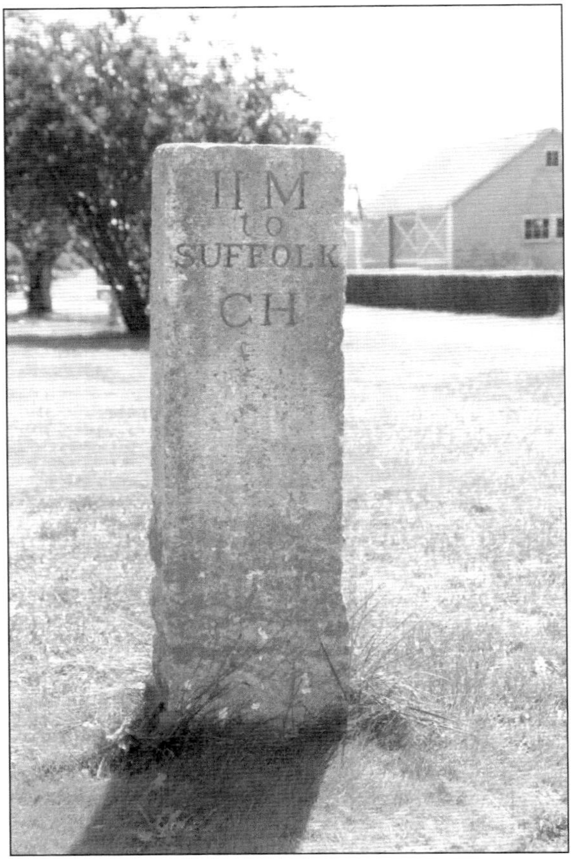

Mile Marker and Odometer, Mid-1700s. The carved granite marker (left) is one of 26 milestones spaced along the Main Road that bisects eastern Long Island's North Fork. Four of the stones can be found in Cutchogue alone; each marks the number of miles from "Suffolk CH" (courthouse), as present-day Riverhead was then known. The last in the series is located at Orient Point, where travelers then, as now, embarked by boat for Connecticut and New England. The mechanism that enabled Benjamin Franklin to measure miles accurately was a sophisticated odometer of French manufacture (below). The device was attached to a carriage wheel; using a system of intricate gearing, distance was determined by multiplying the perimeter of the wheel by the number of rotations that it made. At a time when postage was determined by how far a letter traveled, knowing the distance between major cities was important in standardizing rates. (Left, courtesy Graham Glover; below, courtesy of the historical and interpretive collections of The Franklin Institute, Philadelphia.)

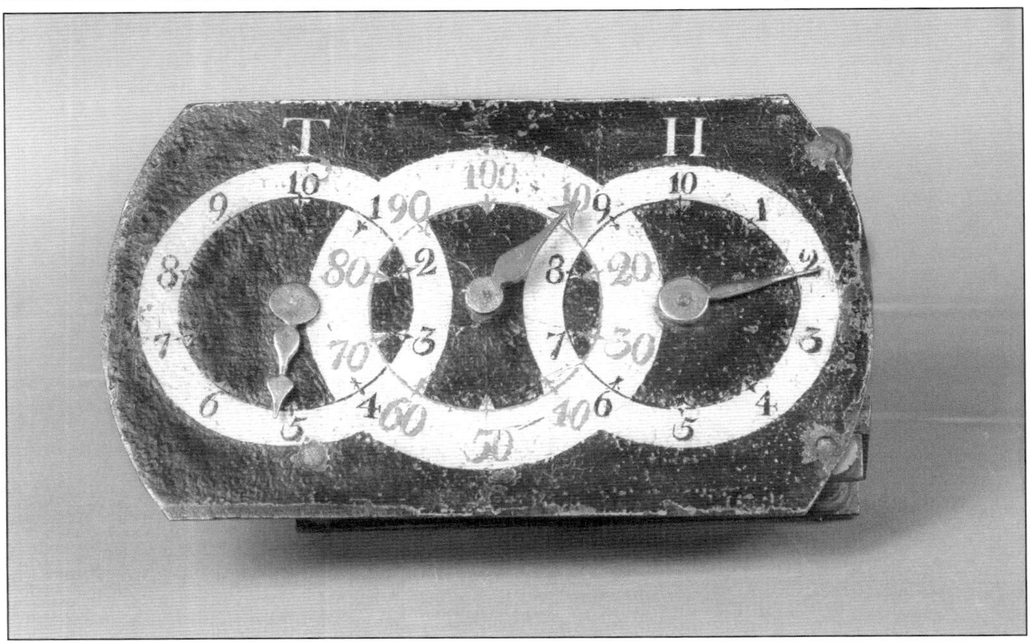

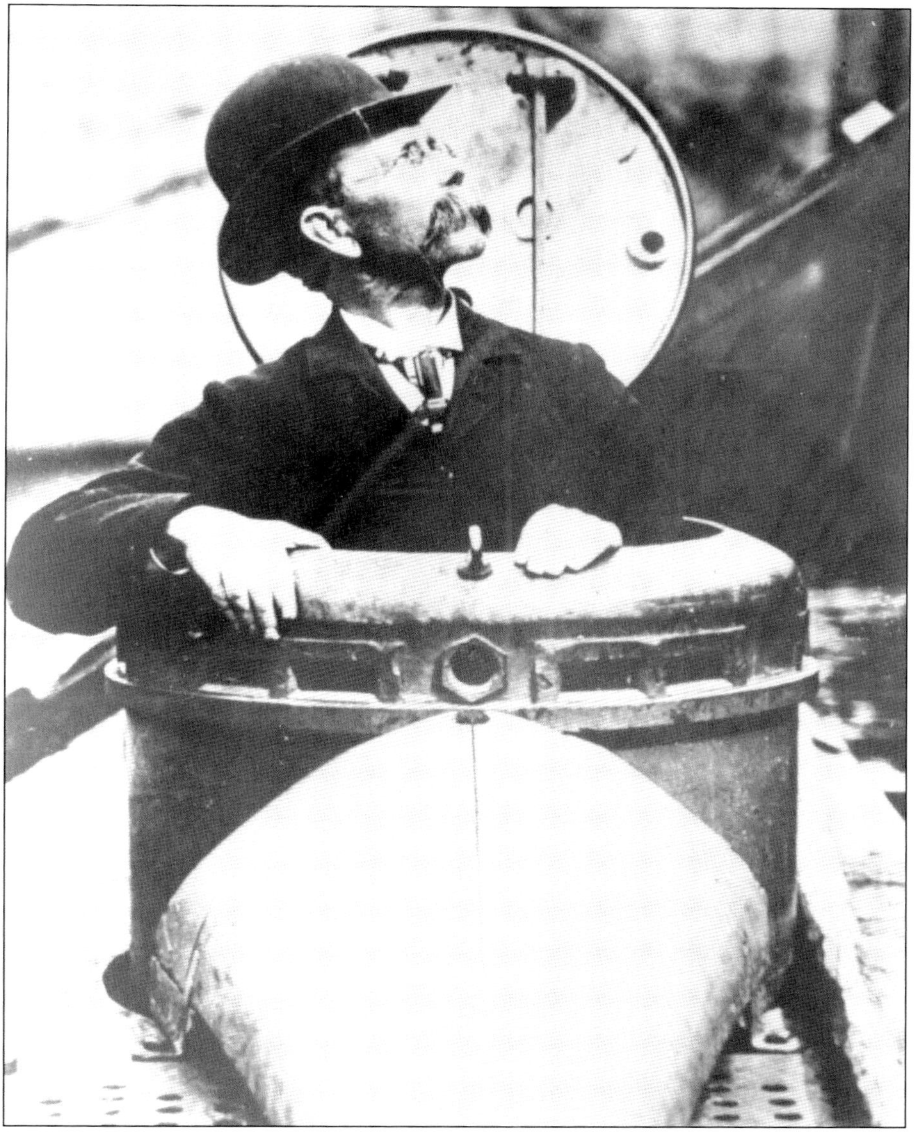

JOHN P. HOLLAND, C. 1900. Irish mathematician, engineer, and inventor John Philip Holland (1840–1914) designed and built the first successful submarine to be commissioned by the US Navy. He perfected his invention in trials in New Suffolk between 1899 and 1905, after discovering that the shipyards at Elizabethport, New Jersey, and New York Harbor were too busy for testing the vessel. A schoolteacher by profession who had immigrated to Paterson, New Jersey, in 1873, Holland developed his first submarine, the *Fenian Ram*, in 1881. It was rejected by the government, but Holland continued to experiment by means of private funding and, in 1897, launched the first submarine capable of operating while submerged for a distance. The innovative craft combined electric batteries for submerged travel and combustion engine power above the surface. It was purchased by the Navy in 1900 and commissioned the USS *Holland*. In all, at least five submarines of Holland's design were tested in New Suffolk, but the inventor lost control of his patents, and his company, the Electric Boat Company, moved to Groton, Connecticut, in 1905. Holland died in poverty and obscurity in 1914. (Courtesy of the Paterson Museum, Paterson, NJ.)

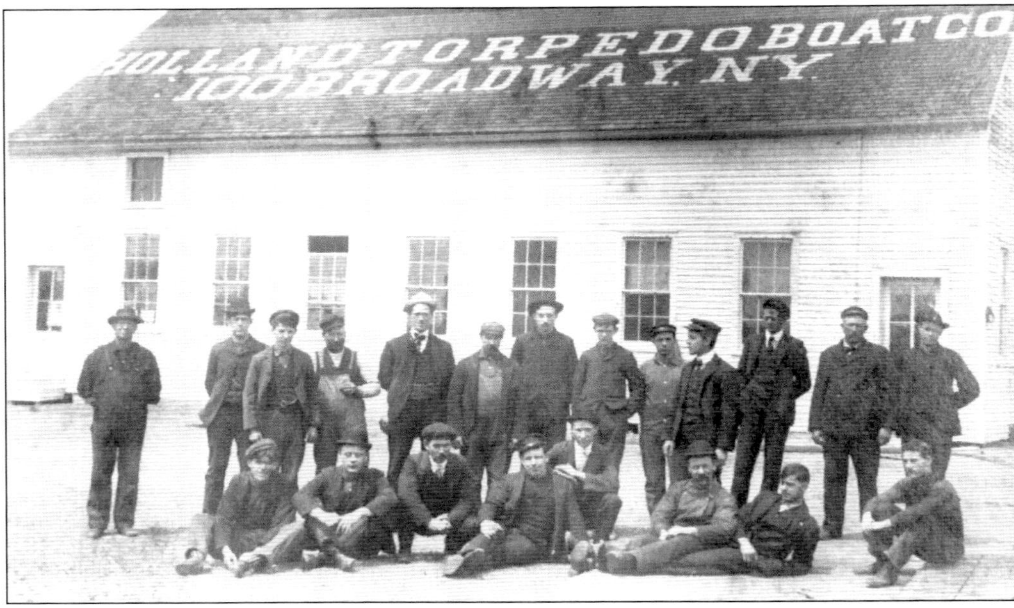

Holland Torpedo Boat Company, c. 1900 and c. 1905. Holland established his base of operations at the Goldsmith & Tuthill boatyard in New Suffolk and laid out a three-mile course for testing the submarines in Little Peconic Bay. His team of machinists, pipe fitters, electricians, and common laborers assembled for the c. 1900 group photograph above. They are, from left to right, (first row) Frank Acker, Charles Bectold, Peter Rehill, Harry Kirby, John Sanders, Charles Berg, Conrad Stick, and Karl Kuester; (second row) Lawrence Sullivan, William Wood, Thomas Delaney, Ben Horton, Harry Morrill, Charles Lewis, Hugo Momm, Terrence Magee, Herman Noblett, Leroy Hammond, John Wilson, Patrick Glenn, and William Deslette. In the below photograph of the harbor, several of Holland's submarines are docked in the shipyard. The five that were tested in New Suffolk were the *Adder*, *Moccasin*, *Porpoise*, *Fulton*, and *Columbia*.

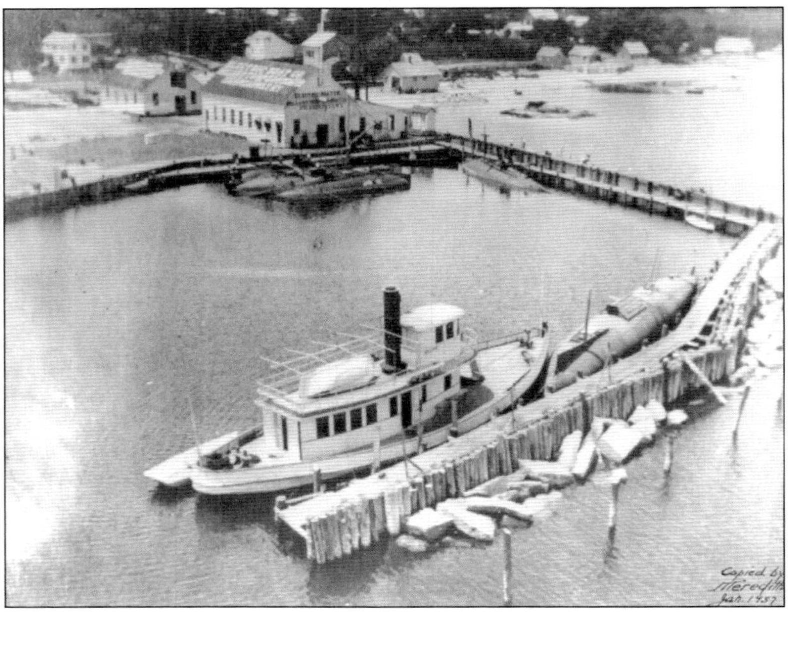

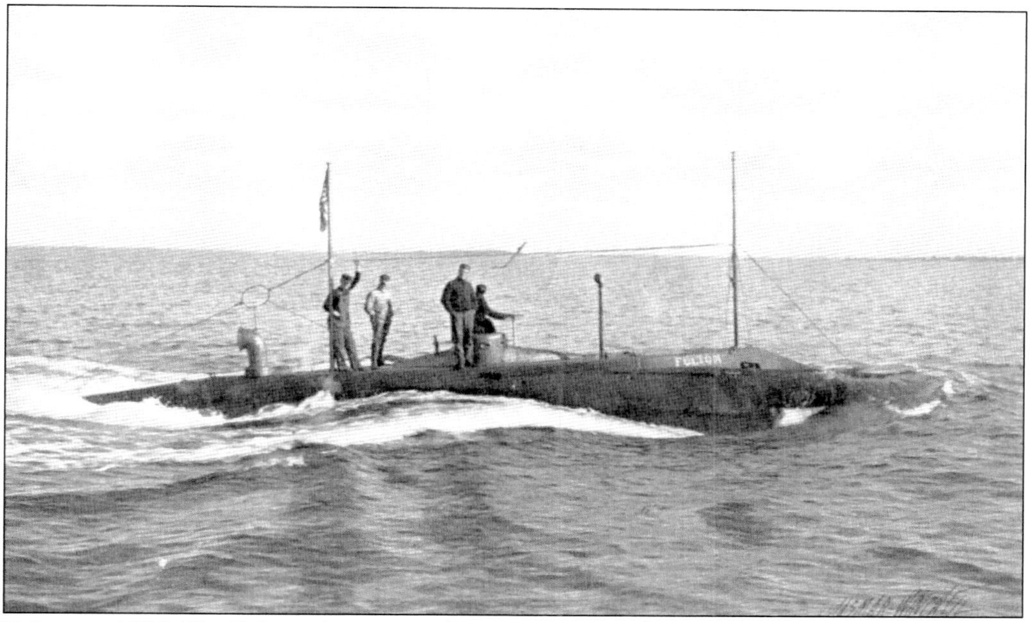

***Fulton*, c. 1905.** The *Fulton* submarine is shown cruising on the surface (above) and rising (below) during trial runs in Little Peconic Bay around 1905. Members of the crew are able to enjoy the ride above the surface. The *Fulton* was Holland's prototype of an A-class (or *Adder*-class) submarine that he developed in cooperation with naval architect Arthur Leopold Busch. Busch and his partner, Lewis Nixon, ran the influential and innovative Crescent Shipyard in Elizabeth, New Jersey, where many of the novel submarines of the period were designed and built. The US Navy never commissioned the *Fulton*, however; it was instead sold to the Imperial Russian Navy in 1905. (Courtesy of a private collection.)

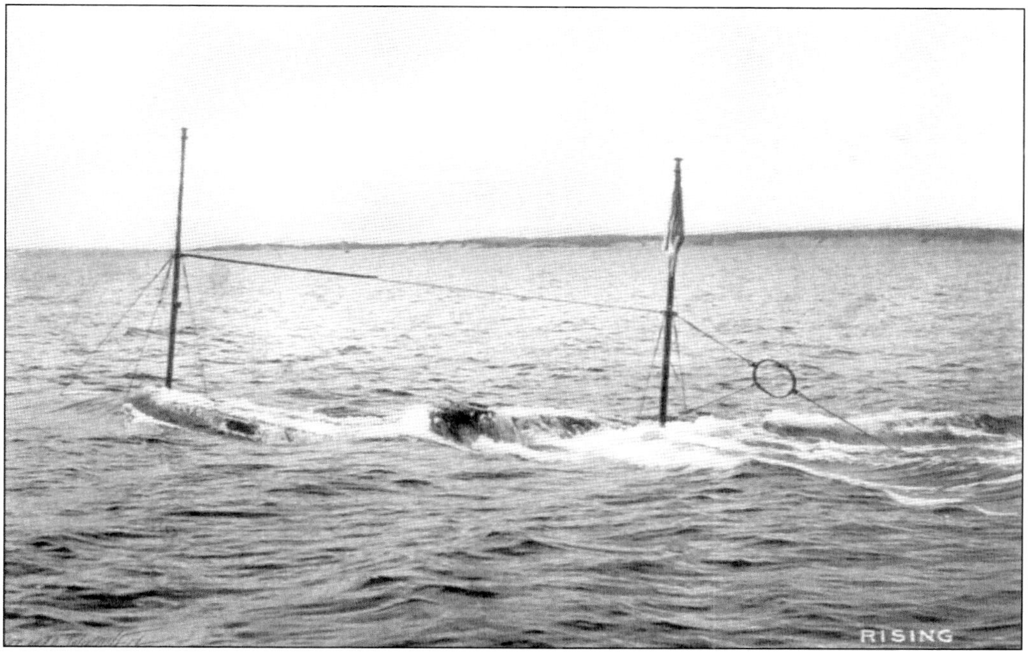

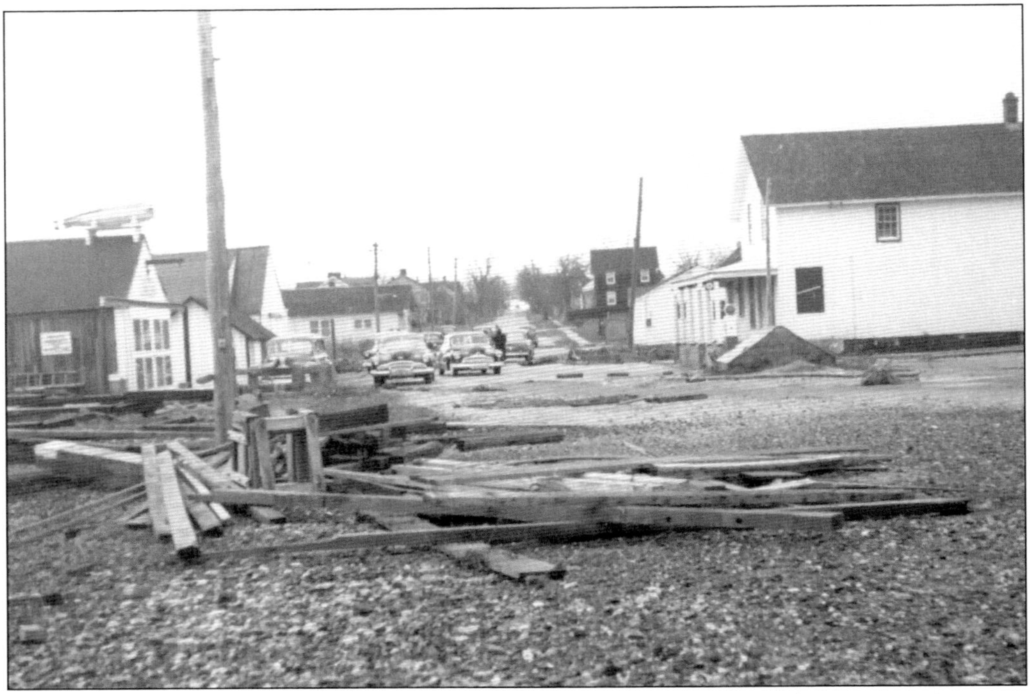

Main Street, New Suffolk, c. 1930. This east-facing photograph shows Main Street in downtown New Suffolk. At left, a wooden model of one of John P. Holland's historic submarines can be seen mounted on the roof of the blacksmith shop. The model was built by the Holland Company and is now displayed in the Carriage House on the Village Green in Cutchogue by the Cutchogue–New Suffolk Historical Council.

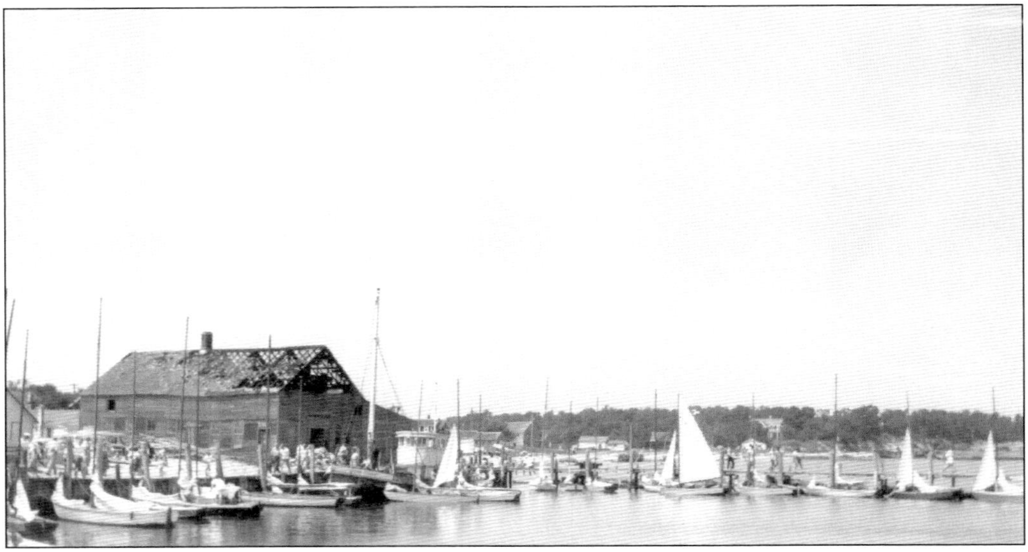

Holland Building, c. 1946. The passage of time was not kind to John P. Holland and his short-lived submarine operations at Goldsmith & Tuthill's boatyard in New Suffolk. Holland's Electric Boat Co. building is on the left, its wooden rafters exposed and clapboard siding badly weathered by the 1940s. The derelict structure continued to fall into disrepair and was later demolished.

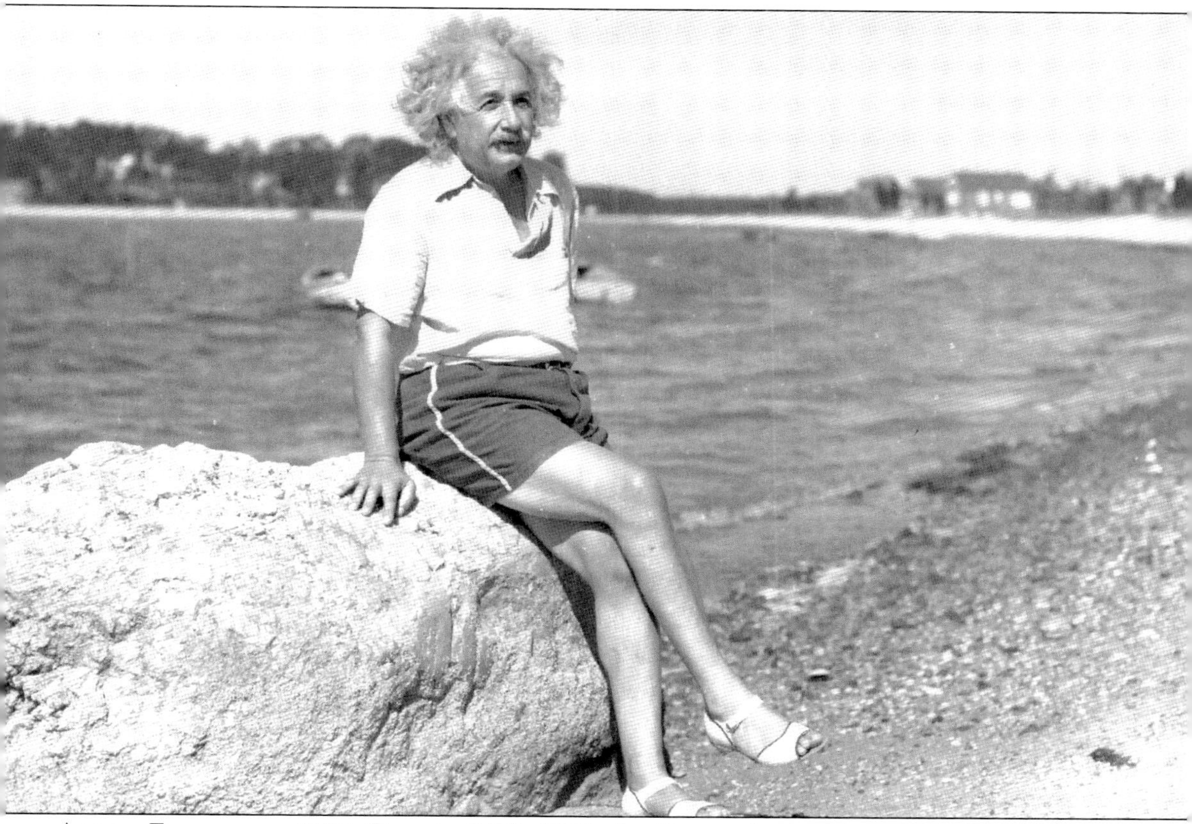

ALBERT EINSTEIN, C. 1938. Einstein (1879–1955), the German-born physicist best known for his theory of relativity, is shown here relaxing on the beach at Nassau Point, Cutchogue, where he rented a cottage in the summers of 1937, 1938, and 1939. It was there that he hosted fellow physicists Leo Szilard and Eugene Wigner on August 2, 1939, to learn of their concerns about Germany's intention to build an atomic bomb. At their urging, Einstein wrote to Pres. Franklin D. Roosevelt and recommended that America quickly adopt its own plan for researching nuclear weapons. The now-famous letter, which Einstein mailed from Richmond's store in East Cutchogue, is viewed as a primary impetus for the Manhattan Project, which produced nuclear weapons and ultimately decided the outcome of World War II. (Courtesy of the Rothman family and the Southold Historical Society.)

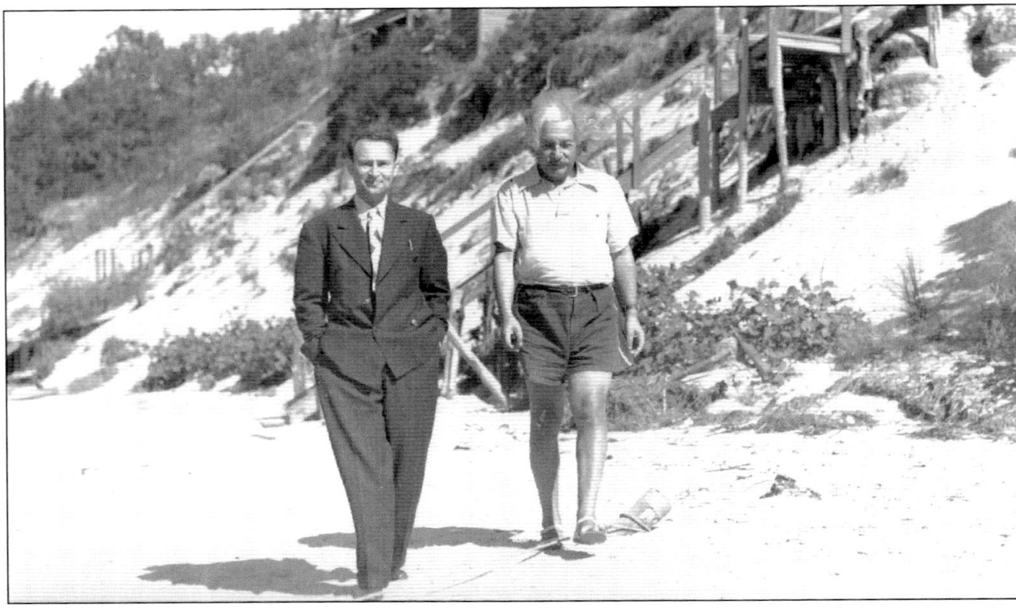

Albert Einstein and David Rothman, Cutchogue, c. 1938. The famous physicist formed an enduring friendship with Southold merchant David Rothman, whose general store was a resource for clothing, supplies, and other "necessities" of a summer vacation. The two men spent many hours in conversation and shared a love of the violin. (Courtesy of the Rothman family and the Southold Historical Society.)

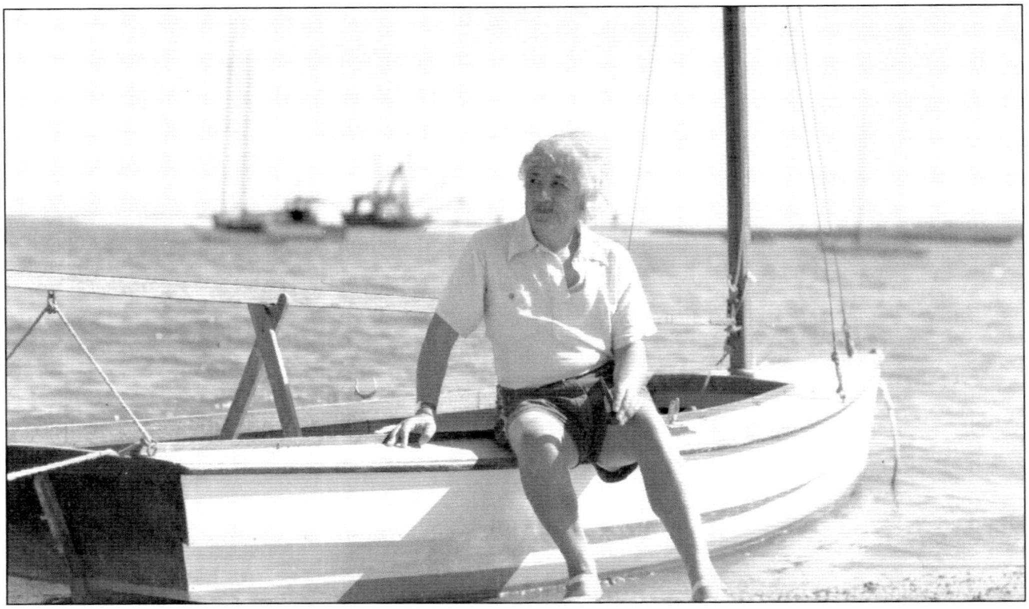

Albert Einstein and *Tineff*, c. 1938. Einstein's summer cottage on Old Cove Road at Nassau Point in Cutchogue was within walking distance of the beach, where he kept a little sailboat named *Tineff* ("worthless" in Yiddish). A novice sailor, he is said to have called Little Peconic Bay "the most beautiful sailing ground I ever experienced." (Courtesy of the Rothman family and the Southold Historical Society.)

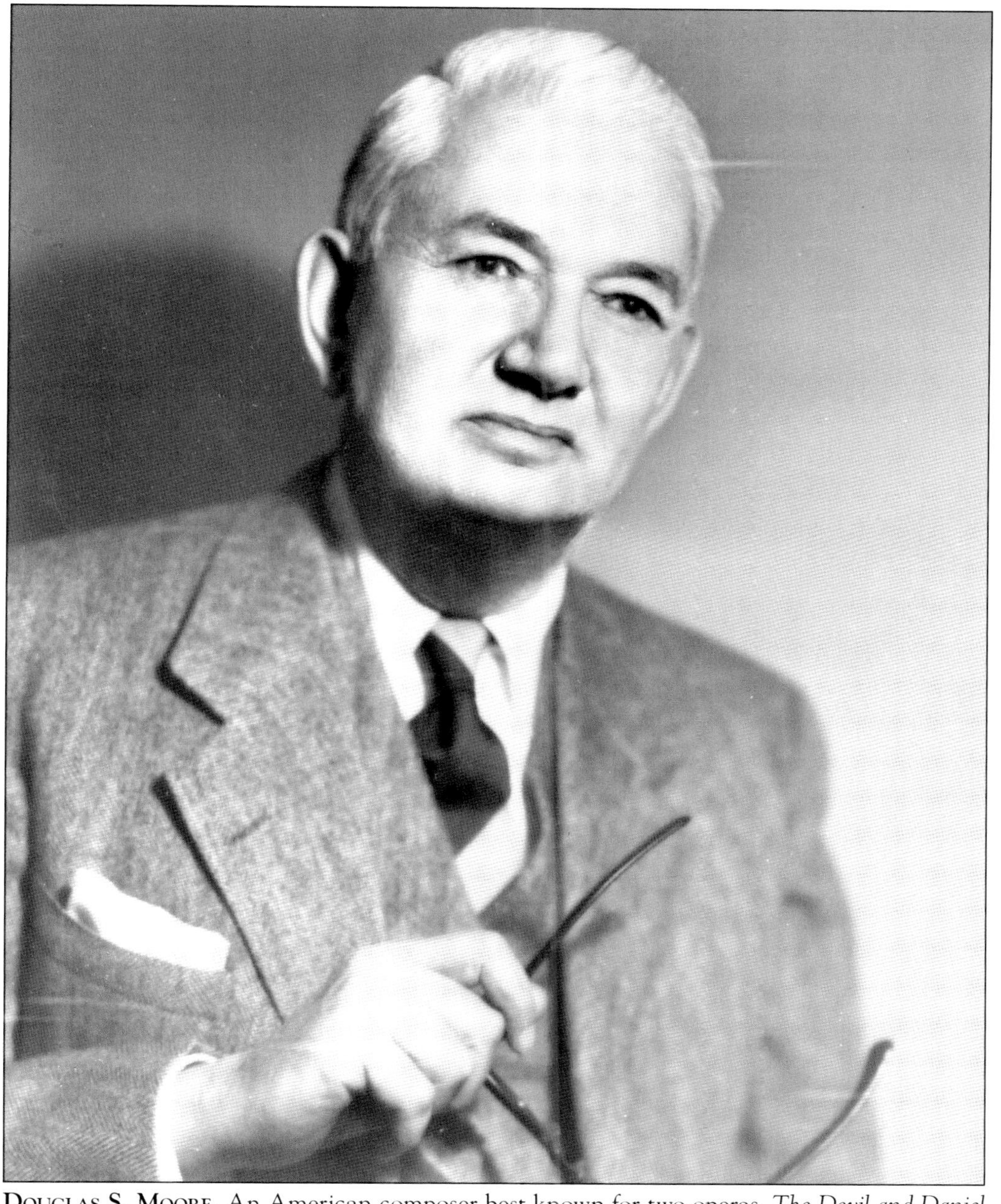

DOUGLAS S. MOORE. An American composer best known for two operas, *The Devil and Daniel Webster* (1938) and *The Ballad of Baby Doe* (1956), Douglas Stuart Moore (1893–1969) was born in Cutchogue and spent much of his life there, composing music in a little studio overlooking a tidal inlet off the bay. Moore descended from early Southold Town settlers, and the Moore family traces its roots to the original settlement of Cutchogue in the 17th century. An alumnus of the Hotchkiss School and Yale University, Moore served as music director at the Cleveland Museum of Art and later taught at Columbia University in New York until his retirement in 1962. (Courtesy of the Southold Historical Society.)

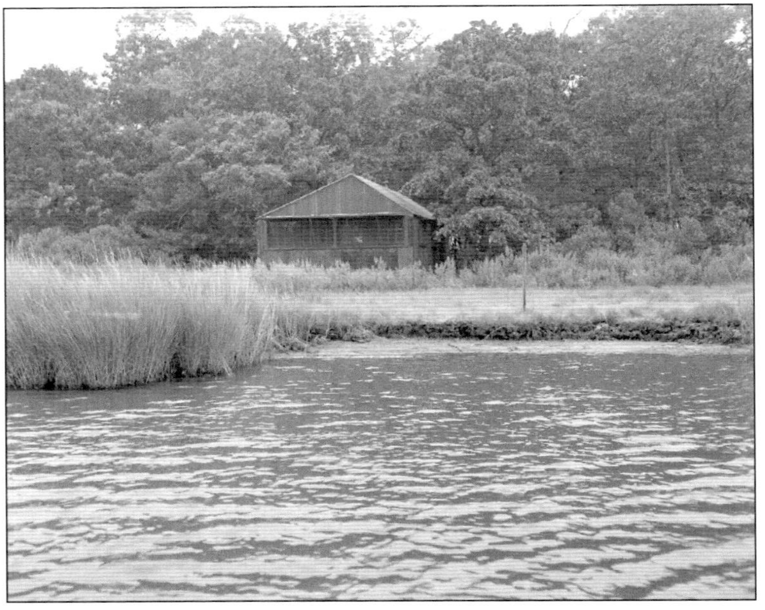

Douglas Moore Studio, Cutchogue. Moore's studio was ideal for composing music: remote from the hustle and bustle of city life, nestled in a bucolic setting, and undisturbed except for the sounds of nature. The modesty and intimacy of Moore's little studio is a reflection of the man and his music, which some critics have compared to that of Aaron Copeland. (Courtesy of the Southold Historical Society.)

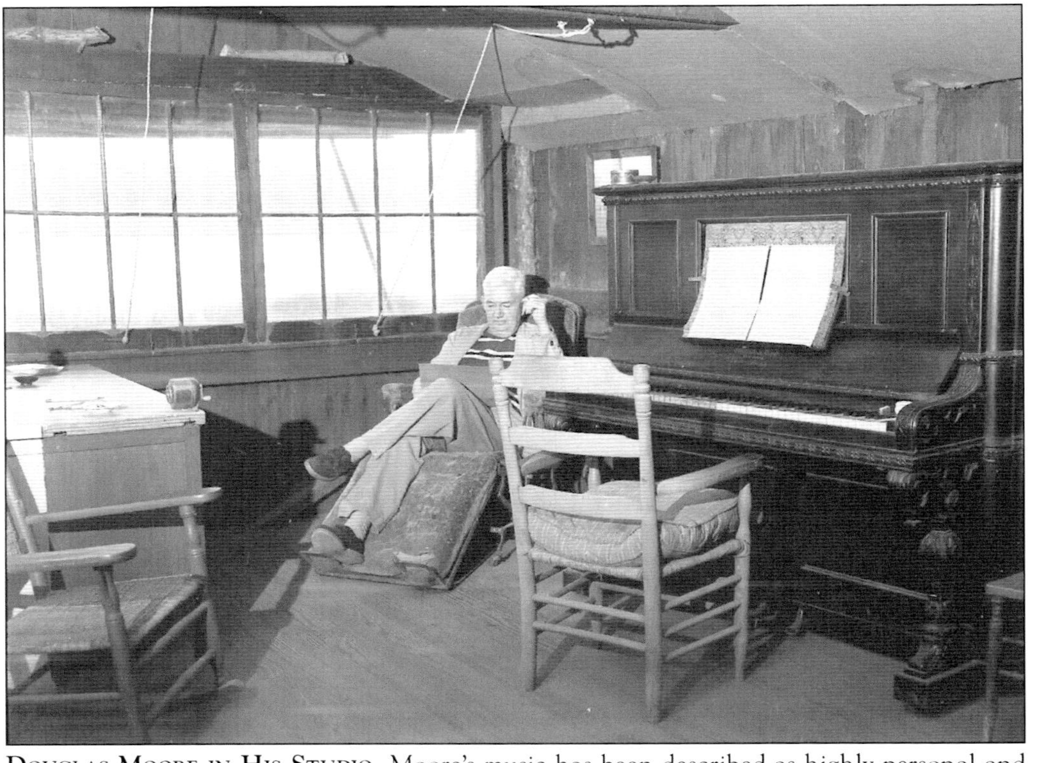

Douglas Moore in His Studio. Moore's music has been described as highly personal and "typically American," with links to folk traditions. His music is distinguished by modesty, grace, and lyricism and reflects influences like jazz and ragtime, as in *The Ballad of Baby Doe*. Despite winning a Pulitzer Prize for the opera *Giants in the Earth* (1949–1950), Moore remains best known for *Baby Doe*, composed in 1956. (Courtesy of the Southold Historical Society.)

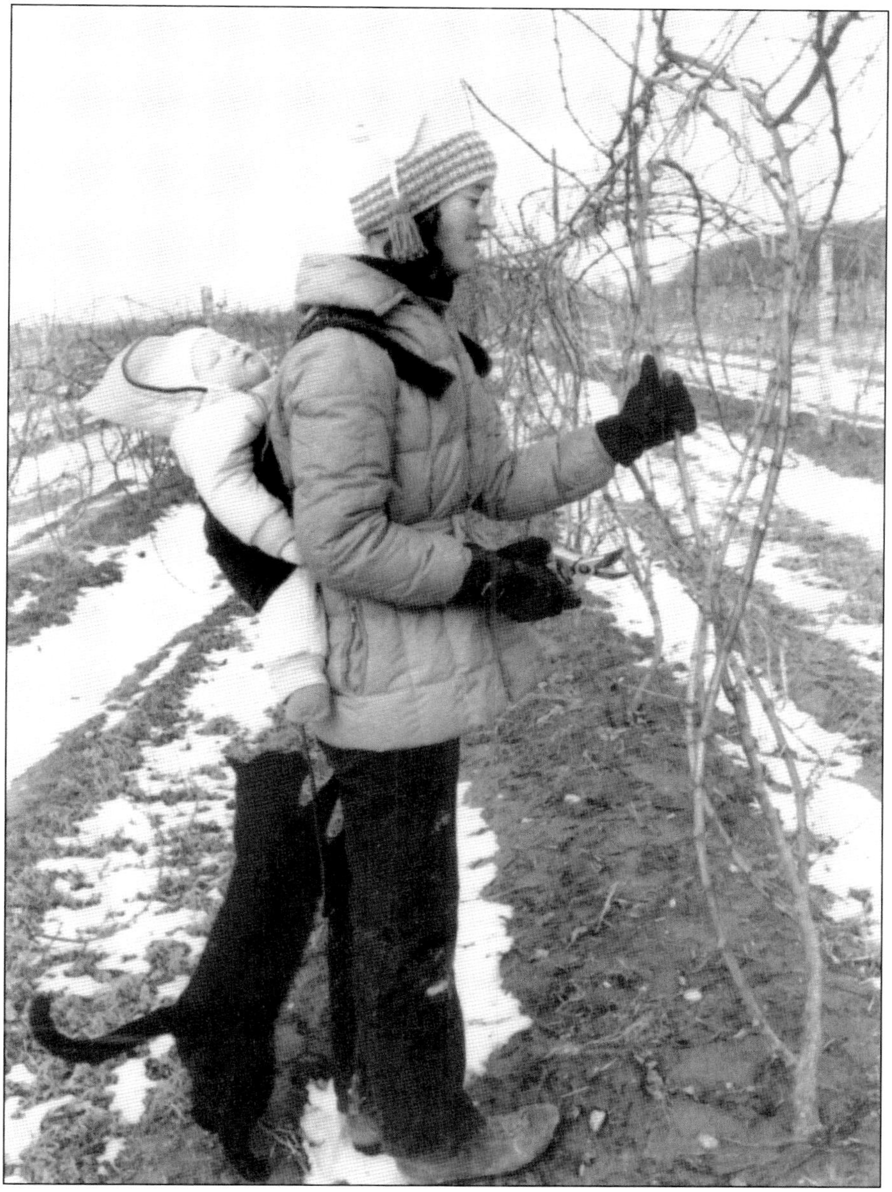

LOUISA HARGRAVE PRUNING GRAPE VINES, 1973. While the exceptional growing conditions of Cutchogue and the surrounding area were praised for centuries, it took the foresight of Alex and Louisa Thomas Hargrave to see that it could rival California and other American wine-growing regions. The Hargraves planted their first *Vitis vinifera* vines in Cutchogue in 1973, hoping that the local climate would support growing grapes that produce the Cabernet Sauvignon and Pinot Noir varieties. They were not disappointed. After 26 years of growing and harvesting grapes and developing the Hargrave Vineyard in Cutchogue—Long Island's first successful commercial vineyard—Alex and Louisa sold the winery in 1999. Louisa, shown here with her daughter Anne and cat Lota, works today as a wine judge, lecturer, and columnist. Over 50 other active vineyards have sprung up on the North Fork since 1973, ranging in size from 200 to 500 acres, all the result of the Hargraves' pioneering efforts, hard work, and vision. (Courtesy of Louisa Hargrave.)

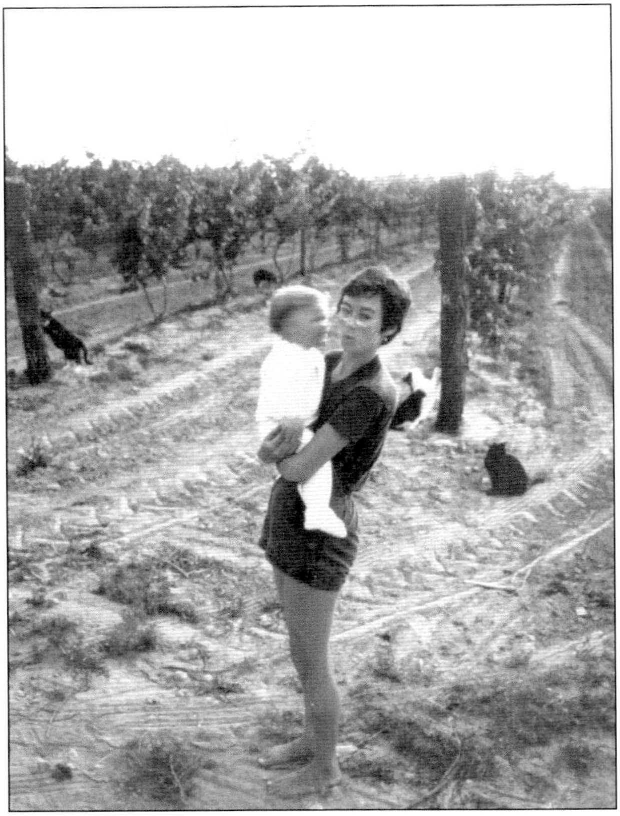

Louisa and Anne Hargrave, 1973. Growing grapes was a family affair! Louisa Hargrave, infant Anne, and the family cats pause for a moment, rows of grapevines stretching behind them. Only time would tell if the growing conditions in Cutchogue were sufficient to produce a wine worthy of bottling. (Courtesy of Louisa Hargrave.)

Planting Grapevines, Cutchogue, 1974. Louisa Hargrave and her helpers plant the vines that will redefine a landscape. Behind them in the near distance, a traditional farm field, barn, and farmhouse defy the Hargraves' experiment in viticulture, which would take decades of labor and perseverance to prove successful. (Courtesy of Louisa Hargrave.)

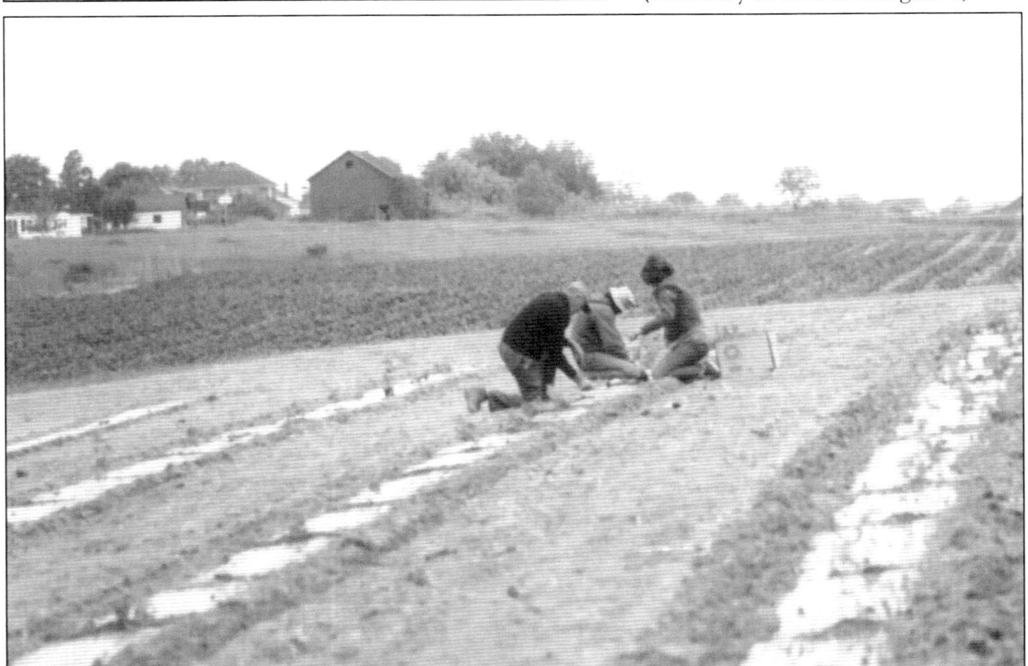

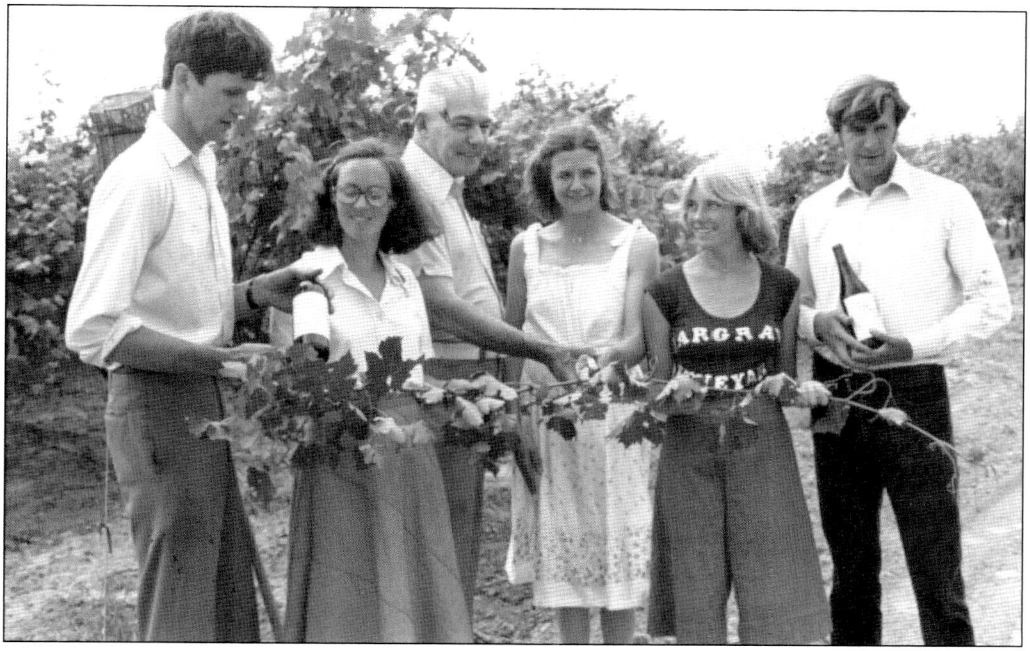

CELEBRATION AND RECOGNITION, CUTCHOGUE, 1977. Hard work has its rewards! After five years of vision and determination, the Hargraves were joined by friends and family to enjoy the grand opening of Hargraves Vineyard (above). Alex Hargrave (far left) stands next to Louisa, while his brother Charlie holds a wine bottle at far right. Later that same year, members of the Suffolk County legislature joined Alex (below, at right) and Louisa (in fur cap) to recognize the momentous occasion of their opening of Hargraves Vineyard, which was seen as an economic boon to the town and the region. Rarely have elected officials been this sensitive to history in the making as here, in the fields of Cutchogue, surrounded by the grapevines of Hargraves Vineyard. *In vino veritas.* (Courtesy of Louisa Hargrave.)

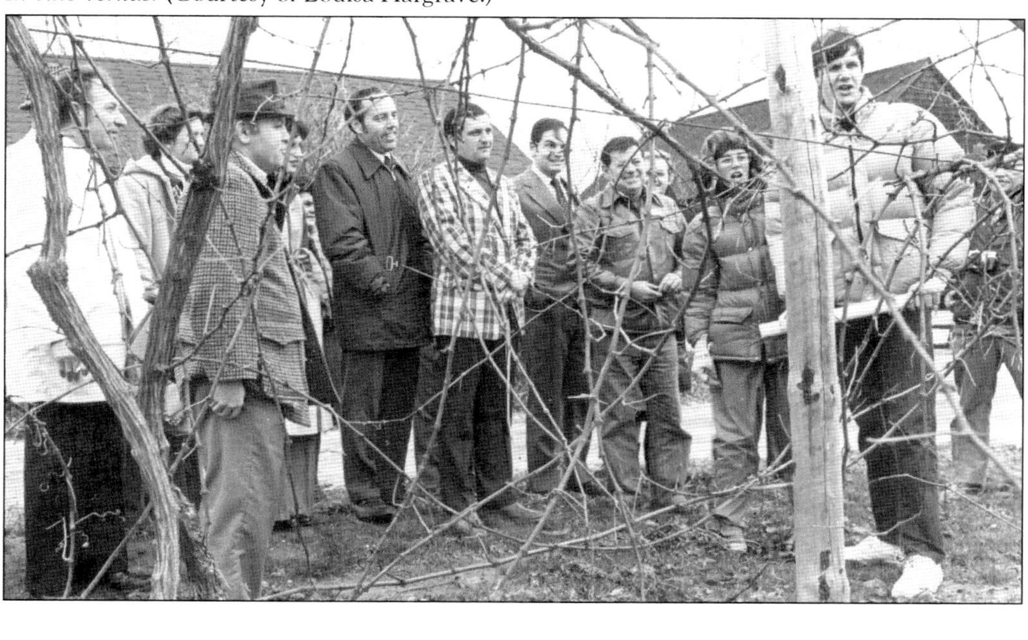

Bibliography

Beers, Frederick W. *Atlas of Long Island, New York*. Beers, Comstock and Cline, 1873.

Butterworth, Marjorie Moore. *The New Suffolk Story*. Cutchogue, NY: Cutchogue–New Suffolk Historical Council, 1983.

Hall, Warren. *Pagans, Puritans and Patriots of Yesterday's Southold*. Cutchogue, NY: Cutchogue–New Suffolk Historical Council, 1975.

Hargrave, Louisa. *The Vineyard: The Pleasures and Perils of Creating an American Family Winery*. New York: The Penguin Group, 2003.

Harris, Bradley L. "John E. Gee and the Early Trucking Industry on Long Island." *Long Island Historical Journal* Vol. 20, Nos. 1–2 (2007): 60–70.

Hedges, Henry P. *An Address Delivered Before the Suffolk County Historical Society*. Sag Harbor, NY: J.H. Hunt, 1889.

Hyde, Merritt B. *Atlas of a Part of Suffolk County, Long Island, New York: North Side–Sound Shore*. New York: E. Belcher Hyde, 1917.

Jefferson, Wayland. *Cutchogue, Southold's First Colony*. Clinton, MA: The Colonial Press Inc., 1940.

Long, Robert P. *Benjamin Franklin's North Fork Milestones*. Robert P. Long, 1991.

MacKay, Robert B., Stanley Lindvall, and Carol Traynor. *AIA Architectural Guide to Nassau and Suffolk Counties, Long Island*. New York: Dover Publications Inc., 1992.

Morris, Richard Knowles. *John P. Holland, 1841–1914: Inventor of the Modern Submarine*. Columbia, SC: University of South Carolina Press, 1998.

Munsell. *History of Suffolk County, New York*. New York: W.W. Munsell & Co., 1882.

Ross, Peter. *A History of Long Island*. New York: The Lewis Publishing Company, 1903.

Thompson, Benjamin F. *History of Long Island*. New York: E. French, 1839.

Wick, Steve. *Heaven and Earth*. New York: St. Martin's Press, 1996.

ABOUT THE ORGANIZATION

The Cutchogue–New Suffolk Historical Council was founded in 1960 to collect, preserve, and interpret the history of Long Island's central North Fork region and to maintain Cutchogue's Village Green for public enjoyment. Nestled between Long Island Sound and Great Peconic Bay and characterized by picturesque farmland, tidal creeks, and vineyards, Cutchogue, New Suffolk, and the surrounding area is unsurpassed in beauty and heritage.

The chief attraction on the Village Green is the Old House, built in Southold by John Budd in 1649 and moved to Cutchogue in 1660. The house is New York State's oldest dwelling and was designated a National Historic Landmark in 1962. Other restored buildings on the green include the 18th-century Wickham Farmhouse and Cutchogue's First District Schoolhouse, built in the 1840s. A mile out of town, the Old Burying Ground, dating from the early 1700s, survives by the side of the Main Road and is owned and maintained by the historical council.

The organization is a nonprofit, educational institution that encourages membership and participation in its many events and programs. All are welcome!